Pro Spring Security

Securing Spring Framework 5 and Boot 2-based Java Applications

Second Edition

Carlo Scarioni
Massimo Nardone

Pro Spring Security: Securing Spring Framework 5 and Boot 2-based Java Applications

Carlo Scarioni
Surbiton, UK

Massimo Nardone
HELSINKI, Finland

ISBN-13 (pbk): 978-1-4842-5051-8
https://doi.org/10.1007/978-1-4842-5052-5

ISBN-13 (electronic): 978-1-4842-5052-5

Managing Director, Apress Media LLC: Welmoed Spahr
Acquisitions Editor: Steve Anglin
Development Editor: Matthew Moodie
Coordinating Editor: Mark Powers

Cover designed by eStudioCalamar

Cover image designed by Freepik (www.freepik.com)

Distributed to the book trade worldwide by Springer Science+Business Media New York, 233 Spring Street, 6th Floor, New York, NY 10013. Phone 1-800-SPRINGER, fax (201) 348-4505, e-mail orders-ny@springer-sbm.com, or visit www.springeronline.com. Apress Media, LLC is a California LLC and the sole member (owner) is Springer Science + Business Media Finance Inc (SSBM Finance Inc). SSBM Finance Inc is a **Delaware** corporation.

For information on translations, please e-mail editorial@apress.com; for reprint, paperback, or audio rights, please email bookpermissions@springernature.com.

Apress titles may be purchased in bulk for academic, corporate, or promotional use. eBook versions and licenses are also available for most titles. For more information, reference our Print and eBook Bulk Sales web page at www.apress.com/bulk-sales.

Any source code or other supplementary material referenced by the author in this book is available to readers on GitHub via the book's product page, located at www.apress.com/9781484250518. For more detailed information, please visit www.apress.com/source-code.

Printed on acid-free paper

I would like to dedicate this book to the memory of my beloved late mother, Maria Augusta Ciniglio. Thanks, Mom, for all the great things you have taught me, for making me a good person, for making me study to become a computing scientist, and for the great memories you left me. You will be loved and missed forever. I love you, Mom. RIP.

—Massimo

Table of Contents

The chapters in the book cover the following:

- **Chapter 1**: Introduces security in general and how to approach security problems at the application level

- **Chapter 2**: Introduces Spring Security v5, how to use it, when to use it, and all of its security functionalities

- **Chapter 3**: Introduces Spring Security with a simple example application that secures web access at the URL level

- **Chapter 4**: Provides a full introduction to the architecture of Spring Security, including the main components and how they interact with each other

- **Chapter 5**: Gives in-depth coverage of the web-layer security options available in Spring Security

- **Chapter 6**: Covers a wide array of authentication providers, including LDAP and JASS, which can be plugged into Spring Security

- **Chapter 7**: Covers access control lists (ACLs), which are used to secure individual domain objects, and how they fit into the general security concerns

- **Chapter 8**: Explains how to extend the core Spring Security functionality by making use of the many extension points supported by its modular architecture

- **Chapter 9**: Shows how to integrate Spring Security with different Java frameworks and some important JVM programming languages

Prerequisites

The examples in this book are all built with Java 11 and Maven 3.6.1. The latest Spring versions are used if possible. Spring Security 5.1.5 was the version used throughout the book. Tomcat Web Server v9 was used for the different web applications in the book, mainly through its Maven plugin, and the laptop used was a ThinkPad Yoga 360 with 8GB of RAM. All the projects were developed using the IntelliJ IDEA Ultimate 2019.2.

You are free to use your own tools and operating system. Because everything is Java based, you should be able to compile your programs on any platform without problems.

Downloading the Code

The code for the examples shown in this book is available via the Download Source Code button located at www.apress.com/9781484250518.

Contacting the Authors

You are more than welcome to send us any feedback regarding this book or any other subject we might help you with. You can contact Carlo Scarioni via his blog at http://cscarioni.blogspot.com, or you can send him email at carlo.scarioni@gmail.com. You can contact Massimo Nardone via email at massimonardonedevchannel@gmail.com.

CHAPTER 1

The Scope of Security

Security. An incredibly overloaded word in the IT world. It means so many different things in so many different contexts, but in the end, it is all about protecting sensitive and valuable resources against malicious usage.

In IT, we have many layers of infrastructure and code that can be subject to malicious attacks, and arguably we should ensure that all these layers get the appropriate levels of protection.

Of course, the growth of the Internet and the pursuit of reaching more people with our applications have opened more and more doors to cyber criminals trying to access these applications in illegitimate ways.

It is also true that good care is not always taken to ensure that a properly secured set of services is being offered to the public. And sometimes, even when good care is taken, some hackers are still smart enough to overcome security barriers that, superficially, appear adequate.

The first step is to define defense in depth (DiD) and its security layers. In general, DiD is a way to define how to develop the cybersecurity of the IT infrastructure by defining how all the defensive mechanisms are layered in order to protect and secure data and information. A failing DiD or too weak development might be a consequence of a cybersecurity attack on the IT infrastructure.

Let's understand a bit more about the mechanisms part of DiD. First of all, DiD is made of three major controls:

- **Administrative controls**: Policies, procedures, guidelines, awareness programs, etc.

- **Technical controls**: Firewalls, antivirus, intrusion prevention systems (IPS), etc.

- **Physical Controls**: Network and server rooms, video surveillance, etc.

1

© Carlo Scarioni and Massimo Nardone 2019
C. Scarioni and M. Nardone, *Pro Spring Security*, https://doi.org/10.1007/978-1-4842-5052-5_1

Figure 1-1 shows the typical DiD mechanisms that define the IT infrastructure security layers.

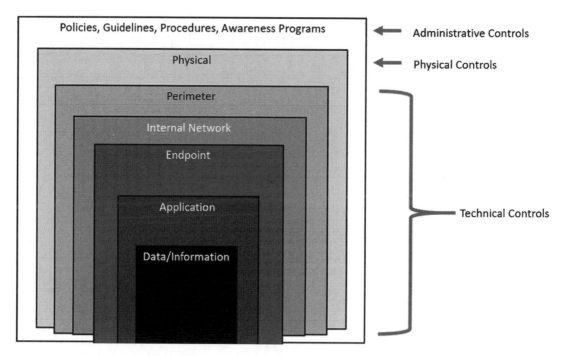

Figure 1-1. *DiD mechanisms and IT infrastruxture layers*

The three major security layers in an IT infrastructure are the network, the operating system (part of the endpoint security layer), and the application itself.

The Network Security Layer

The network security layer is probably the most familiar one in the IT world. When people talk about IT security, they normally think of network-level security—in particular, security that uses firewalls.

Even though people often associate security with the network level, this is only a very limited layer of protection against attackers. Generally speaking, it can do no more than defend IP addresses and filter network packets addressed to certain ports in certain machines in the network.

This is clearly not enough in the vast majority of cases, as traffic at this level is normally allowed to enter the publicly open ports of your various exposed services with no restriction at all. Different attacks can be targeted at these open services, as attackers can execute arbitrary commands that could compromise your security constraints. There are tools like the popular nmap (http://nmap.org/) that can be used to scan a machine to find open ports. The use of such tools is an easy first step to take in preparing an attack, because well-known attacks can be used against such open ports if they are not properly secured.

A very important part of the network-layer security, in the case of web applications, is the use of Secure Sockets Layer (SSL) to encode all sensitive information sent along the wire, but this is related more to the network protocol at the application level than to the network physical level at which firewalls operate.

The Operating System Layer

The operating system layer is probably the most important one in the whole security schema, as a properly secured operating system (OS) environment can at least prevent a whole host machine from going down if a particular application is compromised.

If an attacker is somehow allowed to have unsecured access to the operating system, they can basically do whatever they want—from spreading viruses to stealing passwords or deleting your whole server's data and making it unusable. Even worse perhaps, they could take control of your computer without you even noticing, and use it to perform other malicious acts as part of a botnet. This layer can include the deployment model of the applications since you need to know your operating system's permission scheme to ensure that you don't give your applications unnecessary privileges over your machine. Applications should run as isolated as possible from the other components of the host machine.

The Application Layer

The main focus of this book will be on the application layer. The application security layer refers to all the constraints we establish in our applications to make sure that only the right people can do only the right things when working through the application.

Applications, by default, are open to countless avenues of attack. An improperly secured application can allow an attacker to steal information from the application, impersonate other users, execute restricted operations, corrupt data, gain access to the operating system level, and perform many other malicious acts.

In this book, we will cover application-level security, which is the domain of Spring Security. Application-level security is achieved by implementing several techniques, and there are a few concepts that will help you understand better what the rest of the book will cover. They are the main concerns that Spring Security addresses to provide your applications with comprehensive protection against threats. In the following three subsections, we shall introduce

- Authentication

- Authorization

- ACLs

Authentication

The process of authentication allows an application to validate that a particular user is who they claim they are. In the authentication process, a user presents the application with information about herself (normally, a username and a password) that no one else knows. The application takes this information and tries to match it against information it has stored—normally, in a database or LDAP[1] (Lightweight Directory Access Protocol) server. If the information provided by the user matches a record in the authentication server, the user is successfully authenticated in the system. The application will normally create an internal abstraction representing this authenticated user in the system. Figure 1-2 shows the authentication mechanism.

---

[1]LDAP will be explained in some detail in Chapter 8, where various authentication providers are covered.

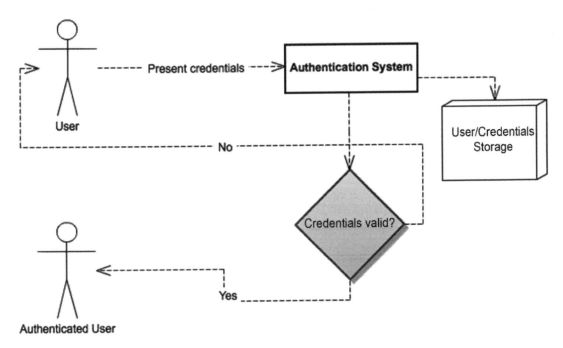

Figure 1-2. *Simple, standard authentication mechanism*

Authorization

When a user is authenticated, that only means that the user is known to the system and has been recognized by it. It doesn't mean that the user is free to do whatever she wants in said system. The next logical step in securing an application is to determine which actions the user is allowed to perform, and which resources she has access to, and make sure that if the user doesn't have the proper permissions she cannot carry out that particular action. This is the work of the authorization process. In the most common case, the authorization process compares the user's set of permissions against the permissions required to execute a particular action in the application, and if a match is found, access is granted. On the other hand, if no match is found, access is denied. Figure 1-3 shows the authorization mechanism.

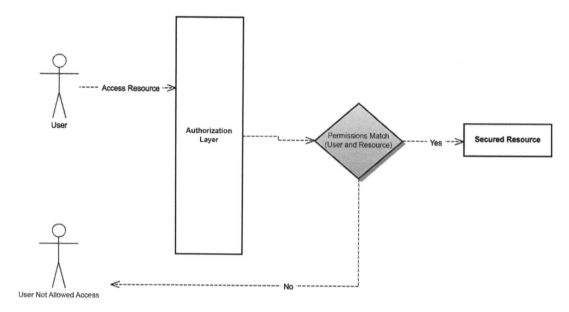

Figure 1-3. *Simple authorization process. The authenticated user tries to access a secured resource*

ACLs

Access control lists (ACLs) are part of the authorization process explained in the previous section. The key difference is that ACLs normally work at a finer grained level in the application. ACLs are simply a collection of mappings between resources, users, and permissions. With ACLs, you can establish rules like "User John has administrative permission on the blog post X" or "User Luis has read permission on blog post X." You can see the three elements: user, permission, and resource. Figure 1-3 shows how ACLs work; they are just a special case of the general authorization process.

Authentication and Authorization: General Concepts

In this section, we shall introduce and explain some fundamental security concepts that you will be coming across frequently in the rest of the book:

- **User:** The first step in securing a system from malicious attackers is to identify legitimate users and allow access to them alone. User abstractions are created in the system and given their own identity. They are the users that will later be allowed to use the system.

- **Credentials**: Credentials are the way a user proves who they are. Normally, in the shape of passwords (certificates are also a common way of presenting credentials), they are data that only the owner of it knows.

- **Role**: In an application security context, a role can be seen as a logical grouping of users. This logical grouping is normally done so the grouped users share a set of permissions in the application to access certain resources. For example, all users with the role of admin will have the same access and permissions to the same resources. Roles serve simply as a way to group permissions to execute determined actions, making users with those roles inherit such permissions.

- **Resource**: By a *resource*, we mean, in this context, any part of the application that we want to access and that needs to be properly secured against unauthorized access—for example, a URL, a business method, or a particular business object.

- **Permissions**: Permissions refer to the access level needed to access a particular resource. For example, two users may be allowed to read a particular document, but only one of them is allowed to write to it. Permissions can apply either to individual users or to users that share a particular role.

- **Encryption**: This allows you to encrypt sensible information (normally passwords, but it can be something else, like cookies) so as to make it incomprehensible to attackers even if they get access to the encrypted version. The idea is that you never store the plain text version of a password, but instead store an encrypted version so that nobody but the owner of such a password knows the original one. There are three main kinds of encryption algorithms:

    - **One-way encryption**: These algorithms, referred as *hashing algorithms*, take an input string and generate an output number known as the *message digest*. This output number cannot be converted back into the original string. This is why the technique is referred to as *one-way encryption*. Here is the way to use it: A requesting client encrypts a string and sends the encrypted string to the server. The server may have access to the original information from a previous registration process, for example, and if it does, it can apply the same hash function to it. Then it compares the output from this hashing to the value sent by the client. If they match, the server validates the information. Figure 1-4 shows this scheme. Usually, the server doesn't even need the original data. It can simply store the hashed version and then compare it with the incoming hash from the client.

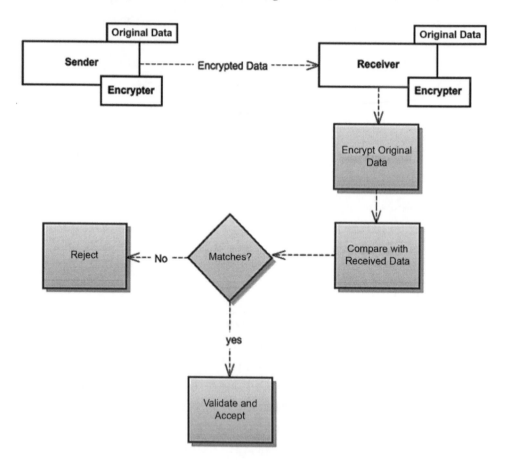

Figure 1-4. *One-way encryption or hashing*

- **Symmetric encryption**: These algorithms provide two functions: encrypt and decrypt. A string of text is converted into an encrypted form and then can be converted back to the original string. In this scheme, a sender and a receiver share the same keys so that they can encrypt and decrypt messages on both ends of the communication.

One problem with this scheme is how to share the key between the endpoints of the communication. A common approach is to use a parallel secure channel to send the keys. Figure 1-5 shows symmetric encryption at work.

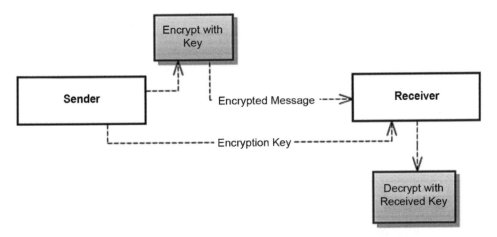

Figure 1-5. *Symmetric encryption. The two endpoints share the same encryption/ decryption key*

- **Public key cryptography**: These techniques are based on asymmetric cryptography. In this scheme, a different key is used for encryption than for decryption. These two keys are referred as the *public key*, which is used to encrypt messages, and the *private key*, which is used to decrypt messages. The advantage of this approach over symmetric encryption is that there is no need to share the decryption key, so no one but the intended receiver of the information is able to decrypt the message. So the normal scenario is the following:

  - The intended recipient of messages shares her public key with everyone interested in sending information to her.

  - A sender encrypts the information with the receiver's public key, and sends a message.

  - The receiver uses her private key to decrypt the message.

  - No one else is able to decrypt the message because they don't have the receiver's private key.

Figure 1-6 shows the public key cryptography scheme.

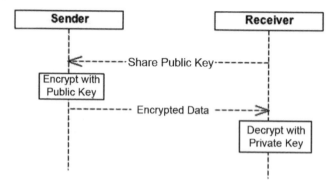

Figure 1-6. *Public key cryptography*

The use of encryption achieves, among other things, two other security goals:

- **Confidentiality**: Potentially sensitive information belonging to one user, or group of users, should be accessible only to this user or group. Encryption algorithms are the main helper in achieving this goal.

- **Integrity**: Data sent by a valid user shouldn't be altered by a third entity on its way to the server, or in its storage. This is normally accomplished through the use of one-way cryptographic algorithms that make it almost impossible to alter an input and produce a corrupted message whose encrypted hash is the same as the original message (thus deceiving the receiver into thinking it is valid).

What to Secure

Not every part of the application requires a strong security model, or even any security at all. If, for example, one part of your application is supposed to serve static content to everyone interested in it, you can simply serve this content. There probably are no security concerns to handle here.

Anyway, when starting to work on a new application, you should think about the security constraints that your application will have. You should think about concerns like those in the following list and whether or not they apply to your particular use case:

- **Identity management**: More than likely, your application will need to establish the identities of the different users that will be using it. Usually, your application will do different things for different users, so you need a way to associate users with certain functionality. You also need to be sure to protect each user's identity information so that it can't be compromised.

- **Secured connections**: In an internet environment, where anyone in the world can potentially access your system and eavesdrop on other users accessing your system, you most likely will want to secure the communication of sensitive data using some kind of transport layer security, such as SSL.

- **Sensitive data protection**: Sensitive data will need to be protected against malicious attacks. This applies to the communication layer and to individual message transmission, as well as to credentials datastores. Encryption should be used in different layers to achieve the most secure application possible.

More Security Concerns

There are many more security concerns than the ones explained so far. Because this is a Spring Security book and not a general application-security book, we will cover only things related to Spring Security. However, we think it is important that you understand that there are many more security concerns than those addressed directly by Spring Security. The following is a quick overview of some of the most common ones. This is only intended to make you aware of their existence, and we recommend you consult a different source (such as a general software security textbook) to gain a better understanding of all these concerns.

- **SQL (and other code) injection**: Validating user input is a very important part of application security. If data is not validated, an attacker could potentially write any kind of string as input (including SQL or server-side code) and send that information to the server. If the server code is not properly written, the attacker could wreak significant havoc because she could execute any arbitrary code on the server.

- **Denial of service attacks**: These attacks consist of making the target system unresponsive to its intended users. This is normally done by saturating the server with requests so that it utilizes all the server's resources and makes it unresponsive to legitimate requests.

- **Cross-site scripting and output sanitation**: A kind of injection can be done where the target is the client part of the application. The idea is that the attacker can make an application return malicious code inside the web pages returned, and thus execute it in the user's browser. This way, the attacker invisibly executes actions using the real user's authenticated session.

Java Options for Security

Java and Java EE out-of-the-box security solutions are very comprehensive. They cover areas ranging from a low-level permission system, through cryptography APIs, to an authentication and authorization scheme.

The list of security APIs offered in Java is very extensive, as the following list of the main ones shows:

- **Java Cryptography Architecture (JCA)**: This API offers support for cryptographic algorithms, including hash-digest and digital-signature support.

- **Java Cryptographic Extensions (JCE)**: This API mainly provides facilities for the encryption and decryption of strings and also secret key generation for symmetric algorithms.

- **Java Certification Path API (CertPath)**: This API provides comprehensive functionality for integrating the validation and verification of digital certificates into an application.

- **Java Secure Socket Extension (JSSE):** This API provides a standardized set of features to offer support for SSL and TLS protocols, both client and server, in Java.

- **Java Authentication and Authorization Service (JAAS):** This API provides service for authentication and authorization in Java applications. It provides a pluggable system where authentication mechanisms can be plugged in independently to applications.

Please refer to this link for the entire list of Java 11 Security APIs: `https://docs.oracle.com/en/java/javase/11/security/java-security-overview1.html#GUID-2EF0B3B8-9F3A-41CF-A7DA-63DB52180084`.

Figure 1-7 shows the Java platform security architecture and elements.

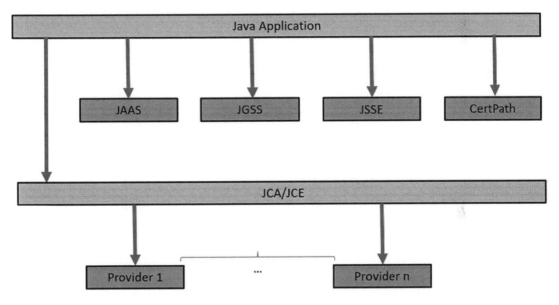

Figure 1-7. *Java platform security architecture and elements*

Spring Security's main concerns are in the authentication/authorization realm. So it overlaps mainly with the JAAS Java API, although they can be used together, as you will see later in the book. Most of the other APIs are leveraged in Spring Security. For example, CertPath is used in X509AuthenticationFilter and JCE is used in the spring-security-crypto module.

Summary

In this chapter, we introduced security from a general point of view down to defense in depth (DiD) and its mechanisms. We explained in a very abstract way the main concerns in IT security and especially from an application point of view. We also described, very briefly, the main Java APIs that support security at different levels.

You can see that this chapter was a very quick overview of security concerns. It is beyond the scope of this book to go any further than this on general topics, although we will study some of them in more depth when they apply to Spring Security. Obviously, this is nothing like a comprehensive software security guide, and if you are interested in learning more about software security in general, you should consult the specialized literature. The next chapter will introduce Spring Security as such.

CHAPTER 2

Introducing Spring Security

In this chapter, you will learn what Spring Security is and how you can use it to address security concerns about your application.

We will also describe what's new in Spring Framework and Security version 5. How to use Spring Security v5 with authentication and authorization will be introduced a bit more in detail since we will be using them a lot in this book.

Finally, we'll take a look at the framework's source code, how to build it, and the different modules that together form the powerful Spring Security project.

What Is Spring Security?

Spring Security is a framework dedicated to providing a full array of security services to Java applications in a developer-friendly and flexible way. It adheres to the well-established practices introduced by the Spring Framework. Spring Security tries to address all the layers of security inside your application. In addition, it comes packed with an extensive array of configuration options that make it very flexible and powerful.

Recall from Chapter 1 that it can be said that Spring Security is simply a comprehensive authentication/authorization framework built on top of the Spring Framework. Although the majority of applications that use the framework are web-based, Spring Security's core can also be used in standalone applications.

Many things make Spring Security immediately attractive to Java developers. To name just a few, consider the following list:

- **It's built on top of the successful Spring Framework.** This is an important strength of Spring Security. The Spring Framework has become "the way" to build enterprise Java applications, and with

© Carlo Scarioni and Massimo Nardone 2019
C. Scarioni and M. Nardone, *Pro Spring Security*, https://doi.org/10.1007/978-1-4842-5052-5_2

good reason. It is built around good practices and two simple yet powerful concepts: dependency injection (DI) and aspect-oriented programming (AOP). Also important is that many developers have experience with Spring, so they can leverage that experience when introducing Spring Security in their projects.

- **It provides out-of-the-box support for many authentication models.** Even more important than the previous point, Spring Security supports out-of-the-box integration with Lightweight Directory Access Protocol (LDAP), OpenID, form authentication, Certificate X.509 authentication, database authentication, Jasypt cryptography, and lots more. All this support means that Spring Security adapts to your security needs—and not only that, it can change if your needs change, without much effort involved for the developer. More info about Jasypt cryptography can be found at `www.jasypt.org/`.

This is important from a business point of view as well because the application can either adapt to the corporate authentication services or implement its own, thus requiring only straightforward configuration changes.

This also means that there is a lot less software for you to write, because you are making use of a great amount of ready-to-use code that has been written and tested by a large and active user community. You can, to a certain point, trust that this code works and use it with confidence. And if it does not work, you can always fix it and send a patch to those in charge of maintaining the project.

- **It offers layered security services.** Spring Security allows you to secure your application at different levels, and to secure your web URLs, views, service methods, and domain model. You can pick and combine these features to achieve your security goals.

This is really flexible in practice. Imagine, for instance, that you offer services exposed through RMI, the Web, JMS, and others. You could secure all of these interfaces, but maybe it's better to secure just the business layer so that all requests are secured when they reach this layer. Also, maybe you don't care about securing individual business objects, so you can omit that module and use just the functionality you need.

- **It is open source software.** As part of the Pivotal portfolio, Spring Security is an open source software tool. It also has a large community and user base dedicated to testing and improving the framework. Having the opportunity to work with open source software is an attractive feature for most developers. The ability to look into the source code of the tools you like and work with is an exciting prospect. Whether our goal is to improve the tools or simply to understand how they work internally, we developers love to read code and learn from it.

Where Does Spring Security Fit In?

Spring Security is without question a powerful and versatile tool. But like anything else, it is not a tool that adapts to everything you want to do. Its offerings have a defined scope.

Where and why would you use Spring Security? Here is a list of reasons and scenarios:

- **Your application is in Java, Groovy, or Kotlin.** The first thing to take into account is that Spring Security can be written in languages like Java, Groovy, or Kotlin and generally in any language supported by the JVM. So if you plan to work in a non-JVM language, Spring Security won't be of any use to you.

- **You need role-based authentication/authorization.** This is the main use case of Spring Security. You have a list of users and a list of resources and operations on those resources. You group the users into roles and allow certain roles to access certain operations on certain resources. That's the core functionality.

- **You want to secure a web application from malicious users.** As mentioned, Spring Security is mostly used in web application environments. When this is the case, the first thing to do is allow only the users that you want to have access to your application, while forbidding all others from even reaching it.

- **You need to integrate with OpenID, LDAP, Active Directory, and databases as security providers.** If you need to integrate with a particular Users and Roles or Groups provider, you should take a look at the vast array of options Spring Security offers because integration might already be implemented for you, saving you from writing lots of unnecessary code. Sometimes you might not be exactly sure what provider your business will require to authenticate against. In this case, Spring Security makes your life easy by allowing you to switch between different providers in a painless way.

- **You need to secure your domain model and allow only certain users to access certain objects in your application.** If you need fine-grained security (that is, you need to secure on a per object, per user basis), Spring Security offers the Access Control List (ACL) module, which will help you to do just that in a straightforward way.

- **You want a nonintrusive, declarative way for adding security around your application.** Security is a cross-cutting concern, not really a core business functionality of your application (unless you work in a security provider firm). As such, it is better if it can be treated as a separate and modular add-on that you can declare, configure, and manage independently of your main business concerns. Spring Security is built with this in mind. By using Servlet Filters, XML configuration, and AOP concepts, the framework tries not to pollute your application with security rules. Even when using annotations, they are still metadata on top of your code. They don't mess with your code logic. You, as a Java developer, must try to isolate the Java Configuration into a configuration library and decouple it from the rest of the application in a similar way you do with XML.

- **You want to secure your service layer the same way you secure your URLs, and you need to add rules at the method level for allowing or disallowing user access.** Spring Security allows you to use a consistent security model throughout the layers of your application because it internally enforces this consistent model itself. You configure users, roles, and providers in just one place, and both the service and web layers make use of this centralized security configuration in a transparent way.

- **You need your application to remember its users on their next visit and allow them access.** Sometimes you don't want or need the users of your application to log in every time they visit your site. Spring supports out-of-the-box, remember-me functionality so that a user can be automatically logged in on subsequent visits to your site, allowing them full or partial access to their profile's functionality.

- **You want to use public/private key certificates to authenticate against your application.** Spring Security allows you to use X.509 certificates to verify the identity of the server. The server can also request a valid certificate from the client for establishing mutual authentication.

- **You need to hide elements in your web pages from certain users and show them to some others.** View security is the first layer of security in a secured web application. It is normally not enough for guaranteeing security, but it is very important from a usability point of view because it allows the application to show or hide content depending on the user that is currently logged in to the system.

- **You need more flexibility than simple role-based authentication for your application.** For example, suppose that you want to allow access only to users over 18 years of age using simple script expressions. Spring Security 3.1 uses the Spring Expression Language (SpEL) to allow you to customize access rules for your application.

- **You want your application to automatically handle HTTP status codes related to authorization errors (401, 403, and others).** The built-in exception-handling mechanism of Spring Security for web applications automatically translates the more common exceptions to their corresponding HTTP status codes; for example, AccessDeniedException gets translated to the 403 status code.

- **You want to configure your application to be used from other applications (not browsers) and allow these other applications to authenticate themselves against yours.** Another application accessing your application should be forced to use authentication mechanisms in order to gain access. For example, you can expose your application through REST endpoints that other applications can access with HTTP security.

- **You are running an application outside a Java EE Server.** If you are running your application in a simple web container like Apache Tomcat, you probably don't have support for the full Java EE security stack. Spring Security can be easily leveraged in these environments.

- **You are running an application inside a Java EE Server.** Even if you are running a full Java EE container, Spring Security is arguably more complete, flexible, and easy to use than the Java EE counterpart.

- **You are already using Spring in your application and want to leverage your knowledge of it.** We explained before some of the great advantages of Spring. If you are currently using Spring, you probably like it a lot. So you will probably like Spring Security as well.

Spring Security Overview

Spring Security v5 is no longer part of SpringSource but instead is now part of Pivotal. Spring by Pivotal includes many projects:

- Spring Security
- Spring Boot
- Spring Framework
- Spring Cloud Data Flow
- Spring Cloud
- Spring Data
- Spring Integration
- Spring Batch
- Spring Hateoas
- Spring Rest Docs
- Spring Amqp
- Spring Mobile
- Spring For Android

- Spring Web Flow

- Spring Web Services

- Spring Ldap

- Spring Session

- Spring Shell

- Spring Flo

- Spring Kafka

- Spring Statemachine

- Spring Io Platform

- Spring Roo

- Spring Scala

- Spring Blazeds Integration

- Spring Loaded

- Spring Xd

- Spring Social

For more information, please refer to the Spring project web page at `https://spring.io/projects`.

All of these projects are built on top of the facilities provided by the Spring Framework itself, which is the original project that started it all. You can think of Spring as the hub of all these satellite projects, providing them with a consistent programming model and a set of established practices. The main points you will see throughout the different projects is the use of DI, XML namespace-based configuration, and AOP, which, as you will see in the next section, are the pillars upon which Spring is built. In the later versions of Spring, annotations have become the most popular way to configure both DI and AOP concerns.

In this book, we will mainly introduce Spring Boot, analyze Spring Framework, and develop Spring Security version 5. Let's start with Spring Boot.

What is Spring Boot?

Spring Boot is an open source Java-based framework which is generally used for developing microservice, enterprise-ready applications. It was developed by the Pivotal Team and helps developers to create stand-alone and production-ready Spring applications.

Spring Boot is considered to be an easy starting point for building all Spring-based applications and running them as quickly as possible, with minimal upfront configuration of Spring.

Note   Remember that a Spring Security application can be developed with Maven or Gradle.

As we said, Spring Security is just one more of the Spring projects, and it is dedicated exclusively to addressing security concerns in your application.

For more information, please refer to the documentation at `https://spring.io/projects/spring-security`.

Spring Security started originally as a non-Spring project. It was originally known as *The Acegi Security System for Spring*, and it was not the big and powerful framework it is today. Originally, it dealt only with authorization and leveraged container-provided authentication. Because of public demand, the project started to get traction, as more people started using it and contributing to its continuously growing code base. This eventually led to it becoming a Spring Framework portfolio project, and then later it was rebranded as "Spring Security."

Here are the Spring Security major releases dates:

- 2.0.0 (April, 2008)

- 3.0.0 (December, 2009)

- 4.0.0 (March, 2015)

- 5.0.0 (November, 2017)

- 5.1.4 (February, 2019)

Notice that Java configuration for Spring Security was added to the Spring framework in Spring 3.1 and extended to Spring Security in Spring 3.2 and is defined in a class annotated @Configuration.

So the project for many years now has been under the Pivotal umbrella of projects, powered by the Spring Framework itself.

But what exactly is the Spring Framework?

Spring Framework 5: A Quick Overview

We have mentioned the Spring Framework project quite a lot. It makes sense to give an overview of it at this point, because many of the Spring Security characteristics we will cover in the rest of the book rely on the building blocks of Spring.

We admit we're biased. We love Spring and have loved it for many years now. We think Spring has so many advantages and so many great things that we can't start a new Java project without using it. Additionally, we tend to carry its concepts around when working with other languages and look for a way to apply them because they now feel so natural.

The Spring Framework 5 overview is shown in Figure 2-1.

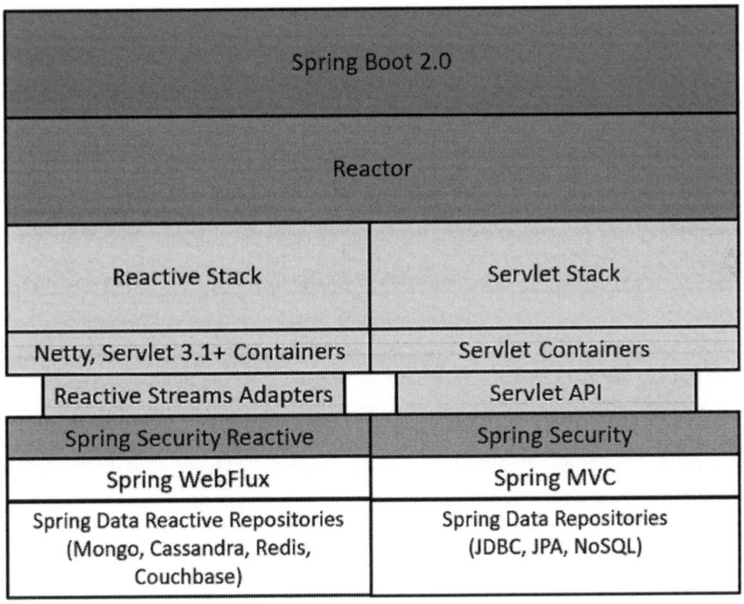

Spring Boot 2.0	
Reactor	
Reactive Stack	Servlet Stack
Netty, Servlet 3.1+ Containers	Servlet Containers
Reactive Streams Adapters	Servlet API
Spring Security Reactive	Spring Security
Spring WebFlux	Spring MVC
Spring Data Reactive Repositories (Mongo, Cassandra, Redis, Couchbase)	Spring Data Repositories (JDBC, JPA, NoSQL)

Figure 2-1. *Spring Framework 5*

Spring Framework 5 was published in September of 2017 and it can be considered the first major Spring Framework release since version 4 was released in December of 2013.

Here is listed of the most important new things in Spring Framework 5:

- JDK baseline update, an upgrade to Java JDK 11

- A reactive programming model. The Spring 5 framework is built on a reactive foundation and is fully asynchronous and nonblocking.

- Programming with annotations. Spring 5 is now an annotation-based programming model.

- New functional programming approach (including Kotlin)

- Reactive-style programming with REST endpoints

- HTTP/2 support

- Kotlin and Spring WebFlux support

- Lambdas support for bean registration

- Spring WebMVC support for latest APIs

- Testing improvements, such as conditional and concurrent testing with JUnit 5

- Integration testing with Spring WebFlux

- Core framework revision

- General updates to the Spring core and container

- Package cleansing and deprecation support

There are many things that attract us to Spring, but the main ones are the two major building blocks of the framework: dependency injection and aspect-oriented programming.

Why are these two concepts so important? They are important because they allow you to develop loosely coupled, single-responsibility, DRY (Don't Repeat Yourself) code practically by default. These two concepts, and Spring itself, are covered extensively in other books and online tutorials; however, we'll give you a brief overview here.

Dependency Injection

The basic idea of DI, a type of Inversion of Control (IoC), is simply that instead of having an object instantiate its needed dependencies, the dependencies are somehow given to the object. In a polymorphic way, the objects that are given as dependencies to the target object that depends on them are known to this target object just by an abstraction (like an interface in Java) and not by the exact implementation of the dependency.

The major advantages of the IoC architecture are

- Easier switching between different implementations

- Offering a good modularity of a program

- A great feature for testing programs by isolating components dependencies and allowing them to communicate through contracts

- Dividing the execution of a certain task from its implementation

It's easier to look at this in code than explain it. See Listing 2-1.

Listing 2-1. The Object Itself Instantiates Its Dependencies (No Dependency Injection)

```
public class NonDiObject {

private Helper helper ;

public NonDiObject ( ) {
 helper = new HelperImpl ( ) ;
 }
public void doStuffWithHelp( ) {
 helper.help( ) ;
 }
}
```

In this example, every instance of NonDiObject is responsible for instantiating its own Helper in the constructor. You can see that it instantiates a HelperImpl, creating a tight, unnecessary coupling to this particular Helper implementation. Now look at Listing 2-2.

Listing 2-2. The Object Receives Its Dependencies from Some External Source (with Dependency Injection)

```
public class DiObject {

private Helper helper ;

public DiObject(Helper helper) {
 this.helper = helper;
 }
public void doStuffWithHelp( ) {
 helper.help( ) ;
 }
}
```

In this version, the Helper is passed to the DiObject at construction time. DiObject is not required to instantiate any dependency. It doesn't even need to know how to do that or what particular implementation type the Helper is, or where it comes from. It just needs a helper and uses it for whatever requirement it has.

The advantage of this approach should be clear. The second version is loosely coupled to the Helper, depending only on the Helper interface, allowing the concrete implementation to be decided at runtime and thus giving lots of flexibility to the design.

Spring dependency injection configuration is normally defined in XML files, although later versions have turned more to annotation-based configuration and Java-based configuration.

Aspect-Oriented Programming

AOP is a technique for extracting cross-cutting concerns from the main application code and applying them in a transverse way across the points where they are needed. Typical examples of AOP concerns are transactions, logging, and security.

The main idea is that you decouple the main business logic of your application from special-purpose concerns that are peripheral to this core logic, and then apply this functionality in a transparent, unobtrusive way through your application. By encapsulating this functionality (which is simply general application logic and not core business logic) in its own modules, they can be used by many parts of the application that need them, avoiding the need to duplicate this code all over the place. The entities that encapsulate this cross-cutting logic are referred to as Aspects in AOP terms.

There are many implementations of AOP in Java. The most popular, perhaps, is AspectJ, which requires a special compilation process. Spring supports AspectJ, but it also includes its own AOP implementation, known simply as *Spring AOP*, which is a pure Java implementation that requires no special compilation process.

Spring AOP using proxies is available only at the public-method level and just when it is called from outside the proxied object. This makes sense because calling a method from inside the object won't call the proxy; instead, it calls the real self object directly (basically a call on the this object). This is very important to be aware of when working with Spring, and sometimes it is overlooked by novice Spring developers.

Even when using its own AOP implementation, Spring leverages the AspectJ syntax and concepts for defining Aspects.

Spring AOP is a fairly big subject, but the principle behind the way it works is not difficult to understand. Spring AOP works with the use of dynamically created proxy objects that take care of the AOP concerns around the invocation of your main business objects. You can think of the proxy and Spring AOP in general simply as a Decorator Pattern implementation, where your business object is the component and the AOP proxy is the decorator. Figure 2-2 shows a simple graphical representation of the concept. Thinking about it this way, you should be able to understand Spring AOP easily. Listing 2-3 shows how the magic happens conceptually.

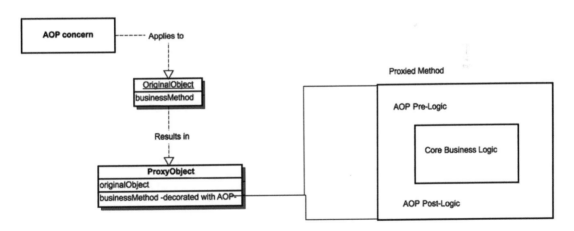

Figure 2-2. Spring AOP in action

Listing 2-3. The Business Object, not Transactional

```
public class Business Object implements BusinessThing {

public void doBusinessThing( ) {
/ / Some business stuff
 }
}
```

Suppose you have an aspect for transactions. Spring creates dynamically at runtime an object that conceptually looks like Listing 2-4.

Listing 2-4. Spring AOP Magic

```
public class BusinessObjectTransactionalDecorator implements BusinessThing {

private BusinessThing componen t ;

public BusinessObjectTransactionalDecorator(BusinessThing component ) {
 t h i s . co mponent = component ;
 }
public void doBusinessThing( ) {
/ / some start transaction code
  component.doBusinessThing( ) ;
/ / some commit transaction code
 }
}
```

Again, remember this simple idea and Spring AOP should be easier to understand.

What's New in Spring Security 5?

The previous version of this book utilizes Spring Security 3. Therefore, it is very important see the most important changes from version 3 to 5. They are the following:

- Pivotal supports Spring Security since v5 because SpringSource does not exist anymore.

- javax.servlet-api is used with v5 is 4.0.1.

- By default now, the ContextPath is /. Use /app_name if you need to define a specific contextPath or use the via properties; for instance, `server.servlet.contextPath=/springbootapp`.

- Spring Security Filter Chain (CSRF): Since after v3 the CSRF token filter is added to the filter chain and turned on by default.

- `j_username`/`j_password` parameters: Starting with v4, we no longer receive the `username` value in the authentication request. Plus, they were updated to `username` and `password`, removing the `j_` prefix.

- CSRF protection was added in v5.

- Password encoding is mandatory in v5.

- `web.xml` files are no longer needed starting with Servlet 3.0.

- Easier Spring Security configurations using Java Configuration.

- Possibility to use a combination with setting the debug level to DEBUG in the Log4J2 configuration file.

If you need to migrate from v3 to v5, we recommend to the following links showing how to migrate:

- `https://docs.spring.io/spring-security/site/migrate/current/3-to-4/html5/migrate-3-to-4-xml.html`

- `https://github.com/spring-projects/spring-framework/wiki/Upgrading-to-Spring-Framework-5.x`

Here are some of the most important new functionalities included in the Spring Security 5.1.4.RELEASE:

- Support for JDK 11

- Automatic password storage upgrades through UserDetailsPasswordService

- Support for OAuth 2.0 Client (for Servlet and WebFlux)

- HTTP Firewall protection introduced

- Support for LDAP Authentication which can now be configured with custom environment variables

- Support for X.509 Authentication for deriving the principal as a strategy

- Support for Graal native image constraints

- Upgraded to Reactor Core 3.2, Reactor Netty 0.8, ASM 7.0, and CGLIB 3.2.8

- Support for Spring's JCL bridge logging

- Support for NIO.2 Path in FileSystemResource

- Improved Core type and annotation resolution performance

- Controller parameter annotations get detected on interfaces as well

- Added Servlet requests parameters with HTTP PUT, PATCH, and DELETE

- Added correlated log messages for HTTP requests and WebSocket sessions and control over DEBUG logging

- More consistently detected method annotations

- Support for HTTP/2 server when running with Reactor Netty 0.8

- Improved DEBUG and TRACE logging

- Support of Hamcrest and XML assertions in WebTestClient

- Support for MockServerWebExchange to be configured with fixed WebSession

- Improved, human-friendly, compact DEBUG and TRACE logging

- Added control over DEBUG logging of potentially sensitive data

- Updated web locale representation (e.g. Language tag, timezone cookies, etc.)

- Added specific MVC exceptions for missing header, cookie, and path variables

- Added base path for sets of annotated controllers (externally configured)

- Centralized handling of "forwarded" type headers

- Support for logical and/or expressions in @Profile conditions

- Support for serving Brotli

- Empty collection/map/array injection in single constructor scenarios

- Support for Hibernate ORM 5.3

- Consistent non-exposure of null beans in the BeanFactory API

- Refined Kotlin beans DSL

- Programmatic ObjectProvider retrieval through the BeanFactory API

- ObjectProvider iterable/stream access for beans-of-type resolution

- Support for reactive clients in @MessageMapping methods

- Support for preserve publication order of messages by STOMP broker

- Supported @SendTo and @SendToUser to be used on the controller method

Spring Security 5 fundamentals include

- Authentication: Confirms truth of credentials

- Authorization: Defines access policy for principal

- AuthenticationManager: Controller in the authentication process

- AuthenticationProvider: Interface that maps to a data store which stores your user data

- Authentication Object: Object that is created upon authentication to hold the login credentials

- GrantedAuthority: Application permission granted to a principal

- Principal: User that performs the action

- SecurityContext: Holds the authentication and other security information

- SecurityContextHolder: Provides access to SecurityContext

- UserDetails: Data object that contains the user credentials, but also the roles of the user

- UserDetailsService: Collects the user credentials and authorities (roles), and builds an UserDetails object

Here are some of the most important technologies Spring Security v5 supports integration with:

- HTTP

- LDAP

- OpenID

- JAAS API

- CAS

Note   The current Spring Security 5.1.4.RELEASE can be downloaded at `https://github.com/spring-projects/spring-security/releases/tag/5.1.4.RELEASE`.

As previously seen, authentication and authorization are some of the fundamental functionalities in Spring Security 5.1. They are very important functionalities because they allow the Spring Security application to identify and authorize user as well as prevent unauthorized access and control the user authorization to access application resources.

In this book, we will present some examples about how to develop application to authorize and authenticate users.

The Spring Security authentication/authorization flow is shown in Figure 2-3.

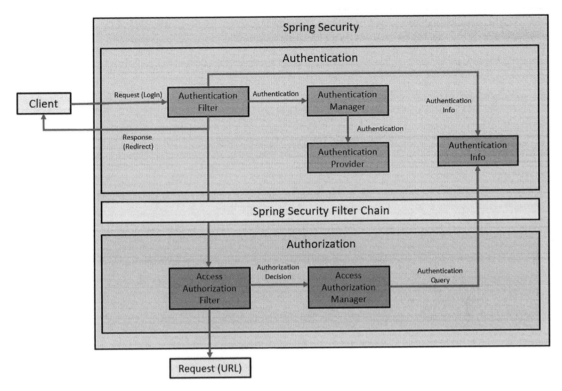

Figure 2-3. *Spring Security authentication/authorization functionalities flow*

Spring Security is utilized via some specific modules as JAR files. The `spring-security-core.jar` file contains the core:

- Authentication and access-control classes and interfaces

- Remoting support and basic provisioning APIs

Here are listed the JAR files required by any application where you will use Spring Security and supports:

- Standalone applications

- Remote clients

- Method (service layer) security

- JDBC user provisioning

The Spring Security v5 project's most important modules (JAR files) include

- Core - `spring-security-core.jar`:
    - `org.springframework.security.core`
    - `org.springframework.security.access`
    - `org.springframework.security.authentication`
    - `org.springframework.security.provisioning`
- Remoting - `spring-security-remoting.jar`
- Web - `spring-security-web.jar`
- Config - `spring-security-config.jar`
- LDAP - `spring-security-ldap.jar`
- OAuth 2.0 Core - `spring-security-oauth2-core.jar`
- ACL - `spring-security-acl.jar`
- CAS - `spring-security-cas.jar`
- OpenID - `spring-security-openid.jar`
- Test - `spring-security-test.jar`

Please notice that both Spring Security XML and Java annotations can be used when developing Spring Security applications.

In this book, both XML and Java annotations will be utilized for our examples.

Summary

Right now, you should have a good idea of what Spring Security is and what it is useful for. You also learned what's new in the Spring Security version 5. Along the way, we introduced some of the major architectural and design principles behind it and how they are layered on top of the great Spring Framework v5. We introduced dependency injection and AOP. In the next chapter, we will set up the development scene and you will build your first Spring Security–powered web application.

CHAPTER 3

Setting Up the Scene

This chapter will guide you through the process of building your first simple Spring Security v5 project using the IntelliJ IDEA Ultimate Edition 2019.2. This involves the following steps:

1. Setting up the development environment

2. Creating a new Java Web Application project without Spring Security

3. Updating the project with Spring Security

4. Running the example

Let's start with setting up the development environment.

Setting Up the Development Environment

Here's the list of software you'll need to download and install in the given order:

- Java SE Development Kit (JDK) 11

- Maven 3.6.1

- IntelliJ IDEA Ultimate Edition 2019.2

- Apache Tomcat Server v9 (External)

Let's go through the steps required to set up everything properly.

Your first step is to set up the Java SE Development Kit.

On most operating systems, the JDK comes in an installer or package, so there shouldn't be any problems.

© Carlo Scarioni and Massimo Nardone 2019
C. Scarioni and M. Nardone, *Pro Spring Security*, https://doi.org/10.1007/978-1-4842-5052-5_3

Note   Remember that the Java SE Development Kit and Java SE Runtime Environment (JRE) require at minimum a Pentium 2 266 MHz processor, 128MB of memory, and 181MB disk for development tools for 64-bit platforms.

Download the JDK version specific to your Windows operating system from the following link:

www.oracle.com/technetwork/java/javase/downloads/jdk11-downloads-5066655.html.

We will use the JDK version 11 in this book. Once you have installed the JDK on your Windows 10 machine, remember to set a JAVA_HOME system variable by following these steps:

1. Open the Windows Environment Variables.

2. Add the JAVA_HOME variable and point it to the JDK installed folder (in my case, C:\Program Files\Java\jdk-11.0.2).

3. Append %JAVA_HOME%\bin to the system PATH variable so that all of the Java commands will be accessible from everywhere.

The result is shown in Figure 3-1.

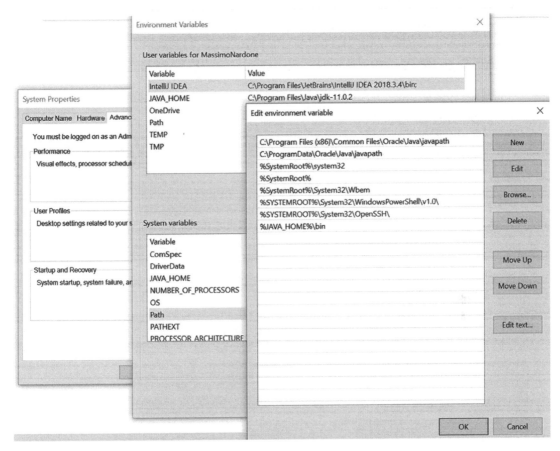

Figure 3-1. *Setting up the JAVA_HOME system variable*

Let's test if the JDK installation was successful. Open a command prompt and type the code shown in Figure 3-2.

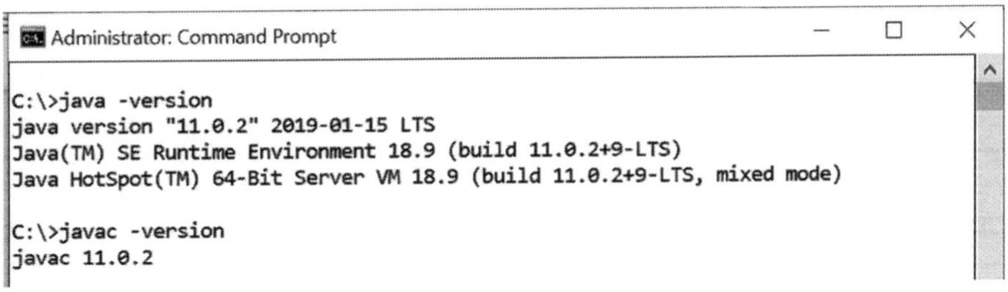

```
Administrator: Command Prompt                    —    □    ×

C:\>java -version
java version "11.0.2" 2019-01-15 LTS
Java(TM) SE Runtime Environment 18.9 (build 11.0.2+9-LTS)
Java HotSpot(TM) 64-Bit Server VM 18.9 (build 11.0.2+9-LTS, mixed mode)

C:\>javac -version
javac 11.0.2
```

Figure 3-2. *Testing the JAVA installation*

Great! Java is now installed and ready to be used for the examples in the book.

Let's now install the IntelliJ IDEA Ultimate Edition 2019.2 for web and enterprise development by following these steps:

1. Download the `.exe` file from `www.jetbrains.com/idea/download /#section=windows`.

2. Install the `.exe` file, which in our case is named `ideaIU-2019.2.exe`.

Once installed, the directory should look like Figure 3-3.

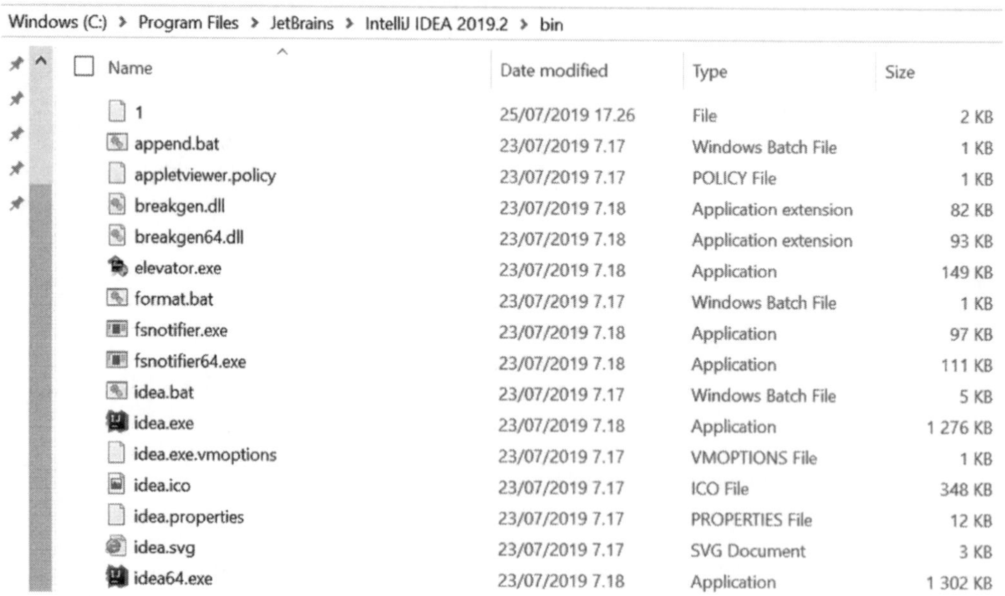

Windows (C:) ⟩ Program Files ⟩ JetBrains ⟩ IntelliJ IDEA 2019.2 ⟩ bin

Name	Date modified	Type	Size
1	25/07/2019 17.26	File	2 KB
append.bat	23/07/2019 7.17	Windows Batch File	1 KB
appletviewer.policy	23/07/2019 7.17	POLICY File	1 KB
breakgen.dll	23/07/2019 7.18	Application extension	82 KB
breakgen64.dll	23/07/2019 7.18	Application extension	93 KB
elevator.exe	23/07/2019 7.18	Application	149 KB
format.bat	23/07/2019 7.17	Windows Batch File	1 KB
fsnotifier.exe	23/07/2019 7.18	Application	97 KB
fsnotifier64.exe	23/07/2019 7.18	Application	111 KB
idea.bat	23/07/2019 7.17	Windows Batch File	5 KB
idea.exe	23/07/2019 7.18	Application	1 276 KB
idea.exe.vmoptions	23/07/2019 7.17	VMOPTIONS File	1 KB
idea.ico	23/07/2019 7.17	ICO File	348 KB
idea.properties	23/07/2019 7.17	PROPERTIES File	12 KB
idea.svg	23/07/2019 7.17	SVG Document	3 KB
idea64.exe	23/07/2019 7.18	Application	1 302 KB

Figure 3-3.   *The IntelliJ IDEA 2019.2 directory*

Now IntelliJ IDEA Ultimate Edition 2019.2 for web and enterprise development tool is ready to be used. Figure 3-4 shows how the dashboard looks when executing it.

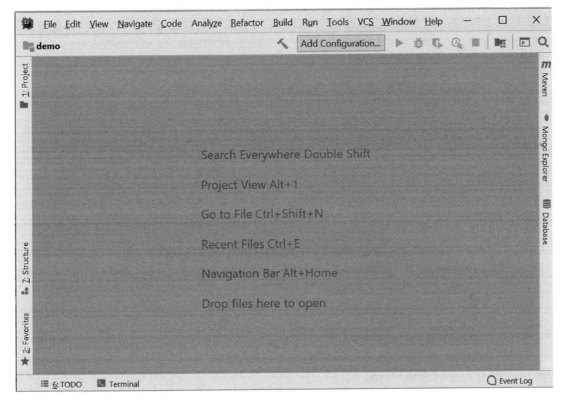

Figure 3-4. *The IntelliJ IDEA Ultimate Edition 2019.2 for web and enterprise development dashboard*

The next step is to install Maven 3.6.1 by downloading the `.zip` file named `apache-maven-3.6.1-bin.zip` at this web page: `https://maven.apache.org/download.cgi`.

Now run the IntelliJ IDEA 2019.2 tool and configure Maven 3.6.1 as shown in Figure 3-5.

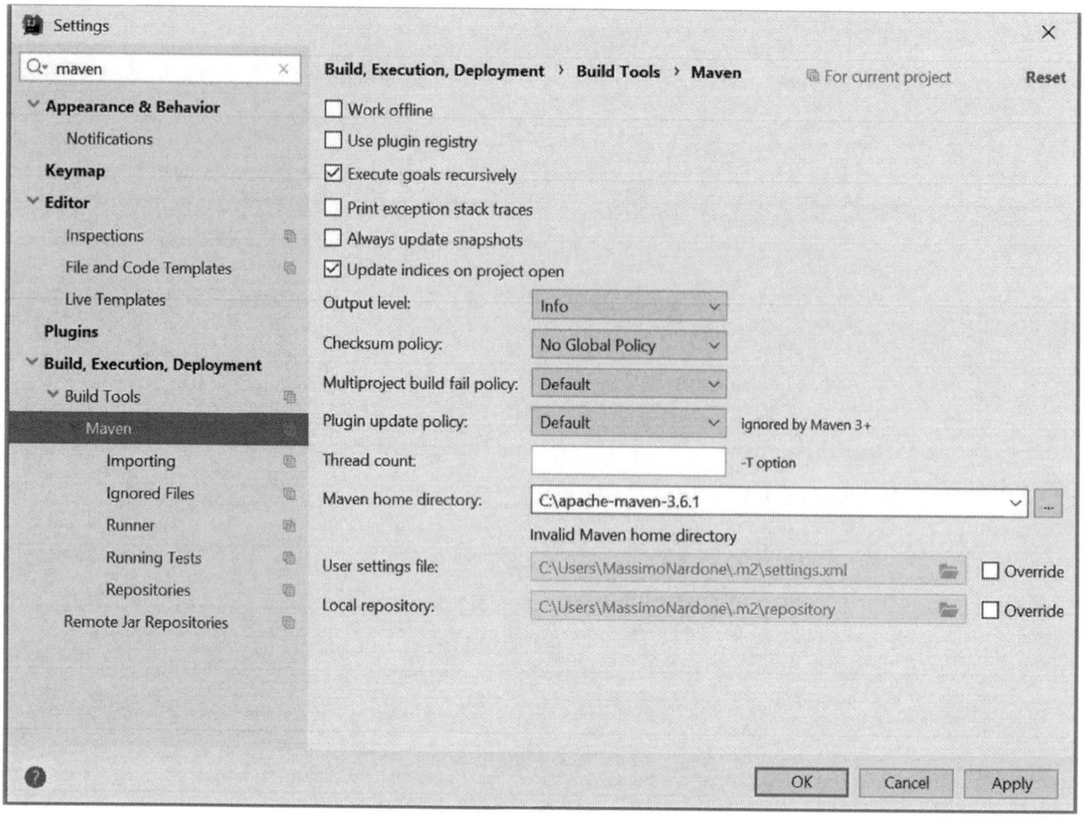

Figure 3-5. *Local Maven 3.6.1 is configured into IntelliJ IDEA 2019.2*

Now Maven 3.6.1 is ready to be used.

The last tool used in this book is the Apache Tomcat Server and plugin v9. The first step is to download and install the Apache Tomcat Server v9 .zip file named apache-tomcat-9.0.16.zip at https://tomcat.apache.org/download-90.cgi.

Unzip the file in a certain directory onto your Windows machine, like C:\Program Files\Apache Software Foundation\apache-tomcat-9.0.22.

Since you need to allow Spring projects to deploy to Tomcat Servers, you need to define Tomcat users to access to Tomcat Manager. Let's open and update the file tomcat-users.xml in the conf directory and add the following XML fragment inside the <tomcat-users> element:

```
<role rolename="manager-gui"/>
<role rolename="manager-script"/>
<user username="tomcat" password="tomcat" roles="manager-gui, manager-script"/>
```

Make sure you add the Tomcat Server to IntelliJ.

Now Apache Tomcat Server and plugin v9 are ready to be used.

Before starting a new spring project, you want to make sure the right JDK package is installed into IntelliJ IDEA 2019.2 IDE tool to compile your examples and avoid the typical compiling issue where the JRE is found instead of JDK. The configuration is shown in Figure 3-6.

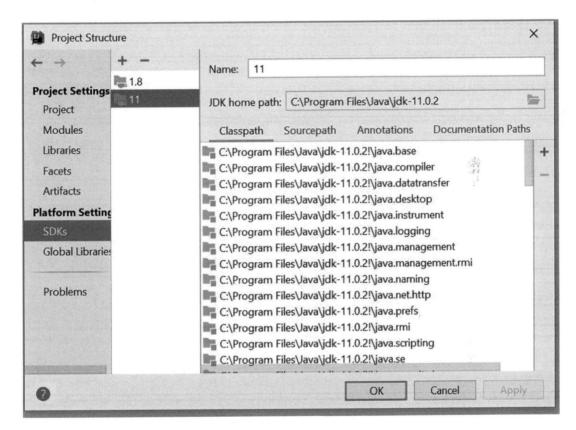

Figure 3-6. *Configuring the JDK to compile your examples*

So now the JDK compiler is set and you are ready to start writing and running your first Spring Web application example.

Creating a New Java Web Application Project

With your development tools set up, you can now create your first Java Web Application project using IntelliJ IDEA 2019.2. The built-in wizard makes creating a new Maven project very easy.

So, let's create your first Java Web application named Pss01, without security, which will just produce the following text: Hello Spring Security!

Here are the steps you will follow to build the simple Maven Web Application project:

1. Create a Java Web Application v4.

2. Create and update the needed .jsp file.

3. Run the Java Web Application using the external Tomcat Server v9.

As first step, launch the IntelliJ IDEA tool and select File ➤ New ➤ Project ➤ Java ➤ Web Application and fill all information about the project, as shown in Figure 3-7.

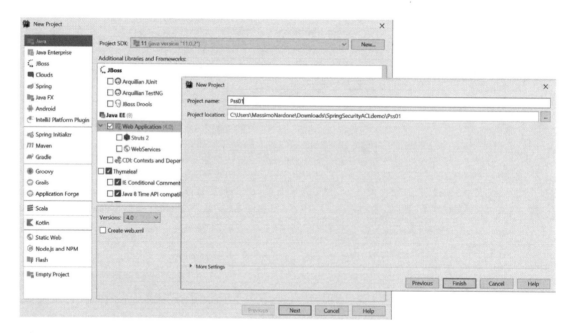

Figure 3-7. *Your first Java Web Application project*

In the Package Explorer, you should now see your Pss01 project. If you expand it and all its children, you'll see something like Figure 3-8.

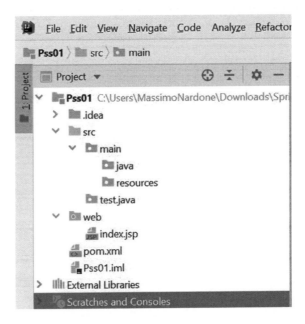

Figure 3-8. *Your first Java Web Application project structure*

In general, the structure of most Java Web Application projects will contain

- The target directory: Used to house all output of the build

- The src directory: Contains all of the source material for building the project, its site, etc.

- src/main/java: Application/library sources

- src/main/resources: Application/library resources

- web: Web application sources

- Pom.xml: File description of the project

Your next step is to update the Java Web Application project's files needed for your first simple application. Please note that for this simple Java Web Application example, you will not need to add any specific dependency to the project file pom.xml, which looks initially like Listing 3-1.

Listing 3-1. The pom.xml File with Servlet Dependencies

```xml
<?xml version="1.0" encoding="UTF-8"?>
<project xmlns="http://maven.apache.org/POM/4.0.0"
         xmlns:xsi="http://www.w3.org/2001/XMLSchema-instance"
         xsi:schemaLocation="http://maven.apache.org/POM/4.0.0
         http://maven.apache.org/xsd/maven-4.0.0.xsd">
    <modelVersion>4.0.0</modelVersion>
    <groupId>com.apress.pss</groupId>
    <artifactId>Pss01</artifactId>
    <version>1.0-SNAPSHOT</version>
</project>
```

The project right now only contains one simple `.jsp` file named `index.jsp`, which you will update to show the text you wish, as shown in Listing 3-2.

Listing 3-2. The index.jsp File

```jsp
<%@ page contentType="text/html;charset=UTF-8" language="java" %>
<html>
  <head>
    <title>$Title$</title>
  </head>
  <body>
    <h2>Hello Spring Security!</h2>
  </body>
</html>
```

Next, click the Add Configuration button, located at the top-right of the IntelliJ tool, to configure how to run your first example.

You can run your project using the external Tomcat Server v9, as shown in Figure 3-9.

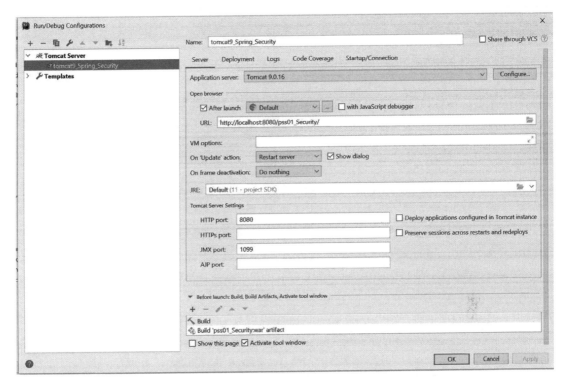

Figure 3-9. *Configure the running steps of your first Maven project*

Now you can open you web browser and type the web address `http://localhost:8080`, as shown in Figure 3-10.

Hello Spring Security!

Figure 3-10. *The Java Web Application project running in a web browser*

Your first Java Web Application project is now ready to be transformed into a Spring Security project.

Creating a New Spring Security v5 Project

Spring Security builds upon the concepts defined in the previous section and integrates nicely into the general Spring ecosystem. You need to understand those concepts well to take maximum advantage of Spring Security v5. However, you can start using Spring Security without really knowing all these details, and then learn them as you progress and look to do more advanced things.

There are two ways to create a new Spring project.

You can either create a Spring project via Spring Boot or via any IDE tool, which in this case is IntelliJ IDEA 2019.2.

So what is Spring Boot? Spring Boot can be used to easily generate standalone, production-grade, Spring-based applications.

To bootstrap your Spring application, you can utilize the Spring Initializr. The Spring Initializr is a browser-based web application and a REST API that will generate a ready skeleton Spring project structure for your Spring application.

To generate a Spring application via Spring Boot, go to the following web page and fill in all the required info: `https://spring.io/projects/spring-boot`.

Please notice that in this book all the Spring code is developed using the IntelliJ IDEA Ultimate Edition 2019.2 tool.

What kind of Spring Security Maven Web Application do you want to create?

Let's create a simple Spring Security example where if the user requests a welcome page, they will not need to authenticate when accessing the Admin page, which would require the admin security credentials via username and password.

If you are using the standalone installation of Spring Security reference release and you decide not to use any IDE tool to build your Maven project, you will find many folders inside the installation directory. Most of the folders in the directory correspond to individual subprojects or modules that split the functionality of Spring Security into more discrete and specialized units.

Spring Security v5 Source

Open source software has an invaluable characteristic for software developers: free access to all source code. With this, we can understand how our favorite tools and frameworks work internally, and we also can learn a lot about the way other (perhaps very good) developers work, including what practices, techniques, and patterns they use. Free access to source code also enables us, in general, to gather ideas and experience for our own development. As a more practical matter, having access to the source code allows us to debug these applications in the context of our application; we can find bugs or simply follow our application's execution through them.

Currently, Spring Security and most Spring projects live in GitHub. You probably know about GitHub (`https://github.com/`). If you don't, you should definitely take a look at it because it has become a standard public source-code repository for many open source projects in a multitude of programming languages.

GitHub is a repository and a hosting service for Git repositories, with a very friendly management interface. The Spring Security project can be found inside the SpringSource general GitHub section at `https://github.com/SpringSource/spring-security`. To get the code, just download and install it as shown previously in this chapter.

If you need to install the Spring Security 5.1.5.RELEASE locally, once unzipped it will include several modules and folders, as shown in Figure 3-11.

.github	02/03/2019 10.40	File folder
acl	02/03/2019 10.40	File folder
aspects	02/03/2019 10.40	File folder
bom	02/03/2019 10.40	File folder
buildSrc	02/03/2019 10.40	File folder
cas	02/03/2019 10.40	File folder
config	02/03/2019 10.40	File folder
core	02/03/2019 10.38	File folder
crypto	02/03/2019 10.38	File folder
data	02/03/2019 10.38	File folder
docs	02/03/2019 10.38	File folder
etc	02/03/2019 10.38	File folder
gradle	02/03/2019 10.38	File folder
itest	02/03/2019 10.38	File folder
ldap	02/03/2019 10.38	File folder
messaging	02/03/2019 10.39	File folder
oauth2	02/03/2019 10.39	File folder
openid	02/03/2019 10.39	File folder
remoting	02/03/2019 10.39	File folder
samples	02/03/2019 10.39	File folder
scripts	02/03/2019 10.39	File folder
taglibs	02/03/2019 10.39	File folder
test	02/03/2019 10.39	File folder
web	02/03/2019 10.40	File folder

Figure 3-11. *The Spring Security v5.1.5.RELEASE folder structure*

Here is a short description of some of the most important modules included in Spring Security v5.1.5.RELEASE:

- Core (spring-security-core): Spring Security's core classes and interfaces on authentication and access control reside here.

- Remoting (spring-security-remoting): In case you need Spring Remoting, this is the module with the necessary classes.

- Aspect (spring-security-aspects): Aspect-oriented programming support within Spring Security.

- Config (spring-security-config): Provides XML and Java configuration support.

- Crypto (spring-security-crypto): Contains cryptography support.

- Data (spring-security-data): Integration with Spring Data.

- Messaging (spring-security-messaging)

- OAuth2: Support for OAuth 2.x support within Spring Security:

  - Core (spring-security-oauth2-core)

  - Client (spring-security-oauth2-client)

  - JOSE (spring-security-oauth2-jose)

- OpenID (spring-security-openid): OpenID web-authentication support.

- CAS (spring-security-cas): CAS (Central Authentication Service) client integration.

- TagLib (spring-security-taglibs): Various tag libraries regarding Spring Security.

- Test (spring-security-test): Testing support.

- Web (spring-security-web): Contains web security infrastructure code, such as various filters and other Servlet API dependencies.

Note   Remember that you are using the IntelliJ IDEA tool where the Spring Security 5.1.5.RELEASE is integrated and configured in it. The usage of Spring Security is done via an XML link at the beginning of the pom.xml file.

Let's build your Spring Security 5 Java Web Application.

Here are the steps you will follow to build the simple Spring Security Maven Web Application project:

- Clone the previous simple Maven project named Pss01.

- Import the required Spring Framework and Spring Security v5 libraries into the project (into the pom.xml file).

- Configure the project to be aware of Spring Security.

- Configure the users and roles that will be part of the system.

- Configure the URLs that you want to secure.

- Create all needed Java and web files.

- Run the Spring Security v5 project using the external Tomcat Server v9.

As a first step, you will clone this project and call it pss01_Security, so you will find both samples when downloading the code.

Once you clone the project from Pss01 to pss01_Security, you add the Maven framework support to the project. All the files and the pss01_Security project structure are shown in Figure 3-12.

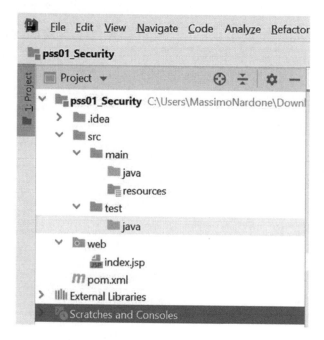

Figure 3-12. *New Maven project to add Spring Security*

Note   It is possible to implement the Spring Security in a Spring application using XML- or Java-based configurations. In this chapter, you will use the Java configuration for your Spring Security Web Application since in general it is hardly suggested to use XML configuration as minimum as possible.

Spring Security Taglibs

The Spring Security Taglibs provides the support for accessing security information and applying security constraints in JSPs pages.

To secure the view layer of the application, you can use

- Authorize Tag

- Authentication Tag

- Accesscontrollist Tag

- Csrfinput Tag

- CsrfMetaTags Tag

You will need to add the spring-security-taglibs dependency to your `pom.xml`:

```
<dependency>
    <groupId>org.springframework.security</groupId>
    <artifactId>spring-security-taglibs</artifactId>
    <version>5.1.5.RELEASE</version>
</dependency>
```

Introducing Cross-Site Request Forgery

With a cross-site request forgery (CSRF) attack a hacker can modify the state of any HTTP method (GET or POST), redirecting the client, for instance, by clicking a modified link to a not-secure web page with the result of stealing a user's sensitive info.

Let's have a look to what CSRF is and how to prevent CSRF attacks using Spring Security. Common CSRF attacks include

- HTTP GET Request: Convincing the victim to click a fake GET link to get sensitive information (e.g. username/password, etc.)

- HTTP POST request: Same as GET but using the POST method

In general, to use the Spring Security CSRF protection, we must ensure the right HTTP methods like (PATCH, POST, PUT, DELETE, etc.) can modify state.

In Spring Security v5, CSRF protection is enabled by default in the Java configuration. If you must disable it, you can add the following: `.csrf().disable().`

If you need to enable the CSRF protection on the server side, you need to include the CSRF token in your requests on the client side by adding this line:

```
<input type="hidden" name="${_csrf.parameterName}" value="${_csrf.token}"/>.
```

Adding Spring Security v5 (and Spring Core Itself) to the Project

In this section, you'll start your journey into the inner workings of the framework and see its main building blocks and how it works. The information will be mostly introductory. We'll conduct a full, in-depth review of the framework in the next chapter. We could just tell you what to add to the project to make the application work, but we think it's better to tell you first what the different components of the framework are so that you can start coding with a better knowledge of how the framework is built. This means that we will tell you how to grab the source code of the project and build it, and then explain in a general way the different modules that make up the framework.

Your next step is to add the Spring Security 5.1.4.RELEASE version, shown in Listing 3-3, in your Maven Web Application by adding to the pom.xml file the following JAR dependencies configuration:

- spring-security-web

- spring-security-config

- spring-security-taglibs

Listing 3-3. Spring Security Maven Dependencies

```
<dependency>
   <groupId>org.springframework.security</groupId>
   <artifactId>spring-security-web</artifactId>
   <version>5.1.5.RELEASE</version>
</dependency>
<dependency>
   <groupId>org.springframework.security</groupId>
   <artifactId>spring-security-config</artifactId>
   <version>5.1.5.RELEASE</version>
</dependency>
<dependency>
   <groupId>org.springframework.security</groupId>
   <artifactId>spring-security-taglibs</artifactId>
   <version>5.1.5.RELEASE</version>
</dependency>
```

The entire updated pom.xml file is shown in Listing 3-4.

Listing 3-4. Adding Spring Security Configuration to the pom.xml File

```xml
<?xml version="1.0" encoding="UTF-8"?>
<project xmlns="http://maven.apache.org/POM/4.0.0"
        xmlns:xsi="http://www.w3.org/2001/XMLSchema-instance"
        xsi:schemaLocation="http://maven.apache.org/POM/4.0.0
        http://maven.apache.org/xsd/maven-4.0.0.xsd">
    <modelVersion>4.0.0</modelVersion>

    <groupId>groupId</groupId>
    <artifactId>pss01_Security</artifactId>
    <version>1.0-SNAPSHOT</version>

    <!-- Spring versions -->
    <properties>
<springframework.version>5.1.5.RELEASE</springframework.version>
<springsecurity.version>5.1.5.RELEASE</springsecurity.version>
    </properties>

    <dependencies>
        <!-- Spring -->
        <dependency>
            <groupId>org.springframework</groupId>
            <artifactId>spring-core</artifactId>
            <version>${springframework.version}</version>
        </dependency>
        <dependency>
            <groupId>org.springframework</groupId>
            <artifactId>spring-web</artifactId>
            <version>${springframework.version}</version>
        </dependency>
        <dependency>
            <groupId>org.springframework</groupId>
            <artifactId>spring-webmvc</artifactId>
            <version>${springframework.version}</version>
        </dependency>
```

```
    <!-- Spring Security -->
    <dependency>
        <groupId>org.springframework.security</groupId>
        <artifactId>spring-security-web</artifactId>
        <version>${springsecurity.version}</version>
    </dependency>
    <dependency>
        <groupId>org.springframework.security</groupId>
        <artifactId>spring-security-config</artifactId>
        <version>${springsecurity.version}</version>
    </dependency>

    <!-- Servlet -->
    <dependency>
        <groupId>javax.servlet</groupId>
        <artifactId>javax.servlet-api</artifactId>
        <version>4.0.1</version>
        <scope>provided</scope>          </dependency>
    <dependency>
        <groupId>javax.servlet.jsp</groupId>
        <artifactId>javax.servlet.jsp-api</artifactId>
        <version>2.3.3</version>
        <scope>provided</scope>
    </dependency>
    <dependency>
        <groupId>javax.servlet</groupId>
        <artifactId>jstl</artifactId>
        <version>1.2</version>
    </dependency>
    <dependency>
        <groupId>taglibs</groupId>
        <artifactId>standard</artifactId>
        <version>1.1.2</version>
    </dependency>
</dependencies>
```

```
<!-- Build -->

<build>
    <sourceDirectory>src</sourceDirectory>
    <plugins>
        <!-- Added for JAVA 11 Support START-->
        <plugin>
            <groupId>org.apache.maven.plugins</groupId>
            <artifactId>maven-compiler-plugin</artifactId>
            <version>3.8.1</version>
            <configuration>
                <release>11</release>
            </configuration>
        </plugin>
    </plugins>
    <finalName>pss01_Security</finalName>
</build>
</project>
```

Please notice that spring-webmvc is the only dependency needed since spring-core and spring-web are transitive dependencies.

The pom.xml file contains the following:

- The dependencies needed for the project, such as Spring, Spring Security, Servlet API, and TagLibs.

- The <build> element containing the plugins used, such as

  - The maven-compiler-plugin, to specify the Java version that will be used in the project

  - The Servlet information

  - The TagLibs

  - The maven-war-plugin needed to build the project into a WAR file, which will be deployed to Tomcat in this case

---

Note   Remember that no Spring Boot dependencies were used in this example.

Configuring the Web Project to Be Aware of Spring Security v5

To activate Spring Security in your Maven Web Application, you need to configure a particular Servlet filter that will take care of preprocessing and postprocessing the requests, as well as managing the required security constraints.

Let's start building your Spring Security Maven Web Application.

As a first step, please make sure that all the tools and directories are created as described previously.

Then update the pom.xml file as shown in Listing 3-4.

Next, create the needed .jsp files under a new project directory called WebContent/ WEB-INF/pages/.

Your project will utilize two .jsp pages:

- welcome.jsp, which is the starting welcome web page of the project

- authenticated.jsp, which is the admin web page to access when the user successfully logs in

The welcome.jsp page is shown in Listing 3-5.

Listing 3-5. welcome.jsp

```
<%@ page language="java" contentType="text/html; charset=ISO-8859-1"
pageEncoding="ISO-8859-1"%>
<%@ taglib prefix="c" uri="http://java.sun.com/jsp/jstl/core"%>
<html>
<head>
    <meta http-equiv="Content-Type" content="text/html; charset=ISO-8859-1">
    <title>Spring Security authentication example.</title>
</head>
<body>
<h2>Welcome to Spring Security authentication example!</h2><br>
<a href="<c:url value="/authenticated" />">Login</a><br>
</body>
</html>
```

The welcome.jsp page will only display a welcoming message and provide the link to the authenticated page, /authenticated.

Let's now create the authenticated.jsp page; see Listing 3-6.

Listing 3-6. authenticated.jsp

```
<%@ page language="java" contentType="text/html; charset=ISO-8859-1"
pageEncoding="ISO-8859-1"%>
<%@ taglib prefix="sec" uri="http://www.springframework.org/security/tags" %>
<%@ taglib prefix="c" uri="http://java.sun.com/jsp/jstl/core"%>
<html>
<head>
    <meta http-equiv="Content-Type" content="text/html; charset=ISO-8859-1">
    <title>Spring Security authentication example</title>
</head>
<body>
<h2>Welcome to Spring Security authentication example!</h2>
Your username is: <strong>${user}</strong><br>
<sec:authorize access="hasRole('ADMIN')">
    You provided Admin authentication credentials!
</sec:authorize>
<br>
<sec:authorize access="hasRole('USER')">
    You provided User authentication credentials!
</sec:authorize>
<br><br>

<a href="<c:url value="/logout" />">Logout</a>
</body>
</html>
```

If the login is successful, the user will access the authenticated.jsp page, which we will explain later.

Next, you need to define the Java classes needed for your example.

Under controller:

- UserController

Under package configuration:

- `AppInitializer`

- `SecurityConfiguration`

- `SpringSecurityInitializer`

- `UserConfiguration`

Let's create the two Java packages where your Java classes will be located:

- `com.apress.pss.springsecurity.controller`

- `com.apress.pss.springsecurity.configuration`

Let's create the `UserController` Java class under the package `com.apress.pss.springsecurity.controller`, as shown in Listing 3-7.

Listing 3-7. UserController Java Class

```
package com.apress.pss.springsecurity.controller;
import javax.servlet.http.HttpServletRequest;
import javax.servlet.http.HttpServletResponse;
import org.springframework.security.core.Authentication;
import org.springframework.security.core.context.SecurityContextHolder;
import org.springframework.security.core.userdetails.UserDetails;
import org.springframework.security.web.authentication.logout.
SecurityContextLogoutHandler;
import org.springframework.stereotype.Controller;
import org.springframework.ui.ModelMap;
import org.springframework.web.bind.annotation.GetMapping;

@Controller
public class UserController {

    @GetMapping ("/")
    public String homePage(ModelMap model) {
        return "welcome";
    }
```

```
@GetMapping ("/welcome")
public String welcomePage(ModelMap model) {
    return "welcome";
}

@GetMapping ("/authenticated")
public String adminPage(ModelMap model) {
    model.addAttribute("user", getPrincipal());
    return "authenticated";
}

@GetMapping ("/logout")
public String logoutPage (HttpServletRequest request,
HttpServletResponse response) {
    Authentication auth = SecurityContextHolder.getContext().
    getAuthentication();
    if (auth != null){
        new SecurityContextLogoutHandler().logout(request, response,
        auth);
    }
    return "welcome";
}

private String getPrincipal(){
    String userName = null;
    Object principal = SecurityContextHolder.getContext().
    getAuthentication().getPrincipal();

    if (principal instanceof UserDetails) {
        userName = ((UserDetails)principal).getUsername();
    } else {
        userName = principal.toString();
    }
    return userName;
}
}
```

This Java class will basically be used to handle and control the requests of your web pages. So, using @GetMapping, this class will handle the web request such as welcome, authenticated, and logout. Additionally, this class via the function named getPrincipal will extract the name of the user logged in to be shown on the authenticated.jsp page. Notice that @GetMapping replaced @RequestMapping.

The next Java class to create is AppInitializer, which initializes Spring classes, such as AnnotationConfigDispatcherServletInitializer to be used in your applications; see Listing 3-8.

Listing 3-8. appInitializer.java

```
package com.apress.pss.springsecurity.configuration;
import org.springframework.web.servlet.support.
AbstractAnnotationConfigDispatcherServletInitializer;

public class AppInitializer extends
AbstractAnnotationConfigDispatcherServletInitializer {

    @Override
    protected Class<?>[] getRootConfigClasses() {
        return new Class[] { UserConfiguration.class };
    }

    @Override
    protected Class<?>[] getServletConfigClasses() {
        return null;
    }

    @Override
    protected String[] getServletMappings() {
        return new String[] { "/" };
    }

}
```

The next Java class to create is SpringSecurityInitializer, which is an empty Java class that initializes the Spring Security classes, such as the AbstractSecurityWebApplicationInitializer, to be used in your applications; see Listing 3-9.

Listing 3-9. SpringSecurityInitializer.java

```
package com.apress.pss.springsecurity.configuration;
import org.springframework.security.web.context.
AbstractSecurityWebApplicationInitializer;
public class SpringSecurityInitializer extends
AbstractSecurityWebApplicationInitializer {
//code is not needed
}
```

The next Java class to create is UserConfiguration, which defines where the Java classes and .jps pages needed for your application are located. In your case, the web resources to handle are located in /WEB-INF/pages/ as .jsp pages. The UserConfiguration Java class is shown in Listing 3-10.

Listing 3-10. UserConfiguration.java

```
package com.apress.pss.springsecurity.configuration;

import org.springframework.context.annotation.Bean;
import org.springframework.context.annotation.ComponentScan;
import org.springframework.context.annotation.Configuration;
import org.springframework.web.servlet.ViewResolver;
import org.springframework.web.servlet.config.annotation.EnableWebMvc;
import org.springframework.web.servlet.view.InternalResourceViewResolver;
import org.springframework.web.servlet.view.JstlView;

@Configuration
@EnableWebMvc
@ComponentScan(basePackages = "com.apress.pss.springsecurity")
public class UserConfiguration {

    @Bean(name="SpringSecurity")
    public ViewResolver viewResolver() {
        InternalResourceViewResolver viewResolver = new
        InternalResourceViewResolver();
        viewResolver.setViewClass(JstlView.class);
        viewResolver.setPrefix("/WEB-INF/views/");
        viewResolver.setSuffix(".jsp");
```

```
        return viewResolver;
    }

}
```

The last Java class to create is SecurityConfiguration, which defines the security configuration for your Spring Security v5 application; see Listing 3-11.

Listing 3-11. SecurityConfiguration.java

```
package com.apress.pss.springsecurity.configuration;

import org.springframework.beans.factory.annotation.Autowired;
import org.springframework.context.annotation.Bean;
import org.springframework.context.annotation.Configuration;
import org.springframework.security.config.annotation.authentication.
builders.AuthenticationManagerBuilder;
import org.springframework.security.config.annotation.web.builders.
HttpSecurity;
import org.springframework.security.config.annotation.web.configuration.
EnableWebSecurity;
import org.springframework.security.config.annotation.web.configuration.
WebSecurityConfigurerAdapter;
import org.springframework.security.crypto.bcrypt.BCryptPasswordEncoder;
import org.springframework.security.crypto.password.PasswordEncoder;

@Configuration
@EnableWebSecurity
public class SecurityConfiguration extends WebSecurityConfigurerAdapter {

    @Autowired
    PasswordEncoder passwordEncoder;

    @Override
    protected void configure(AuthenticationManagerBuilder auth) throws
    Exception {
        auth.inMemoryAuthentication()
                .passwordEncoder(passwordEncoder)
```

```
.withUser("user").password(passwordEncoder.encode("user123")).roles("USER")
                .and()
.withUser("admin").password(passwordEncoder.encode("admin123")).roles("USER",
"ADMIN");
    }

    @Bean
    public PasswordEncoder passwordEncoder() {
        return new BCryptPasswordEncoder();
    }

    @Override
    protected void configure(HttpSecurity http) throws Exception {

        http.authorizeRequests()
                .antMatchers("/", "/welcome", "/login").permitAll()
.antMatchers("/authenticated/**").hasAnyRole("ADMIN", "USER")
                .and().formLogin()
.and().logout().logoutSuccessUrl("/welcome").permitAll()

.and().csrf().disable();

    }

}
```

Let's analyses this Java class in detail. You define all security configuration needed in SecurityConfiguration and then you define the PasswordEncoder, which returns the BCryptPassword. You then define the page seen by, like welcome.jsp, and then the security role needed to access the authenticated.jsp page, such as admin and user. The logout will redirect to the welcome.jsp page and finally the csrf will be disabled.

The structure of your new Spring Security v5 project should look like Figure 3-13.

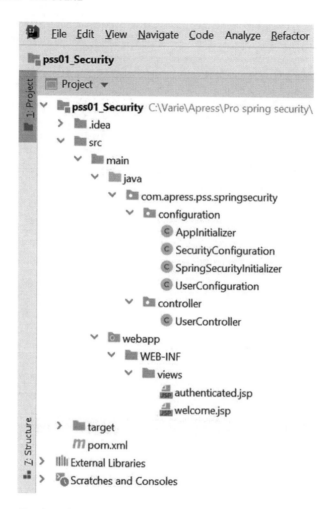

Figure 3-13. *New Spring Security v5 project structure*

Next, build and run the Spring Security v5 project as shown in Figure 3-14.

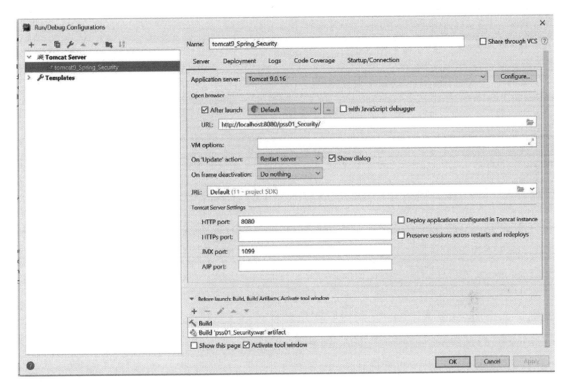

Figure 3-14. *Project running configuration*

You can now build the project, deploy the WAR file, start the application running on the standalone Tomcat Server v9, and deploy the WAR file automatically.

Your application is deployed successfully. Open the web browser and type the following link: `http://localhost:8080/pss01_Security/`. The outcome is shown in Figure 3-15.

Welcome to Spring Security authentication example!

Login

Figure 3-15. *Browsing the new Spring Security project*

You can now access the security `authenticated.jsp` by clicking the Login link. The outcome is shown in Figure 3-16.

Figure 3-16. *Accessing the Spring Security login web page*

Now, if you access with the wrong credentials, you will receive an error message like the one in Figure 3-17.

Figure 3-17. *Accessing with wrong login credentials*

As you can see, Spring Security will directly produce the login error and remind the user that the credentials provided are not correct.

If you next provide the right user or admin credentials, you will receive the content defined in the authenticated.jsp page which, using the taglibs, identifies if an admin or user credential is provided, displays a welcome message, and provides the username using ${user}, who logged in.

If you log in as the correct admin, you will see the result shown in Figure 3-18.

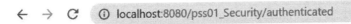

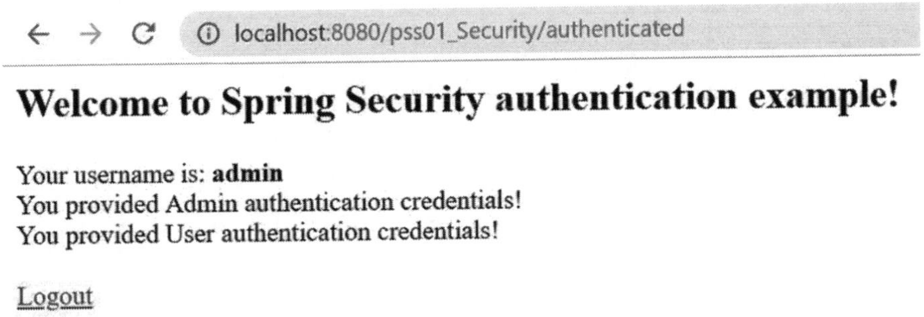

Welcome to Spring Security authentication example!

Your username is: **admin**
You provided Admin authentication credentials!
You provided User authentication credentials!

Logout

Figure 3-18. *Accessing with the right admin credentials*

If you log in as a correct user, you will receive the result shown in Figure 3-19.

Welcome to Spring Security authentication example!

Your username is: **user**

You provided User authentication credentials!

Logout

Figure 3-19. *Accessing with the right user credentials*

Notice that when you log in as a user, the text saying that "You provided User authentication credentials!" is shown, while when you log in as an admin, the text saying, "You provided Admin authentication credentials!" is shown. This was controlled via the Spring Security Taglibs.

The admin login iteration flow is shown in Figure 3-20.

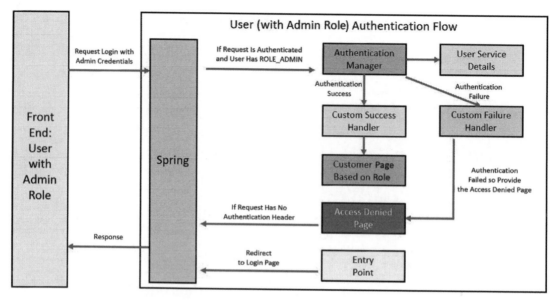

Figure 3-20. *Spring Security user with Admin role authentication request flow*

Great! You have built your first Spring Security web application. We will dive deeply into how all this works internally when we look at the architecture of Spring Security.

Summary

We introduced all the tools needed to create the environment to develop Spring Security Java Web Applications. You learned how to install and configure all the tools needed for these examples and you should have a good idea of what is needed to build a Spring Security v5 project. You learned how to build your first Java Web Application project without Spring Security and then you added the security dependencies to update it as a Spring Security v5 application. In the next chapter, we'll go deep into the architecture and design of the Spring Framework.

CHAPTER 4

Spring Security Architecture and Design

In the previous chapter, you developed an initial application secured with Spring Security. You got an overview of the way this application worked and looked in detail at some of the Spring Security components that are put into action in common Spring Security–secured applications. In this chapter, we are going to extend those explanations and delve deeply into the framework.

We'll look at the main components of the framework, explain the work of the servlet filters for securing web applications, look at how Spring aspect-oriented programming helps you add security in an unobtrusive way, and in general, show how the framework is designed internally.

What Components Make Up Spring Security?

In this section, we'll take a look at the major components that make Spring Security work. We'll offer a big-picture overview of the framework and then delve deeper into each major component.

The 10,000-Foot View

Spring Security is a relatively flexible framework that aims to make it easy for the developer to implement security in an application. At the most general level, it's a framework composed of intercepting rules for granting, or not granting, access to resources. Figure 4-1 illustrates this.

© Carlo Scarioni and Massimo Nardone 2019
C. Scarioni and M. Nardone, *Pro Spring Security*, https://doi.org/10.1007/978-1-4842-5052-5_4

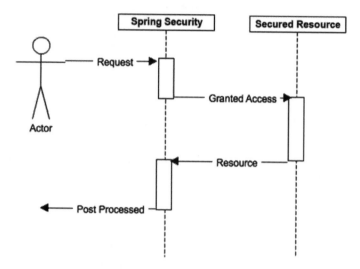

Figure 4-1. *Spring Security 10,000-foot overview*

From this view, you can think of Spring Security simply as an extra layer built on top of your application, wrapping specific entry points into your logic with determined security rules.

The 1,000-Foot View

Going into a little more detail, we arrive at AOP and servlet filters.

Spring Security's interception model of security applies to two main areas of your application: URLs and method invocations. Spring Security wraps around these two *entry points* of your application and allows access only when the security constraints are satisfied. Both the method call and the filter-based security depend on a central *Security Interceptor*, where the main logic resides to make the decision whether or not access should be granted. In Figure 4-2, you can see this more detailed overview of the framework.

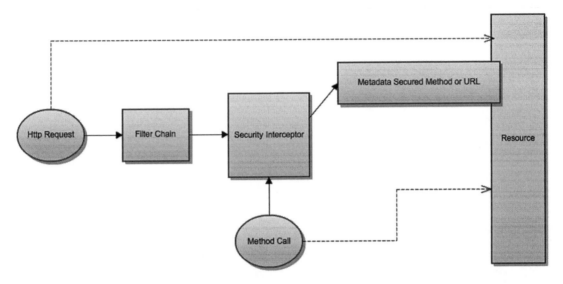

Figure 4-2. *In this view, both method calls and HTTP requests try to access a resource, but first they must go through the Security Interceptor*

The 100-Foot View

Spring Security might seem simple conceptually, but internally there is a lot going on in a very well-built software tool. This next overview will show you the main collaborating parts that participate in the general process of ensuring that your security constraints are enforced. This is particularly achievable with an open source project like Spring Security which allows you to get into the framework itself and appreciate its design and architecture by accessing the source code directly. After that, we'll delve deeper into the implementation details.

For us, what follows is the best way to understand Spring Security from the inside. The enumeration of what we consider to be the main components of the framework will help you know where everything belongs and how your application is enforcing the security rules that you specify for it.

The most important Spring Security internal architecture core modules are

- Authentication

- Authorization

The process of the Authentication and Authorization modules were introduced in Chapter 1.

Figure 4-3 provides an illustration of all the concept/components.

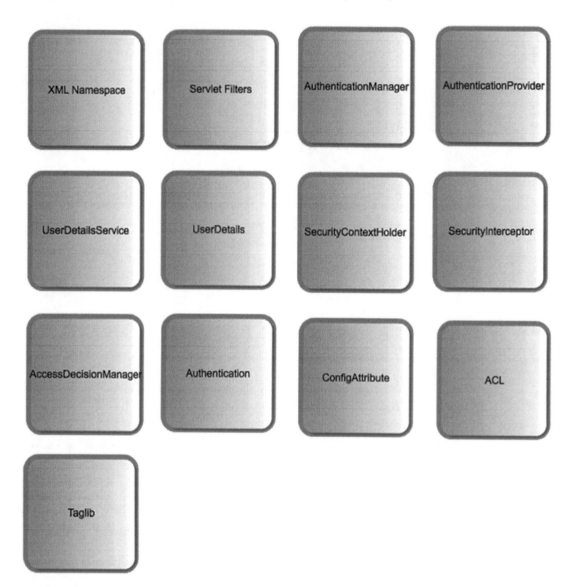

Figure 4-3. *The key components of Spring Security*

The Security Interceptor

One of the most important components of the framework is the Security Interceptor. With the main logic implemented in AbstractSecurityInterceptor and with two concrete implementations in the form of FilterSecurityInterceptor and

MethodSecurityInterceptor (as shown in Figure 4-4), the Security Interceptor is in charge of deciding whether a particular petition should be allowed to go through to a secured resource. MethodSecurityInterceptor, as its name should tell you, deals with petitions directed as method calls, while FilterSecurityInterceptor deals with petitions directed to web URLs.

The Security Interceptor works with a preprocessing step and a postprocessing step. In the preprocessing step, it looks to see whether the requested resource is secured with some metadata information (or ConfigAttribute). If it is not, the request is allowed to continue its way either to the requested URL or method. If the requested resource is secured, the Security Interceptor retrieves the Authentication object from the current SecurityContext. If necessary, the Authentication object will be authenticated against the configured AuthenticationManager with the following method:

```
public interface AuthenticationManager {

  Authentication authenticate(Authentication authentication)
    throws AuthenticationException;

}
```

An AuthenticationManager can do mainly three things with its method:

- Return an Authentication with value authenticated=true if the input represents a valid principal and can be verified

- Throw an AuthenticationException if the input represents an invalid principal

- Return null if it can't decide

Notice that ProviderManager (which delegates to a chain of AuthenticationProvider instances) is the most commonly used implementation of AuthenticationManager.

An example of the AuthenticationManager hierarchy using ProviderManager is shown in Figure 4-4.

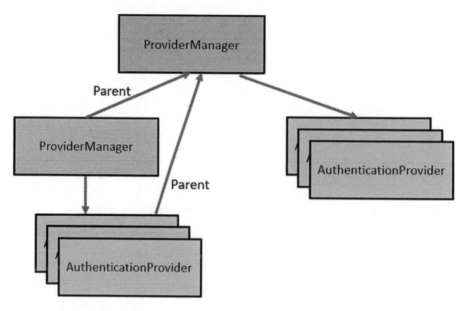

Figure 4-4. *AuthenticationManager hierarchy using ProviderManager*

After the object is authenticated, AccessDecisionManager is called to determine if the authenticated entity is able to finally access the resource. AccessDecisionManager throws an AccessDeniedException if the authenticated entity is not allowed to access the resource. If AccessDecisionManager decides that the Authentication entity is allowed to access the resource, the Authentication object is passed to RunAsManager if this is configured. If RunAsManager is not configured, a no-op implementation is called. RunAsManager returns either null (if it's not configured to be used) or a new Authentication object containing the same principal, credentials, and granted authorities as the original Authentication object, plus a new set of authorities based on the RUN_AS that is being used. This new Authentication object is put into the current SecurityContext.

After this processing, and independently of whether or not a RUN_AS Authentication object is used, the Security Interceptor creates a new InterceptorStatusToken with information about the SecurityContext and the ConfigAttributes. This token will be used later in the postprocessing step of the Security Interceptor. At this point, the Security Interceptor is ready to allow access to the secured resource, so it passes the invocation through and the particular secured entity (either a URL or a method) is invoked. After the invocation returns, the second phase of the Security Interceptor comes into play, and the postprocessing begins. The postprocessing step is considerably simpler, and it involves only calling an AfterInvocationManager's decide method if there is one configured. In its current implementation, AfterInvocationManager delegates to instances of PostInvocationAuthorizationAdvice, which ultimately filters the returned objects or throws an AccessDeniedException if necessary. This is the case if you are using the postinvocation filters in method-level security, as you will see in the following chapter. In the case of web security, the AfterInvocationManager is null.

That is a lot of work for the Security Interceptor. However, because the framework is nicely modular at the class level, you can see that the Security Interceptor simply delegates most of the task to a series of well-defined collaborators, which in a very SRP (Single Responsibility Principle) way focus on single, narrowly scoped responsibilities. This is good software design and an example you should emulate. As shown in Listing 4-1, you paste the main parts of the code from the AbstractSecurityInterceptor itself so that you can see the things we've been talking about. We include some comments in the code so that you can understand better what it does; they start with // ----.

Please notice that the entire AbstractSecurityInterceptor course code can be found on the GitHub address at https://github.com/spring-projects/spring-security/blob/master/core/src/main/java/org/springframework/security/access/intercept/AbstractSecurityInterceptor.java.

Listing 4-1. AbstractSecurityInterceptor

```
protected InterceptorStatusToken beforeInvocation(Object object) {
Assert.notNull(object, "Object was null");
final boolean debug = logger.isDebugEnabled();

// --- Here we are checking if this filter is able to process a particular
type of object. For example FilterSecurityInterceptor is able to process
FilterInvocation objects. MethodSecurityInterceptor is able to process
MethodInvocation objects.
if (!getSecureObjectClass().isAssignableFrom(object.getClass())) {
throw new IllegalArgumentException("Security invocation attempted for
object "
                + object.getClass().getName()
                + " but AbstractSecurityInterceptor only configured to
                support secure objects of type: "
                + getSecureObjectClass());
    }
```

```
// ---- Here we are retrieving the security metadata that maps to the
object we are receiving. So if we are receiving a FilterInvocation, the
request is extracted from it and used to find the ConfigAttribute (s) that
match the request path pattern
        Collection<ConfigAttribute> attributes = this.
        obtainSecurityMetadataSource().getAttributes(object);

if (attributes == null || attributes.isEmpty()) {
if (rejectPublicInvocations) {
throw new IllegalArgumentException("Secure object invocation " + object +
" was denied as public invocations are not allowed via this interceptor. "
                                + "This indicates a configuration error
                                because the " + "rejectPublicInvocations
                                property is set to 'true'");
            }

if (debug) {
logger.debug("Public object - authentication not attempted");
            }

publishEvent(new PublicInvocationEvent(object));

return null; // no further work post-invocation
        }

if (debug) {
logger.debug("Secure object: " + object + "; Attributes: " + attributes);
        }

if (SecurityContextHolder.getContext().getAuthentication() == null) {
credentialsNotFound(messages.getMessage("AbstractSecurityInterceptor.
authenticationNotFound",
                "An Authentication object was not found in the
                SecurityContext"), object, attributes);
        }
```

```
        Authentication authenticated = authenticateIfRequired();
```

// ---- Here we are calling the decision manager to decide if authorization is granted or not. This will trigger the voting mechanism, and in case that access is not granted an exception should be thrown.

```
try {
this.accessDecisionManager.decide(authenticated, object, attributes);
        }
catch (AccessDeniedException accessDeniedException) {
publishEvent(new AuthorizationFailureEvent(object, attributes,
authenticated, accessDeniedException));

throw accessDeniedException;
        }

if (debug) {
logger.debug("Authorization successful");
        }

if (publishAuthorizationSuccess) {
publishEvent(new AuthorizedEvent(object, attributes, authenticated));
        }
```

   // ---- Here it will try to use the run-as functionality of Spring
   Security that allows a user
// --to impersonate another one acquiring its security roles, or more precisely, its
//--GrantedAuthority (s)

```
Authentication runAs = this.runAsManager.buildRunAs(authenticated, object,
attributes);

if (runAs == null) {
if (debug) {
logger.debug("RunAsManager did not change Authentication object");
            }
```

```
            // no further work post-invocation
return new InterceptorStatusToken(SecurityContextHolder.getContext(),
false, attributes, object);
        } else {
if (debug) {
logger.debug("Switching to RunAs Authentication: " + runAs);
            }

SecurityContext origCtx = SecurityContextHolder.getContext();
SecurityContextHolder.setContext(SecurityContextHolder.
createEmptyContext());
SecurityContextHolder.getContext().setAuthentication(runAs);

            // need to revert to token.Authenticated post-invocation
return new InterceptorStatusToken(origCtx, true, attributes, object);
        }
// ---- If the method has not thrown an exception at this point, it is safe
to continue
// ---- the invocation through to the resource. Authorization has been
granted.
    }

protected Object afterInvocation(InterceptorStatusToken token, Object
returnedObject) {
if (token == null) {
            // public object
return returnedObject;
        }

if (token.isContextHolderRefreshRequired()) {
if (logger.isDebugEnabled()) {
logger.debug("Reverting to original Authentication: " + token.
getSecurityContext().getAuthentication());
        }

SecurityContextHolder.setContext(token.getSecurityContext());
    }
```

```
// ---- If there is an afterInvocationManager configured, it will be
called.
// ---- It will take care of filtering the return value or actually
throwing an exception
//----- if it is relevant to do so.

if (afterInvocationManager != null) {
            // Attempt after invocation handling
try {
returnedObject = afterInvocationManager.decide(token.getSecurityContext().
getAuthentication(),
token.getSecureObject(),
token.getAttributes(), returnedObject);
            }
catch (AccessDeniedException accessDeniedException) {
AuthorizationFailureEvent event = new AuthorizationFailureEvent(token.
getSecureObject(), token .getAttributes(), token.getSecurityContext().
getAuthentication(), accessDeniedException);
publishEvent(event);

throw accessDeniedException;
            }
        }

// ---- Here is the full authorization cycled finished. The response is
returned to the caller.
return returnedObject;
    }
```

The Security Interceptor lies at the core of the Spring Security framework. Every call to a secured resource in Spring Security passes through this interceptor. The AbstractSecurityInterceptor shows its versatility when you realize that two not-very-related kinds of resources (URL endpoints and methods) leverage most of the functionality of this abstract interceptor. This, once again, shows the effort put into the design and implementation of the framework.

Figure 4-5 shows the interceptor in a UML (Unified Modeling Language) class diagram. And Figure 4-6 shows a simplified sequence diagram.

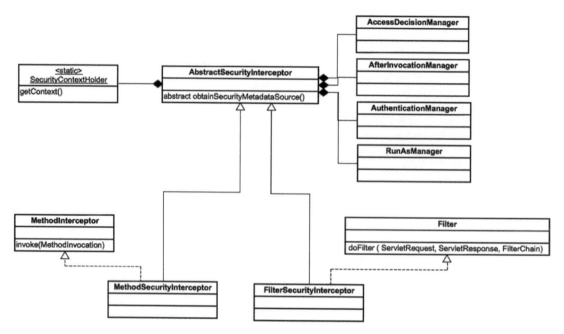

Figure 4-5. *SecurityInterceptor UML class diagram, simplified*

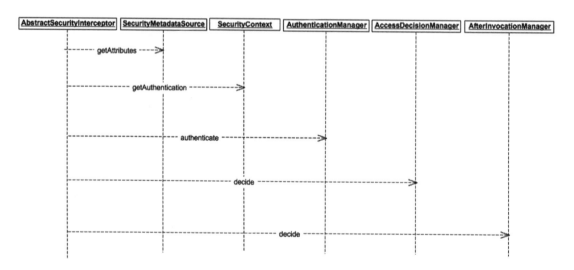

Figure 4-6. *AbstractSecurityInterceptor sequence diagram, simplified*

We know how the Security Interceptors work, but how do they come to be? How do they know what to intercept? The answer to that lies in the next few components, so keep reading.

The XML Namespace

The XML namespace is of extreme importance to the general appeal and usability of the framework, yet it is, in theory, not strictly necessary. If you know how the Spring Framework's namespaces work, you probably have a good idea of what is going on when you define your security-specific XML configuration in your application context definition files. If you don't know how they work, maybe you think Spring is somehow made aware of how to treat these specific elements and how to load them in the general Spring application context. Either way, here we will explain in some detail the process behind the definition of a custom namespace in Spring, and particularly, the elements in the Spring Security namespace.

Originally, Spring did not support custom XML. All that Spring understood was its own classes defined in the standard Spring Core namespace, where you can define <bean>s on a bean-to-bean basis and can't really define anything conceptually more complex without adding that complexity yourself to the configuration.

This <bean>-based configuration was, and still is, very good for configuring general-purpose bean instances, but it can get messy really fast for defining more domain-specific utilities. And beyond being messy, it is also very poor at expressing the business domain of the beans you are defining.

We'll explore this manual configuration later in the book, but for standard cases it is not needed, and you should simply use the namespace. However, keep in mind that under the hood the namespace is nothing more than syntactic sugar. At the end of the day, you still end up with standard Spring beans and objects.

Spring 2.0 introduced support for defining custom XML namespaces. Since then, a lot of projects have made use of this facility, making them more attractive to work with.

An XML custom namespace is simply an XML-based Domain Specific Language (DSL), guided by the rules of an XML schema (.xsd) file that allows developers to create Spring beans using concepts and a syntax more in synch with the programming concerns they are trying to model.

Note   A DSL is a language customized to represent the concepts of a particular application domain. Sometimes, a whole new language is created to support the new domain, which is referred to as an *external DSL*. Some other times, an existing language is tweaked to allow for new expressions that represent the concepts of the domain, and this is referred to as an *internal DSL*. In the case presented in this chapter, you are using a general-purpose language (XML); however, you are defining certain constraints about the elements (using XSD) and thus are creating an internal DSL to represent security concepts.

Making Spring aware of a new namespace is really simple. (That's not to say it is simple to actually parse the information of the XML and convert it to beans—this depends on the complexity of your DSL.) All you need is the following:

- An `.xsd` file defining your particular XML structure

- A `spring.schemas` file where you specify the mapping between a URL-based schema location and the location of your `.xsd` file in your classpath

- A `spring.handlers` file where you specify which class is in charge of handling everything related to your namespace

- A bunch of parser classes that will be in charge of parsing each of the top elements defined in your XML file

In Chapter 8, you will see some examples of how to create a new namespace element and integrate it with Spring Security.

For Spring Security, all the namespace configuration-related information resides in the `config` module. In Figure 4-7, you can see the expanded structure of the `config` module as seen in the Eclipse integrated development environment (IDE), in this case Spring tool Suite v4 for Eclipse.

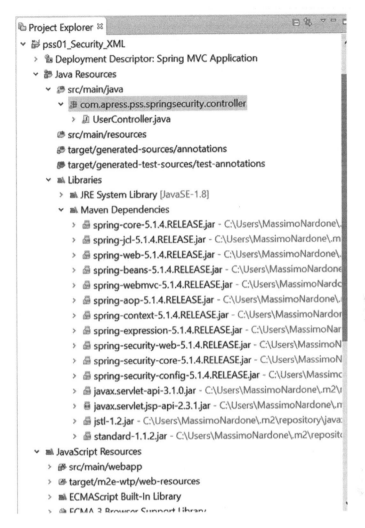

Figure 4-7. *Spring Security's file structure*

The files `spring.handlers` and `spring.schemas` should reside in the `META-INF` directory in the classpath so that Spring can find them there.

OK, so enough of the general namespace information. More specifically, how does the Spring Security namespace work?

When you create a Spring-based application using XML-defined application context configuration with some of the Spring Security namespace definitions, and you run the application, when it starts to load up, it looks in the application context's namespace definitions at the top of the XML configuration file. It will find the reference to the

Spring Security namespace (normally a reference like xmlns:security="http://www.springframework.org/schema/security"). Using the information from the spring.handlers mapping file, it will see that the file to handle the security elements is the final class, org.springframework.security.config.SecurityNamespaceHandler. Spring calls the parse method of this class for every top element in the configuration file that uses the security namespace. Figure 4-8 shows the load-up sequence for this process.

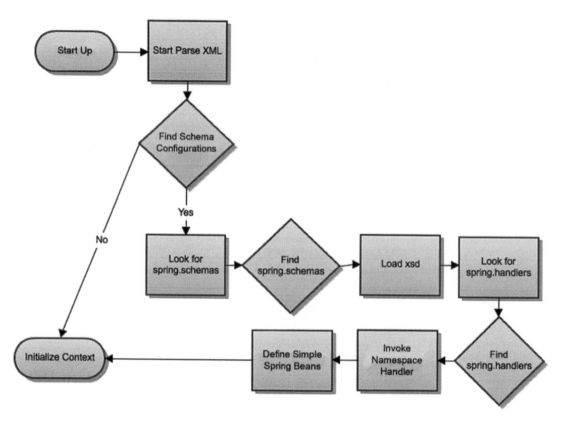

Figure 4-8. *Sequence of loading up a Spring namespace*

SecurityNamespaceHandler delegates to a series of BeanDefinitionParser objects for the individual parsing of each top-level element. The whole list of elements supported in the Spring Security namespace configuration are defined in the class org.springframework.security.config.Elements as constants. This class is shown in Listing 4-2.

Listing 4-2. Constants for All the Spring Security Namespace Elements

```
package org.springframework.security.config;
public abstract class Elements {

public static final String ACCESS_DENIED_HANDLER = "access-denied-handler";
public static final String AUTHENTICATION_MANAGER = "authentication-manager";
public static final String AFTER_INVOCATION_PROVIDER = "after-invocation-provider";
public static final String USER_SERVICE = "user-service";
public static final String JDBC_USER_SERVICE = "jdbc-user-service";
public static final String FILTER_CHAIN_MAP = "filter-chain-map";
public static final String INTERCEPT_METHODS = "intercept-methods";
public static final String INTERCEPT_URL = "intercept-url";
public static final String AUTHENTICATION_PROVIDER = "authentication-provider";
public static final String HTTP = "http";
public static final String LDAP_PROVIDER = "ldap-authentication-provider";
public static final String LDAP_SERVER = "ldap-server";
public static final String LDAP_USER_SERVICE = "ldap-user-service";
public static final String PROTECT_POINTCUT = "protect-pointcut";
public static final String EXPRESSION_HANDLER = "expression-handler";
public static final String INVOCATION_HANDLING = "pre-post-annotation-handling";
public static final String INVOCATION_ATTRIBUTE_FACTORY = "invocation-
attribute-factory";
public static final String PRE_INVOCATION_ADVICE = "pre-invocation-advice";
public static final String POST_INVOCATION_ADVICE = "post-invocation-advice";
public static final String PROTECT = "protect";
public static final String SESSION_MANAGEMENT = "session-management";
public static final String CONCURRENT_SESSIONS = "concurrency-control";
public static final String LOGOUT = "logout";
public static final String FORM_LOGIN = "form-login";
public static final String OPENID_LOGIN = "openid-login";
public static final String OPENID_ATTRIBUTE_EXCHANGE = "attribute-exchange";
public static final String OPENID_ATTRIBUTE = "openid-attribute";
public static final String BASIC_AUTH = "http-basic";
public static final String REMEMBER_ME = "remember-me";
public static final String ANONYMOUS = "anonymous";
```

```
public static final String FILTER_CHAIN = "filter-chain";
public static final String GLOBAL_METHOD_SECURITY = "global-method-security";
public static final String PASSWORD_ENCODER = "password-encoder";
public static final String SALT_SOURCE = "salt-source";
public static final String PORT_MAPPINGS = "port-mappings";
public static final String PORT_MAPPING = "port-mapping";
public static final String CUSTOM_FILTER = "custom-filter";
public static final String REQUEST_CACHE = "request-cache";
public static final String X509 = "x509";
public static final String JEE = "jee";
public static final String FILTER_SECURITY_METADATA_SOURCE = "filter-
security-metadata-source";
public static final String METHOD_SECURITY_METADATA_SOURCE = "method-
security-metadata-source";
    @Deprecated
public static final String FILTER_INVOCATION_DEFINITION_SOURCE = "filter-
invocation-definition-source";
public static final String LDAP_PASSWORD_COMPARE = "password-compare";
public static final String DEBUG = "debug";
public static final String HTTP_FIREWALL = "http-firewall";
}
```

From the list of elements presented in the previous class, the top-level ones as used
in the XML configuration files are as follows (in the previous listing, we refer to them by
the name of the constant and not by the XML element name):

- LDAP_PROVIDER: This element is used to configure the Lightweight
  Directory Access Protocol (LDAP) authentication provider for your
  application in case you require one.

- LDAP_SERVER: This element is used to configure an LDAP server in
  your application.

- LDAP_USER_SERVICE: This element configures the service for
  retrieving user details from an LDAP server and populating that
  user's authorities (Spring Security uses the term "authorities" to refer
  to the permission names that are granted to a particular user. For
  example, ROLE_USER is an authority).

- USER_SERVICE: This element defines the in-memory user service where you can store user names, credentials, and authorities directly in the application context definition file. Notice that this type of configuration is specific for test environments and academic purposes because it is easy to set up and fast.

- JDBC_USER_SERVICE: This element allows you to set up a database-driven user service, where you specify a DataSource and the queries to retrieve the user information from a database.

- AUTHENTICATION_PROVIDER: This element defines a DaoAuthenticationProvider, which is an authentication provider that delegates to an instance of UserDetailsService. The UserDetailsService can be any of the ones defined in the previous three bullet points, or a reference to a customized one.

- GLOBAL_METHOD_SECURITY: This element is in charge of setting up the global support in your application to the annotations @Secured, @javax.annotation.security.RolesAllowed, @PreAuthorize, and @PostAuthorize. This element is the one that will handle the registration of a method interceptor that will be aware of all the metadata of the bean's methods in order to apply the corresponding security advice.

- AUTHENTICATION_MANAGER: This element registers a global ProviderManager in the application and sets up the configured AuthenticationProviders on it.

- METHOD_SECURITY_METADATA_SOURCE: This element registers a MapBasedMethodSecurityMetadataSource in the application context. It will hold a Map<RegisteredMethod, List<ConfigAttribute>>. It does this so that when a request is made to a method, the method can be retrieved and its security constraints can be checked.

- DEBUG: For development purposes, this element registers a DebugFilter in the security filter chain.

- HTTP: This is the main element for a web-based secure application. The HTTP element is really powerful. It allows for the definition of URL-based security-mapping strategies, the configuration of the filters, the Secure Sockets Layer (SSL) support, and other HTTP-related security configurations.

- HTTP_FIREWALL: This element uses a firewall element and adds it to the filter chain if it is configured. The firewall referenced should be an implementation of Spring's own HttpFirewall interface.

- FILTER_INVOCATION_DEFINITION_SOURCE: This element has been deprecated. See the following one.

- FILTER_SECURITY_METADATA_SOURCE: This element wraps a list of <intercept-url> elements. These elements map the relationship between URLs and the ConfigAttributes required for accessing those URLs.

- FILTER_CHAIN: This element allows you to configure the Spring Security filter chain that will be used in the application, which filters you want to add to the chain, and a request matcher if you want to customize how the chain matches requests. The most important request matchers are ant-based and regexp-based.

You will be using the Spring Security namespace thoroughly throughout the book, so many of the elements described here will be revisited in later chapters.

The Filters and Filter Chain

The filter chain model is what Spring Security uses to secure web applications. This model is built on top of the standard *servlet filter* functionality. Working as an Intercepting Filter Pattern, the filter chain in Spring Security is built of a few single-responsibility filters that cover all the different security constraints required by the application.

The filter chain in Spring Security preprocesses and postprocesses all the HTTP requests that are sent to the application and then applies security to URLs that require it.

A typical filter for a single HTTP request is shown in Figure 4-9.

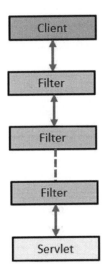

Figure 4-9. *Spring Security filter example for a single HTTP request*

The Spring Security filter chain is made up of Spring beans; however, standard servlet-based web applications don't know about Spring beans.

From the point of view of the container, Spring Security is actually a single filter, which internally contains a lot of filters with different purposes.

Spring Security is installed as a single filter in the chain named FilterChainProxy, which is a chain of filters containing all the security needed, as shown in Figure 4-10.

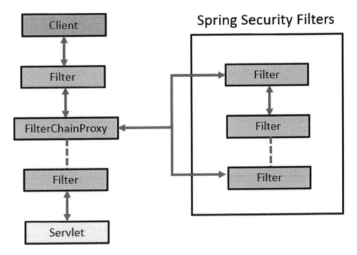

Figure 4-10. *Spring Security filters overview*

In the security filter, there is also a special layer of indirection installed in the container named DelegatingFilterProxy. DelegatingFilterProxy does not need to be a Spring Bean.

The flow works so that the DelegatingFilterProxy filter will delegate to a FilterChainProxy, which instead is always a bean with a fixed name of springSecurityFilterChain which at the end will be responsible, within your application, for

- Protecting the application URLs

- Validating the submitted username and passwords

- Redirecting to the login form

The DelegatingFilterProxy process containing the FilterChainProxy is shown in Figure 4-11.

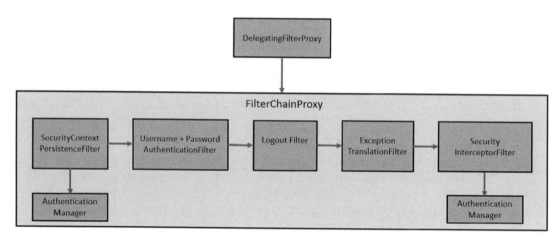

Figure 4-11. *Spring Security filter chain overview*

The Spring Security filter configuration is achieved via a special servet and two main XML files, web.xml and applicationContext.xml. Please notice that starting with Servlet 3.0, web.xml is no longer necessary.

This special servlet filter is needed to cross the boundaries between the standard servlet API and life cycle and the Spring application where the bean filters will reside. This is the job of the org.springframework.web.filter.DelegatingFilterProxy defined in the web.xml, which uses under the hood the WebApplicationContextUtils. getWebApplicationContext utility method to retrieve the root application context of the application. These two classes are from the Spring Framework, not from Spring Security.

Figure 4-12 shows the configuration of the filter chain.

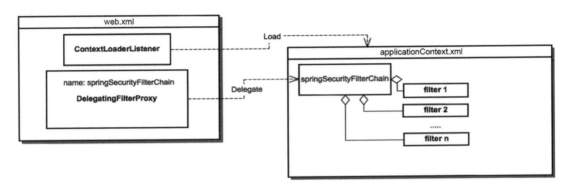

Figure 4-12. *Understanding the Spring Security filter configuration. The filter in the web.xml file has the same name as the bean in the Spring application context so that the listener can find it*

Full information about how migrating from Spring Security 3.x to 4.x and from 4.x to 5.x (Java Configuration) can be found at `https://docs.spring.io/spring-security/site/migrate/current/3-to-4/html5/migrate-3-to-4-jc.html` and `https://github.com/spring-projects/spring-security/issues/4874`.

The filter chain will be fully explained in Chapter 5. However, here we'll provide an overview of which filters are available and what they do. The available filters are defined as enums in the file named `org.springframework.security.config.http.SecurityFilters`. The enums are then referenced later in the startup process when instantiating the bean definitions for each filter. Here are the defined filters:

- `CHANNEL_FILTER`: This filter ensures that the request is handled by the correct channel—meaning, in most cases, it determines whether or not the request is handled by HTTPS.

- `CONCURRENT_SESSION_FILTER`: This filter is part of the concurrent session-handling mechanism. Its main function is to query the session to see if it has expired (which happens mainly when the maximum number of concurrent sessions per user are reached) and to log out the user if that is the case.

- `SECURITY_CONTEXT_FILTER`: This filter populates `SecurityContextHolder` with a new or existing security context to be used by the rest of the framework.

- LOGOUT_FILTER: This filter is based, by default, on a particular URL invocation (/logout). It takes care of the logout process, including tasks such as clearing the cookies, removing the "remember me" information, and clearing the security context.

- X509_FILTER: This filter extracts the principal and credentials from an X509 certificate using the class java.security.cert. X509Certificate and attempts to authenticate with these preauthenticated values.

- PRE_AUTH_FILTER: This filter is used with the J2EE authentication mechanism. The J2EE authenticated principal will be used as the preauthenticated principal in the framework.

- FORM_LOGIN_FILTER: This filter is used when a user name and password is required on a login form. This filter takes care of authenticating with the requested user name and password. It handles, from Spring v4, requests to a particular URL (/login) with a particular set of user-name and password parameters (username, password).

- OPENID_FILTER: This filter processes OpenId authentication requests, handling both the initial request with the OpenId identity to the external server and the redirect from the OpenId server back to the application. All this interaction is managed when the filter detects requests to the preconfigured URL /openid since Spring v4.

- LOGIN_PAGE_FILTER: This filter generates a default login page when the user doesn't provide a custom one. It is activated when the URL / spring_security_login is requested.

- DIGEST_AUTH_FILTER: This filter processes HTTP Digest authentication headers. It looks for the presence of both Digest and Authorization HTTP request headers. It can be used to provide Digest authentication to standard user agents, like browsers, or to application clients like SOAP. On successful authentication, the SecurityContext will be populated with the valid Authentication object.

- BASIC_AUTH_FILTER: This `filter` processes the BASIC authentication headers in an HTTP request. It looks for the header `Authorization` and tries to authenticate with these credentials.

- REQUEST_CACHE_FILTER: This filter retrieves a request from the request-cache that matches the current request, and it sends the cached one through the rest of the filter chain.

- SERVLET_API_SUPPORT_FILTER.: This filter wraps the request in a request wrapper that implements the Servlet API security methods, like `isUserInRole`, and delegates it to `SecurityContextHolder`. This allows for the convenient use of the request object itself to get the security information. For example, you can use `request.getAuthentication` to retrieve the `Authentication` object.

- JAAS_API_SUPPORT_FILTER: This filter tries to obtain and use `javax.security.auth.Subject`, which is a final class, and continue the filter chain execution with this subject.

- REMEMBER_ME_FILTER: If no user is logged in, this filter will look to see whether there is any "remember me" functionality active and any "remember me" `Authentication` available. If there is, this filter will try to login automatically and authenticate with this "remember me" information.

- ANONYMOUS_FILTER: This filter checks to see whether there is already an `Authentication` in the context. If there is not, it creates a new Anonymous one and sets it on the security context.

- SESSION_MANAGEMENT_FILTER: This filter passes the `Authentication` object that corresponds to the authenticated user who is logged in to the system to some configured session management processors in order to do session-related handling of the `Authentication`. Mainly, these processors will do some kind of validation and throw `SessionAuthenticationException` if appropriate. Currently, these processors (or strategies) include only one main class in the form of `org.springframework.security.web.authentication.session.ConcurrentSessionControlStrategy`, dealing with both session fixation and concurrent sessions.

- EXCEPTION_TRANSLATION_FILTER: This filter handles the translation between Spring Security exceptions (like AccessDeniedException) and the corresponding HTTP status code. It also redirects to the application entry point in case the exception is thrown because there is not yet an authenticated user in the system.

- FILTER_SECURITY_INTERCEPTOR: This filter handles the authorization mechanism for defined URLs. It delegates to its parent class' (AbstractSecurityInterceptor) functionality (which we'll cover later in the chapter) the actual workflow logic of granting or not granting the access to the specific resource.

- SWITCH_USER_FILTER: This filter allows a user to impersonate another one by visiting a particular URL, which since Spring v4 was updated from from /j_spring_security_switch_user to /login/impersonate. This URL should be secured to allow just certain users access to this functionality. Also, the method attemptSwitchUser in the implementing class SwitchUserFilter can be overridden to add constraints, so that you can use more finely grained information to decide if certain users are allowed or not allowed to impersonate other users.

ConfigAttribute

The interface org.springframework.security.access.ConfigAttribute encapsulates the access information metadata present in a secured resource. For example, for your study purposes, ROLE_ADMIN is a ConfigAttribute. There are a few implementations of ConfigAttribute, as you can see in Figure 4-13.

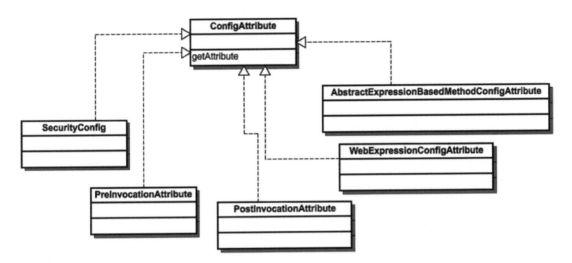

Figure 4-13. *ConfiAttribute hierarchy*

When you annotate a method with @Secured("ROLE_ADMIN") or something similar, or specify a URL with <security:intercept-url pattern="/hello" access="ROLE_ SIMPSON_MEMBER" />, Spring Security does the following. On startup, as normal Spring functionality, all the bean postprocessors in the ApplicationContext get invoked. And in the case of Spring Security, the process is the following.

What happens in the case of web requests is not really that complex. Web requests don't really use the postprocessor infrastructure.

When you use the element <security:intercept-url pattern="/x" access= "ROLE_XX" />, Spring Security uses the class FilterInvocationSecurityMetadataSource Parser to parse this XML. In the parsing process, the private method parseInterceptUrls ForFilterInvocationRequestMap will be invoked. This method maps the information contained in each of the URL patterns in the XML element into a map of Ant-style request paths, like /*, ROLE_USER. Here /* is an Ant pattern and ROLE_USER is a config attribute (this says that basically this config attribute is needed to access any URL with this pattern). This map, ultimately, will be set up in an instance of an implementation of the interface org.springframework.security.web.access.intercept. FilterInvocationSecurityMetadataSource inside the FilterSecurityInterceptor, which uses it when each request comes to match the requested URL against the keys in the map to find out if the URL is secured and then extracts the ConfigAttributes against which to check the authorities of the requesting Authentication object. This setup process is shown in Figure 4-14.

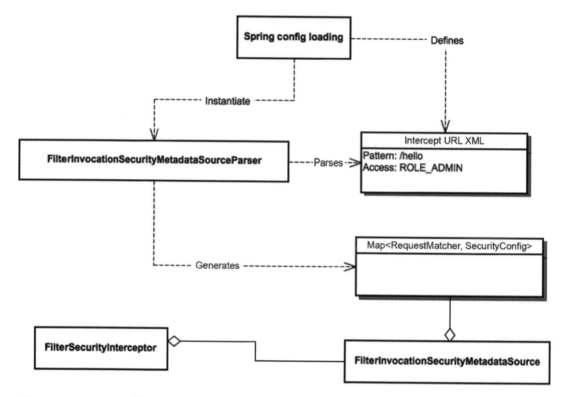

Figure 4-14. `ConfigAttribute` *setup for web applications*

For method-level security, you have many options—the most common one being the configurations performed through the use of annotations. There are a few different annotations available in the framework; however, the setup treatment by the framework is very similar. In the case of the @Secured annotation, for instance, you need to make Spring aware that this special annotation needs a special security treatment. To do that, you register the following in the security application context XML file:

```
<global-method-security secured-annotations = "enabled"/>
```

When you set up that definition in the application context XML configuration, Spring Security creates a new MethodSecurityMetadataSourceAdvisor and registers it in the application context. This advisor is marked as an infrastructure advisor and is picked up by Spring Core's InfrastructureAdvisorAutoProxyCreator, which is a BeanPostProcessor that Spring initializes automatically. It processes all the beans in the application context and determines if any of the configured advisors can be applied to any of the beans and their methods. If so, it wraps the bean with the required advisor or advisors. The postprocessor finds the

MethodSecurityMetadataSourceAdvisor and eventually calls an implementation of the MethodSecurityMetadataSource.getAttributes method for each bean and all its methods, to determine if they have any ConfigAttribute configured as metadata in them. If the MethodSecurityMetadataSource finds ConfigAttributes in the bean, the InfrastructureAdvisorAutoProxyCreator, from Spring Core, calls its own method (createProxy) to apply MethodSecurityMetadataSourceAdvisor, which internally contains the Security Interceptor as the org.aopalliance.aop.Advice to apply to the bean. Figure 4-15 shows this interaction graphically.

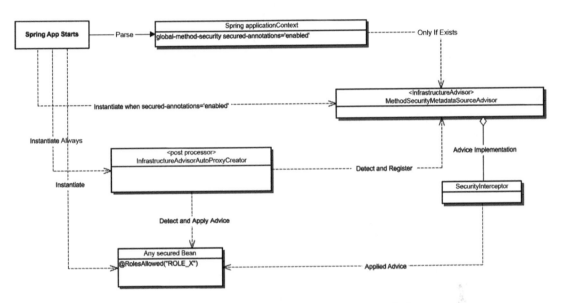

Figure 4-15. *Decorating annotated beans with security advice*

At first sight, this looks like simple magic, but it takes a lot of hard work from Spring to do it. And you have to thank the Spring and Spring Security developers for taking care of all this and giving you a simple and powerful API for resolving your security concerns.

The Authentication Object

The Authentication object is an abstraction that represents the entity that logs in to the system—most likely, a user. Because it is normally a user authenticating, we'll assume so and use the term "user" in the rest of the book. There are a few implementations of the Authentication object in the framework, as you can see in Figure 4-16.

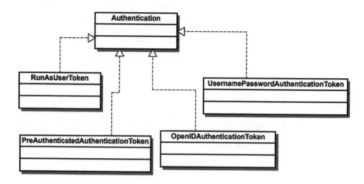

Figure 4-16. *Authentication hierarchy*

An Authentication object is used both when an authentication request is created (when a user logs in), to carry around the different layers and classes of the framework the requesting data, and then when it is validated, containing the authenticated entity and storing it in SecurityContext.

The most common behavior is that when you log in to the application, a new Authentication object will be created, storing your user name, password, and permissions, which are technically known as Principal, Credentials, and Authorities, respectively.

Authentication is an interface, and it is pretty simple, as Listing 4-3 shows.

Note   There are many implementations of the Authentication interface, and in this book we will refer most of the time to the general Authentication interface when we are not interested in the particular implementation type. Of course, when we need to talk about the specifics of an implementation detail, we will refer to the concrete classes.

Listing 4-3. The Authentication Interface

```
package org.springframework.security.core;

import java.io.Serializable;

import java.security.Principal;
import java.util.Collection;
```

```
import org.springframework.security.authentication.AuthenticationManager;
import org.springframework.security.core.context.SecurityContextHolder;

public interface Authentication extends Principal, Serializable {
Collection<? extends GrantedAuthority> getAuthorities();
    Object getCredentials();
    Object getDetails();
    Object getPrincipal();
Boolean isAuthenticated();
Void setAuthenticated(boolean isAuthenticated) throws IllegalArgumentException;
}
```

As Figure 4-16 shows, currently there are a few implementations of Authentication in the framework:

- UsernamePasswordAuthenticationToken: This is a simple implementation that contains, as its name clearly specifies, the user name and password information of the authenticated (or pending authentication) user. It is the most common Authentication implementation used throughout the system, as many of the AuthenticationProvider objects depend directly on this class.

- PreAuthenticatedAuthenticationToken: This implementation exists for handling preauthenticated Authentication objects. Preauthenticated authentications are those where the actual authentication process is handled by an external system, and Spring Security deals only with extracting the principal (or user) information out of the external system's messages.

- OpenIDAuthenticationToken: This is an Authentication implementation used specifically for OpenID authentication schemes. It is used by both the OpenID filter and the OpenID authentication provider.

- RunAsUserToken: This implementation is used by the RunAsManager, which is called by the Security Interceptor when the accessed resource contains a ConfigAttribute that starts with the prefix RUN_AS_. If there is a ConfigAttribute with this value, RunAsManager adds new GrantedAuthorities to the authenticated user corresponding to the RUN_AS value.

SecurityContext and SecurityContextHolder

The interface org.springframework.security.core.context.SecurityContext
(actually, its implementation is SecurityContextImpl) is the place where Spring
Security stores the valid Authentication object, associating it with the current thread.
The org.springframework.security.core.context.SecurityContextHolder is
the class used to access SecurityContext from many parts of the framework. It is
built mainly of static methods to store and access SecurityContext, delegating to
configurable strategies the way to handle this SecurityContext—for example, one
SecurityContext per thread (default), one global SecurityContext, or a custom
strategy. The class diagram for these classes can be seen in Figure 4-17, and Listings 4-4
and 4-5 show the two classes.

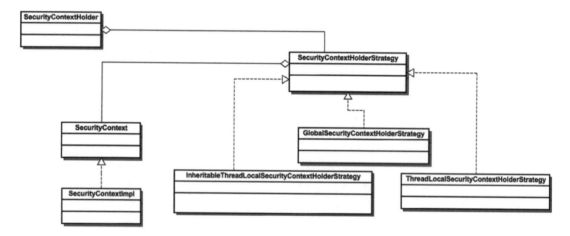

Figure 4-17. SecurityContext and SecurityContextHolder

Listing 4-4. SecurityContext Interface

```
package org.springframework.security.core.context;
import org.springframework.security.core.Authentication;
import java.io.Serializable;

public interface SecurityContext extends Serializable {
    Authentication getAuthentication();
void setAuthentication(Authentication authentication);
}
```

Notice that the entire SecurityContextHolder reference can be found on GigHub at https://github.com/spring-projects/spring-security/blob/master/core/src/main/java/org/springframework/security/core/context/SecurityContext.java.

Listing 4-5. SecurityContextHolder Class

```java
package org.springframework.security.core.context;
import org.springframework.util.ReflectionUtils;
import java.lang.reflect.Constructor;

public class SecurityContextHolder {
public static final String MODE_THREADLOCAL = "MODE_THREADLOCAL";
public static final String
  MODE_INHERITABLETHREADLOCAL = "MODE_INHERITABLETHREADLOCAL";
public static final String MODE_GLOBAL = "MODE_GLOBAL";
public static final String SYSTEM_PROPERTY = "spring.security.strategy";
private static String strategyName = System.getProperty(SYSTEM_PROPERTY);
private static SecurityContextHolderStrategy strategy;
private static int initializeCount = 0;

static {
initialize();
    }
public static void clearContext() {
strategy.clearContext();
    }
public static SecurityContext getContext() {
return strategy.getContext();
    }
public static int getInitializeCount() {
return initializeCount;
    }

private static void initialize() {
if ((strategyName == null) || "".equals(strategyName)) {
strategyName = MODE_THREADLOCAL;
        }
```

```java
if (strategyName.equals(MODE_THREADLOCAL)) {
strategy = new ThreadLocalSecurityContextHolderStrategy();
        } else if (strategyName.equals(MODE_INHERITABLETHREADLOCAL)) {
strategy = new InheritableThreadLocalSecurityContextHolderStrategy();
        } else if (strategyName.equals(MODE_GLOBAL)) {
strategy = new GlobalSecurityContextHolderStrategy();
        } else {
try {
                Class<?> clazz = Class.forName(strategyName);
                Constructor<?> customStrategy = clazz.getConstructor();
strategy = (SecurityContextHolderStrategy) customStrategy.newInstance();
            } catch (Exception ex) {
ReflectionUtils.handleReflectionException(ex);
            }
        }
initializeCount++;
    }
public static void setContext(SecurityContext context) {
strategy.setContext(context);
    }
public static void setStrategyName(String strategyName) {
SecurityContextHolder.strategyName = strategyName;
initialize();
    }
public static SecurityContextHolderStrategy getContextHolderStrategy() {
return strategy;
    }
public static SecurityContext createEmptyContext() {
return strategy.createEmptyContext();
    }

public String toString() {
        return "SecurityContextHolder[strategy='" + strategyName + "';
        initializeCount=" + initializeCount + "]";
    }
}
```

AuthenticationProvider

AuthenticationProvider is the main entry point for authenticating an Authentication object. This interface has only two methods, as Listing 4-6 shows. This is one of the major extension points of the framework, as you can tell by the many classes that currently extend this interface. Each of the implementing classes deals with a particular external provider to authenticate against. So if you come across a particular provider that is not supported and you need to authenticate against it, you probably need to implement this interface with the required functionality. You will see examples of this later in the book.

AuthenticationProvider (see Figure 4-18) is very similar to AuthenticationManager but it has an extra method which can be used to call a query if it supports a given Authentication type, as shown here:

```
public interface AuthenticationProvider {

        Authentication authenticate(Authentication authentication)
                        throws AuthenticationException;

        boolean supports(Class<?> authentication);

}
```

Here are some of the existing providers that come with the framework:

```
CasAuthenticationProvider
JaasAuthenticationProvider
DaoAuthenticationProvider
OpenIDAuthenticationProvider
RememberMeAuthenticationProvider
LdapAuthenticationProvider
```

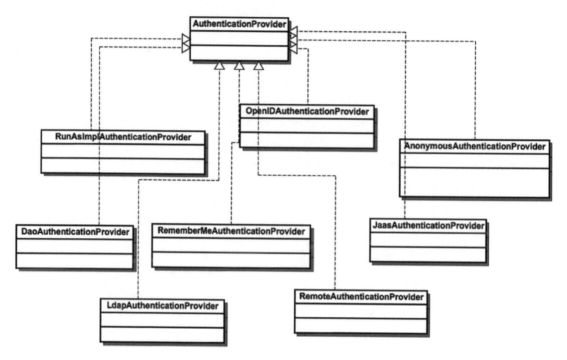

Figure 4-18. *AuthenticationProvider hierarchy*

The entire AuthenticationProvider reference can be found on GitHub at https://github.com/spring-projects/spring-security/blob/master/core/src/main/java/org/springframework/security/authentication/AuthenticationProvider.java.

Listing 4-6. AuthenticationProvider Interface

```
package org.springframework.security.authentication;

import org.springframework.security.core.Authentication;
import org.springframework.security.core.AuthenticationException;

public interface AuthenticationProvider {
    Authentication authenticate(Authentication authentication) throws
    AuthenticationException;
boolean supports(Class<?> authentication);
}
```

AccessDecisionManager

AccessDecisionManager is the class in charge of deciding if a particular Authentication object is allowed or not allowed to access a particular resource. In its main implementations, it delegates to AccessDecisionVoter objects, which basically compare the GrantedAuthorities in the Authentication object against the ConfigAttribute(s) required by the resource that is being accessed, deciding whether or not access should be granted. They emit their vote to allow access or not. The AccessDecisionManager implementations take the output from the voters into consideration and apply a determined strategy on whether or not to grant access. Voters, however, also can abstain from voting.

The AccessDecisionManager interface can be seen in Listing 4-7. Its UML class diagram is shown in Figure 4-19.

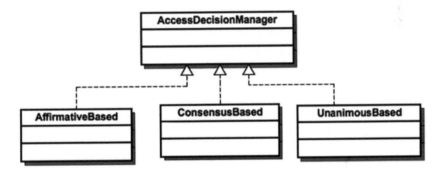

Figure 4-19. *AccessDecisionManager hierarchy*

The entire AccessDecisionManager reference can be found on GitHub at https://github.com/spring-projects/spring-security/blob/master/core/src/main/java/org/springframework/security/access/AccessDecisionManager.java.

Listing 4-7. AccessDecisionManager

```
package org.springframework.security.access;

import java.util.Collection;
import org.springframework.security.authentication.
InsufficientAuthenticationException;
import org.springframework.security.core.Authentication;
```

```
public interface AccessDecisionManager {
void decide(Authentication authentication, Object object,
Collection<ConfigAttribute> configAttributes)
throws AccessDeniedException, InsufficientAuthenticationException;
boolean supports(ConfigAttribute attribute);
boolean supports(Class<?> clazz);
}
```

The current AccessDecisionManager implementations all delegate to voters, but they work in slightly different ways. The current voters, which are described in the following sections, are defined in the package org.springframework.security.access.vote.

AffirmativeBased

This access decision manager calls all its configured voters, and if any of them vote that access should be granted, this is enough for the access decision manager to allow access to the secured resource. If no voters vote to grant access and there is at least one who votes not to grant it, the access decision manager throws an AccessDeniedException denying access. If there are only abstaining voters, a decision is made based on the AccessDecisionManager's instance variable allowIfAllAbstainDecisions, which is a Boolean that defaults to false, determining if access should be granted or not when all voters abstain.

ConsensusBased

This access decision manager implementation calls all its configured voters to make a decision to either grant or deny access to a resource. The difference with the AffirmativeBased decision manager is that the ConsensusBased decision manager decides to grant access only if there are more voters granting access than voters denying it. So the majority wins in this case. If there are the same number of granting voters as denying voters, the value of the instance variable allowIfEqualGrantedDeniedDecisions is used to decide. By default, this variable's value is true, and access is granted. When all voters abstain, the access decision will be decided the same way as it is for the AffirmativeBased manager.

UnanimousBased

As you probably guessed, this access decision manager will grant access to the resource only if all the configured voters vote in favor of allowing access to the resource. If any voter votes to deny the access, the AccessDeniedException will be thrown. The "all abstain" case is handled the same way as with the other implementations of AccessDecisionManager.

AccessDecisionVoter

This discussion of the AccessDecisionManager and its current implementations should have made clear the importance of the Access Decision Voters, because they are the ones, working as a team, who ultimately determine if a particular Authentication object has enough privileges to access a particular resource.

The org.springframework.security.access.AccessDecisionVoter interface is very simple as well, and you can see it in Listing 4-8.

The main method is vote, and as can be deduced from the interface, it will return one of three possible responses (ACCESS_GRANTED, ACCES_ABSTAIN, ACCESS_DENIED), depending on whether the required conditions are satisfied.

The satisfaction or not of the conditions is given by analyzing the Authentication object's rights against the required resource. In practice, this basically means that the Authentication's authorities are compared against the resource's security attributes looking for matches.

The following are the current AccessDecisionVoter implementations:

- org.springframework.security.access.annotation.Jsr250Voter:
  This voter votes on resources that are secured with JSR 250
  annotations—namely, DenyAll, PermitAll, and RolesAllowed.
  Their names are very descriptive. DenyAll won't allow any access at
  all to the resource, independent of the security information carried
  by the Authentication object trying to access it. PermitAll will
  allow access to everyone, regardless of what roles they have. The
  RolesAllowed annotation can be configured with a series of roles. If
  an Authentication object tries to access the resource, it must have
  one of the roles configured in the RolesAllowed annotation in order
  to get access granted by this voter.

- `org.springframework.security.access.prepost.`
  `PreInvocationAuthorizationAdviceVoter`: This voter votes on
  resources with expression configurations based on @PreFilter
  and @PreAuthorize annotations. @PreFilter and @PreAuthorize
  annotations support a `value` attribute that can have a SpEL expression.
  The `PreInvocationAuthorizationAdviceVoter` is the one in charge
  of evaluating the SpEL expressions (of course with the help of Spring's
  SpEL evaluation mechanism) provided in these annotations. We will be
  explaining and using SpEL expressions in several parts of the book so
  this concept will become clearer as the book advances.

- `org.springframework.security.access.vote.AbstractAclVoter`:
  This is the abstract class that has the skeleton to write voters dealing
  with domain ACL rules so that other implementing class builds on
  its functionality to add voting behavior. Currently, it is implemented
  in `AclEntryVoter`, which votes on users' permissions on domain
  objects. This voter will be covered in the chapter dedicated to ACL.

- `org.springframework.security.access.vote.`
  `AuthenticatedVoter`: This voter votes whenever a `ConfigAttribute`
  referencing any of the three possible levels of authentication
  is present on the secured resource. The three levels are IS_
  AUTHENTICATED_FULLY, IS_AUTHENTICATED_REMEMBERED, and
  IS_AUTHENTICATED_ANONYMOUSLY. The voter emits a positive vote
  if the `Authentication` object's authentication level matches (or is
  a stronger level in the hierarchy IS_AUTHENTICATED_FULLY > IS_
  AUTHENTICATED_REMEMBERED > IS_AUTHENTICATED_ANONYMOUSLY) the
  authentication level configured in the resource.

- `org.springframework.security.access.vote.RoleVoter`: This is
  perhaps the most commonly used voter of them all. This voter, by
  default, is able to vote on resources that have `ConfigAttribute(s)`
  containing security metadata starting with the prefix ROLE_ (which
  can be overridden). When an `Authentication` object tries to access
  the resource, its `GrantedAuthorities` are matched against the
  relevant `ConfigAttributes`. If there is a match, access is granted. If
  there isn't, access is denied.

- org.springframework.security.access.expression.
  WebExpressionVoter: This is the voter in charge of evaluating SpEL
  expressions in the context of web requests in the filter chain—
  expressions like 'hasRole' in the <intercept-url> element. To
  make use of this voter, and in general to support SpEL expressions
  in web security, the use-expressions="true" attribute needs to be
  added to the <http> element.

The voters model is yet another one in the framework that is open for extension
and customization. You can easily create your own implementation and add it to the
framework. You will see how to do this in Chapter 8.

The entire AccessDecisionVoter reference can be found on GitHub at https://
github.com/spring-projects/spring-security/blob/master/core/src/main/java/
org/springframework/security/access/AccessDecisionVoter.java.

Listing. 4-8. AccessDecisionVoter Interface

```
package org.springframework.security.access;
import java.util.Collection;
import org.springframework.security.core.Authentication;

public interface AccessDecisionVoter<S> {
int ACCESS_GRANTED = 1;
int ACCESS_ABSTAIN = 0;
int ACCESS_DENIED = -1;
boolean supports(ConfigAttribute attribute);
boolean supports(Class<?> clazz);
int vote(Authentication authentication, S object,
Collection<ConfigAttribute> attributes);
}
```

UserDetailsService and AuthenticationUserDetailsService

The interface org.springframework.security.core.userdetails.
UserDetailsService is in charge of loading the user information from the underlying
user store (in-memory, database, and so on) when an authentication request arrives in

the application. UserDetailsService makes use of the provided user name for looking up the rest of the required user data from the datastore. It defines just one method, as you can see in Listing 4-9. You can see its hierarchy in Figure 4-20.

Listing 4-9. UserDetailsServicepackage org.springframework.security.core. userdetails

```
public interface UserDetailsService {
  UserDetails loadUserByUsername(String username) throws
  UsernameNotFoundException;
}
```

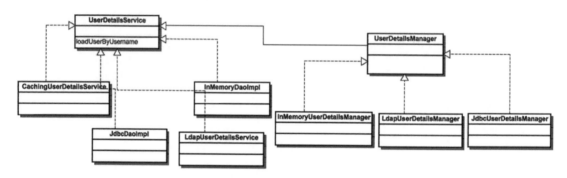

Figure 4-20. UserDetailsService *hierarchy*

The interface org.springframework.security.core.userdetails. AuthenticationUserDetailsService is more generic. It allows you to retrieve a UserDetails using an Authentication object instead of a user name String, making it more flexible to implement. Actually, there is an implementation of AuthenticationUserDetailsService (UserDetailsByNameServiceWrapper) that simply delegates to a UserDetailsService extracting the user name from the Authentication object.

Listing 4-10 shows the AuthenticationUserDetailsService interface. These are the two main strategies (AuthenticationUserDetailsService and UserDetailsService) used for retrieving the user information when attempting authentication. They are usually called from the particular AuthenticationProvider that is being used in the application. For example, the OpenIDAuthenticationProvider and CasAuthenticationProvider delegate to an AuthenticationUserDetailsService to obtain the user details, while the DaoAuthenticationProvider delegates directly to a UserDetailsService. Some other providers don't use a user details service of any kind (for example, JaasAuthenticationProvider uses its own mechanism to retrieve the principal from a javax.security.auth.login.LoginContext), and some others use a completely custom one (for example, LdapAuthenticationProvider uses a UserDetailsContextMapper).

Listing 4-10. AuthenticationUserDetailsService

```
package org.springframework.security.core.userdetails;
    public interface AuthenticationUserDetailsService<T extends Authentication> {
    UserDetails loadUserDetails(T token) throws UsernameNotFoundException;
}
```

UserDetails

The interface org.springframework.security.core.userdetails.UserDetails object is the main abstraction in the system, and it's used to represent a full user in the context of Spring Security. It is also made available to be accessed later in the system from any point that has access to SecurityContext. Normally, developers create their own implementation of this interface to store particular user details they need or want (like email, telephone, address, and so on). Later, they can access this information, which will be encapsulated in the Authentication object, and they can be obtained by calling the getPrincipal method on it.

Some of the current UserDetailsService (for example, InMemoryUserDetailsManager) implementations use the class org.springframework.security.core.userdetails.User, which is available in the core of the framework, as the UserDetails implementation returned by the method loadUserByUsername. However, this is another of those configurable points of the framework, and you can easily create your own UserDetails implementation and use that in your application. Listing 4-11 shows the UserDetails interface.

Listing 4-11. UserDetails Interface

```
package org.springframework.security.core.userdetails;

import org.springframework.security.core.Authentication;
import org.springframework.security.core.GrantedAuthority;

import java.io.Serializable;
import java.util.Collection;

public interface UserDetails extends Serializable {
Collection<? extends GrantedAuthority> getAuthorities();
String getPassword();
String getUsername();
boolean isAccountNonExpired();
boolean isAccountNonLocked();
boolean isCredentialsNonExpired();
boolean isEnabled();
}
```

ACL

The ACL is the module in charge of securing your application at the individual domain object level with a fine level of granularity. This means, in a general way, assigning an ID to each domain object in your application and creating a relationship between these objects and the different users of the application. These relationships determine whether or not a determined user is allowed access to a particular domain. The ACL model offers a fine-grained, access-level configuration you can use to define different rules for accessing the objects depending on who is trying to access it. (For example, a user might be allowed read access while another user will have write/read access over the same domain object.)

The current support for ACLs is configured to get the configuration rules from a relational database. The DDL (Data Definition Language) for configuring the database comes along with the framework itself, and it can be found in the ACL module.

ACL security will be fully covered in Chapter 7.

JSP Taglib

If you are working to secure a Java web application, the `taglib` component of the framework is the one you use to hide or show certain elements in your pages according to your users' permissions.

The tags are simple to use and, at the same time, very convenient for making a more usable web site. They help you adapt the UI of your application on a per-user (or more commonly, per-role) basis.

Good Design and Patterns in Spring Security

We said it before, but we will repeat it here: One of the great aspects of working with open source software is that you can (and we say *you should*) look at the source code and understand the software at a new, deeper level. Also, you can look at the way the software is built, what is good, and what is bad (at least by your own subjective standards) and just learn how other developers work. This can have a great impact on the way you work, because you might discover a way of doing things that you couldn't have learned on your own.

The code for Spring Security is publicly available on GitHub at `https://github.com/spring-projects/spring-security`.

Sometimes, of course, you will find things you don't like, but that is good as well. You can learn from other people's mistakes as much as you can learn from their successes.

For us, Spring in general and Spring Security in particular have achieved something that we found invaluable in the Java development space—that is, they can make us better developers even without us noticing it. For instance, we often ask ourselves, "How many people would be using a template pattern for accessing databases if they weren't using Spring, instead of a more awkward DB access layer?" or "How many people would be just programming against implementation classes all the time, creating unnecessary coupling if it wasn't for Spring's DI support?" or "How many people would have cross-cutting concerns, like transactions, all over their code base if it wasn't for how easily Spring brings AOP into the development process?"

We think helping good practices almost without noticing is really a great achievement of Spring. It won't create great developers by itself for sure, but it helps the average developer to not make mistakes that they might make if they didn't have the support of the framework and its principles to adhere to.

As you might see from the description of the main components of the framework, Spring Security itself is built with good design principles and patterns in mind. Let's have a brief look here at some of the things we find interesting in the framework, and from which you can learn.

This section won't really help you to do more with Spring Security, but it will serve as a way to appreciate the good work that has been done in constructing this fantastic framework.

Strategy Pattern

A big part of the pluggability and modularity of the framework is achieved thanks to the wide use of the Strategy pattern. You can find it, for example, in the type of SecurityContext to be used, the AuthenticationProvider hierarchy, the AccessDecisionVoters, and many other elements. Covering design patterns is outside the scope of this book but as a reminder of the strategy pattern's power, we leave you with this definition from Wikipedia: "The strategy pattern defines a family of algorithms, encapsulates each one, and makes them interchangeable. Strategy lets the algorithm vary independently from clients that use it."

That definition shows a great deal of the power that comes with working with interfaces. You can have different implementations of the same interface and pass any of them to a client class for doing different kinds of work. The client classes don't need to know or care about the implementation details they are working with. Knowing the interface or contract is enough to leverage its job.

Decorator Pattern

Built into Spring's core AOP framework, you can find the Decorator pattern—mostly in the way that your annotated business classes and methods get security constraints applied to them. Basically, your objects have only certain meta information related to the security constraints that should be applied to them, and then by some "Spring magic" they get wrapped with security handling. Listing 4-12 shows the invoke method of MethodSecurityInterceptor. In the listing, you can see how the objects are decorated with prefunctionality and postfunctionality that surrounds the invocation of the actual method.

Listing 4-12. `MethodSecurityInterceptor`'s Invoke Method

```
public Object invoke(MethodInvocation mi) throws Throwable {
InterceptorStatusToken token = super.beforeInvocation(mi);
        Object result = mi.proceed();
returnsuper.afterInvocation(token, result);
    }
```

SRP

Spring Security's code seems to take very seriously the Single Responsibility Principle. There are many examples of it around the framework, because any object you choose seems to have one and only one responsibility. For example, the `AuthenticationProvider` deals only with the general concern of authenticating a principal with its credentials in the system. The `SecurityInterceptor` is simply in charge of intercepting the requests, and it delegates all security-checking logic to collaborating objects. A lot more examples like this can be extracted from the framework.

DI

Again, this is built into the Spring Framework itself, and of course as everything in the Spring architecture, this means that it is also inherited by the rest of the Spring projects, including Spring Security. Dependency injection (DI) is one of Spring's most important features. Almost every component in Spring Security is configured through the use of dependency injection. The `AccessDecisionManager` is injected into the `AbstractSecurityInterceptor`, and `AccessDecisionVoter` implementations are injected into the `AccessDecisionManager`. And like this, most of the framework is built by composing components together through dependency injection.

Summary

This was a complex chapter, but going through the inner workings of a software tool is definitely the best way to understand it and take advantage of it. And that is what you did. You got an in-depth explanation of Spring Security's architecture, its major components, and the way it works from the inside.

You should now understand how the XML namespace works, how AOP fits into the framework, and how, in general, the Servlet Filter functionality is used to enforce web-level security.

We demystified the "Spring magic" by going through all the components that help you add security to your applications in a seemingly simple way.

You looked at some code snippets from the framework itself to get a greater appreciation of the work done in it, as well as to understand better why things work the way they do.

You also studied the modularity inherent in the framework and saw how it helps to create software that is both flexible and extensible.

Even with all we covered in this chapter, this was basically an introduction and a reference to have in hand when you read the upcoming chapters and you start looking at the options to secure your applications. From now on, you will understand where everything fits in the framework and how the different components link to each other.

In the next chapter, you will start developing an example application. In the beginning, it will be a simple web application, and you will see how to secure it. You will use all your current knowledge of the framework to tweak the configuration and test different ways of implementing security at the web level.

CHAPTER 5

Web Security

In this chapter, we will continue explaining how to apply security at the web layer for the Java Web-Based Applications you started in Chapter 3. You will see in detail the inner work of the security filter chain and the different metadata options at your disposal to define security constraints in your application. We will also explain in detail the taglib facility for enforcing security constraints at the view level, which was also introduced in Chapter 3.

Introducing the Simple Example Application

In this chapter, you will be working on a simple test web application named favoritesmovies. The application itself will be very simple. (It won't have any really useful functionality). However, we will try to cover most of the options available for securing web applications with Spring Security, even if some of the options don't seem realistic for an application of this kind.

First, you will set up the application. As in Chapter 3, you will create a Java Web Application and include Maven as the framework. Again, you will assume certain versions of the different tools you need. Mainly, you will use Java 11 and Maven 3.6.0 as you did in Chapter 3.

Create the project as shown in Figure 5-1.

© Carlo Scarioni and Massimo Nardone 2019
C. Scarioni and M. Nardone, *Pro Spring Security*, https://doi.org/10.1007/978-1-4842-5052-5_5

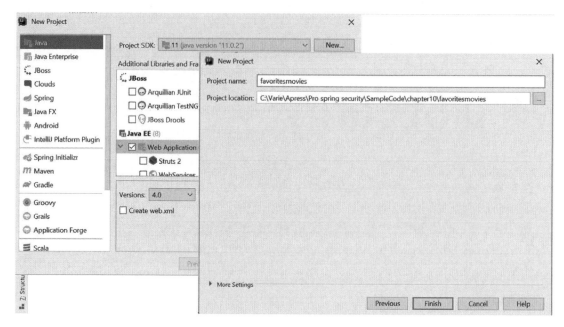

Figure 5-1. *Creating a new dynamic web application*

Now you have an empty web project. The next step will be to convert it to Maven project. At the moment, you will use the same dependencies you had in your program from Chapter 3. So make sure your pom.xml file has the content from Listing 5-1.

Listing 5-1. First pom.xml for favoritesmovies

```
<?xml version="1.0" encoding="UTF-8"?>
<project xmlns="http://maven.apache.org/POM/4.0.0"
xmlns:xsi="http://www.w3.org/2001/XMLSchema-instance"
xsi:schemaLocation="http://maven.apache.org/POM/4.0.0
http://maven.apache.org/maven-v4_0_0.xsd">

  <modelVersion>4.0.0</modelVersion>
  <packaging>war</packaging>

  <name>pss01_favoritesmovies</name>
  <groupId>com.apress.pss</groupId>
  <artifactId>favoritesmovies</artifactId>
  <version>1.0-SNAPSHOT</version>
    <!-- Build -->
    <build>
```

```
    <pluginManagement>
        <plugins>
            <plugin>
                <groupId>org.apache.maven.plugins</groupId>
                <artifactId>maven-compiler-plugin</artifactId>
                <version>3.2</version>
                <configuration>
                    <source>11</source>
                    <target>11</target>
                </configuration>
            </plugin>
            <plugin>
                <groupId>org.apache.maven.plugins</groupId>
                <artifactId>maven-war-plugin</artifactId>
                <version>2.4</version>
                <configuration>
                    <warSourceDirectory>src/main/webapp</
                    warSourceDirectory>
                    <warName>pss01_Security</warName>
                    <failOnMissingWebXml>false</failOnMissingWebXml>
                </configuration>
            </plugin>
        </plugins>
    </pluginManagement>
    <finalName>favoritesmovies</finalName>
    </build>
</project>
```

As shown previously, when creating a new Java Web Application project, a new index.jsp page is automatically generated under the WEB-INF folder.

Just to test that it works, update the .jsp file to show simple "Hello World!" text, and then compile and execute the application running on the external Tomcat v9, as you did in Chapter 3.

If you open your browser and go to http://localhost:8080/favoritesmovies, you will see the message "Hello World!" as the output of the index.jsp web page, as shown in Figure 5-2.

Figure 5-2. *The first iteration of the application displays the simple Hello World! page*

Let's start adding the security to this example.

First, you need to configure pom.xml with the Spring Security 5 dependencies shown and explained in Chapter 3, such as

- spring-security-web

- spring-security-config

- spring-security-taglibs

Update your pom.xml file as shown in Listing 5-2.

Listing 5-2. pom.xml with All the Security and Framework Dependencies

```xml
<?xml version="1.0" encoding="UTF-8"?>
<project xmlns="http://maven.apache.org/POM/4.0.0"
xmlns:xsi="http://www.w3.org/2001/XMLSchema-instance"
xsi:schemaLocation="http://maven.apache.org/POM/4.0.0
http://maven.apache.org/maven-v4_0_0.xsd">

  <modelVersion>4.0.0</modelVersion>
  <packaging>war</packaging>

  <name>pss01_favoritesmovies</name>
  <groupId>com.apress.pss</groupId>
  <artifactId>favoritesmovies</artifactId>
  <version>1.0-SNAPSHOT</version>

    <properties>
        <springframework.version>5.1.5.RELEASE</springframework.version>
        <springsecurity.version>5.1.5.RELEASE</springsecurity.version>
    </properties>
```

```xml
<dependencies>
    <!-- Spring -->
    <dependency>
        <groupId>org.springframework</groupId>
        <artifactId>spring-core</artifactId>
        <version>${springframework.version}</version>
    </dependency>
    <dependency>
        <groupId>org.springframework</groupId>
        <artifactId>spring-web</artifactId>
        <version>${springframework.version}</version>
    </dependency>
    <dependency>
        <groupId>org.springframework</groupId>
        <artifactId>spring-webmvc</artifactId>
        <version>${springframework.version}</version>
    </dependency>

    <!-- Spring Security -->
    <dependency>
        <groupId>org.springframework.security</groupId>
        <artifactId>spring-security-web</artifactId>
        <version>${springsecurity.version}</version>
    </dependency>
    <dependency>
        <groupId>org.springframework.security</groupId>
        <artifactId>spring-security-config</artifactId>
        <version>${springsecurity.version}</version>
    </dependency>

    <dependency>
        <groupId>javax.servlet</groupId>
        <artifactId>javax.servlet-api</artifactId>
        <version>4.0.1</version>
    </dependency>
```

```xml
        <dependency>
            <groupId>javax.servlet.jsp</groupId>
            <artifactId>javax.servlet.jsp-api</artifactId>
            <version>2.3.3</version>
        </dependency>
        <dependency>
            <groupId>javax.servlet</groupId>
            <artifactId>jstl</artifactId>
            <version>1.2</version>
        </dependency>
        <dependency>
            <groupId>taglibs</groupId>
            <artifactId>standard</artifactId>
            <version>1.1.2</version>
        </dependency>

        <dependency>
            <groupId>org.springframework.security</groupId>
            <artifactId>spring-security-taglibs</artifactId>
            <version>5.1.5.RELEASE</version>
        </dependency>
    </dependencies>

    <!-- Build -->
    <build>
        <pluginManagement>
            <plugins>
                <plugin>
                    <groupId>org.apache.maven.plugins</groupId>
                    <artifactId>maven-compiler-plugin</artifactId>
                    <version>3.2</version>
                    <configuration>
                        <source>11</source>
                        <target>11</target>
                    </configuration>
                </plugin>
```

```
        <plugin>
            <groupId>org.apache.maven.plugins</groupId>
            <artifactId>maven-war-plugin</artifactId>
            <version>2.4</version>
            <configuration>
                <warSourceDirectory>src/main/webapp</
                warSourceDirectory>
                <warName> favoritesmovies </warName>
                <failOnMissingWebXml>false</failOnMissingWebXml>
            </configuration>
        </plugin>
      </plugins>
    </pluginManagement>
    <finalName>favoritesmovies</finalName>
  </build>
</project>
```

Create a new folder named `view` under the `WEB-INF` folder. It will hold all your `.jsp` web pages.

Next, import all the Java classes you used in Chapter 3.

Under the Java package `com.apress.pss.springsecurity.controller`, copy

- `UserController`

Under the Java package `com.apress.pss.springsecurity.configuration`, copy

- `AppInitializer`

- `SecurityConfiguration`

- `SpringSecurityInitializer`

- `UserConfiguration`

Note that, for the purposes of web security, it doesn't really matter if you use a Spring MVC controller, like you do here, or if you use simple servlets, as you did in Chapter 3, or for that matter, if you use any other Servlet-based framework for developing your application. Remember that, at the core, the web part of Spring Security basically attaches itself to the standard Java servlet filter architecture. So if your application uses servlets and filters, you can leverage Spring Security's web support.

Since Spring Framework 4.3, there are some new HTTP mapping annotations based on @RequestMapping:

- @GetMapping

- @PostMapping

- @PutMapping

- @DeleteMapping

- @PatchMapping

For instance, @GetMapping is a specialized version of the @RequestMapping annotation, which will act as a shortcut for @RequestMapping(method = RequestMethod.GET). @GetMapping annotated methods to handle the HTTP GET requests matched with a certain given URI expression.

Now that you've copied the Java classes from Chapter 3, you can start making changes to them.

Let's start with the Java controller file, where using @GetMapping you define the controls with values /, /index, and /movies, which will trigger the index.jsp and movies.jsp pages.

The UserController Java class can be found in Listing 5-3.

Listing 5-3. The UserController Controller

```
package com.apress.pss.springsecurity.controller;

import javax.servlet.http.HttpServletRequest;
import javax.servlet.http.HttpServletResponse;
import org.springframework.security.core.Authentication;
import org.springframework.security.core.context.SecurityContextHolder;
import org.springframework.security.web.authentication.logout.
SecurityContextLogoutHandler;
import org.springframework.stereotype.Controller;
import org.springframework.ui.ModelMap;
import org.springframework.web.bind.annotation.GetMapping;
```

```
@Controller
public class UserController {

@GetMapping ("/")
    public String home() {
        return "index";
    }
@GetMapping ("/index")
    public String index() {
        return "index";
    }

@GetMapping ("/movies")
    public String movies() {
        return "movies";
    }
}
```

You can see that in this controller you specified the URL, the HTTP method, and the body of the request you will receive. The URL is built with a combination of the class-level RequestMapping annotation's value concatenated with the method-level RequestMapping annotation's value. So your URL is movies. The HTTP method is specified as POST in the RequestMapping annotation on the method. The RequestBody annotation in the method parameter simply tells Spring to populate the movie parameter with the string that comes in the body of the request. And the ResponseBody annotation at the method level tells Spring to use the return value of the method as the body content of the response.

Next, let's create a simple .jsp page named movies.jsp, as shown in Listing 5-4.

Listing 5-4. The movies.jsp Page

```
<html>
    <body>
      <h2>My favorites list of movies:</h2>
        <br>Il Postino
        <br>La vita e' bella
        <br>NottingHill
</body>
</html>
```

With no user authentication yet required, you can test your new functionality by building the application, opening the URL http://localhost:8080/favoritesmovies/ movies, and seeing the result in Figure 5-3.

Figure 5-3. *Executing the project using a .jsp web page*

As you can see, the application using the control /movies will trigger the movies.jsp page and show the list of the movies.

Let's configure it now so that the /movies control will require an authenticated user with the ADMIN role. Update the SecurityConfiguration Java class from Chapter 3 to the code shown in Listing 5-5.

Listing 5-5. SecurityConfiguration Java Class

```
package com.apress.pss.springsecurity.configuration;

import org.springframework.beans.factory.annotation.Autowired;
import org.springframework.context.annotation.Bean;
import org.springframework.context.annotation.Configuration;
import org.springframework.security.config.annotation.authentication.
builders.AuthenticationManagerBuilder;
import org.springframework.security.config.annotation.web.builders.
HttpSecurity;
import org.springframework.security.config.annotation.web.configuration.
EnableWebSecurity;
import org.springframework.security.config.annotation.web.configuration.
WebSecurityConfigurerAdapter;
import org.springframework.security.crypto.bcrypt.BCryptPasswordEncoder;
import org.springframework.security.crypto.password.PasswordEncoder;
```

```java
@Configuration
@EnableWebSecurity
public class SecurityConfiguration extends WebSecurityConfigurerAdapter {

    @Autowired
    PasswordEncoder passwordEncoder;

    @Override
    protected void configure(AuthenticationManagerBuilder auth) throws
    Exception {
        auth.inMemoryAuthentication()
                .passwordEncoder(passwordEncoder)
                .withUser("admin").password(passwordEncoder.
                encode("admin123")).roles("ADMIN");
    }

    @Bean
    public PasswordEncoder passwordEncoder() {
        return new BCryptPasswordEncoder();
    }

    @Override
    protected void configure(HttpSecurity http) throws Exception {

        http.authorizeRequests()
                .antMatchers("/", "/index", "/login").permitAll()
                .antMatchers("/**").hasRole("ADMIN")
                .and().formLogin()
                .and().logout().logoutSuccessUrl("/index").permitAll()
                .and().csrf().disable();

    }

}
```

The code is very simple, as basically the /, /index, and /login controls are permitted without authentication, while any other page via the /** will require an authenticated user with ADMIN as role. You will use the default login page generated automatically by Security Spring v5. Logout is needed when the logout link is used; this will be explained later. Finally, cross-site request forgery is disabled as discussed in Chapter 3.

Next, update the movies.jsp page to

```
<%@ page language="java" contentType="text/html; charset=ISO-8859-1"
pageEncoding="ISO-8859-1"%>
<%@ taglib prefix="c" uri="http://java.sun.com/jsp/jstl/core"%>
<html>
<head>
    <meta http-equiv="Content-Type" content="text/html;
    charset=ISO-8859-1">
    <title>Spring Security authentication example</title>
</head>
<body>
<h2>My favorites list of movies:</h2>
<br>Il Postino
<br>La vita e' bella
<br>NottingHill
<br><br>
<a href="<c:url value="/logout" />">Logout</a>
</body>
</html>
```

Now you have all the files needed and configured for this example. You want know to access the same URL as before to reach the movies.jsp page but this time Spring Security will ask you to provide admin credentials to access it. Restart the application and paste the following URL in your browser's address bar: http://localhost:8080/favoritesmovies/movies.

This time, your browser should get redirected to the URL http://localhost:8080/favoritesmovies/login and should show you the familiar login form from Chapter 3, which you can see in Figure 5-4. Log in as admin/admin123 and you can access the movies.jsp page as an admin.

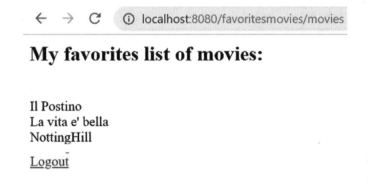

Figure 5-4. *Spring Security v5 login form*

Once the admin credential is correct, Spring Security will provide access to the movies.jsp page, as shown in Figure 5-5.

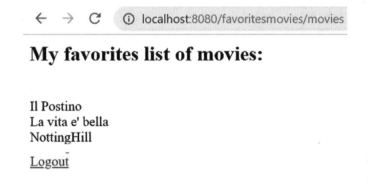

Figure 5-5. *The movies page accessed with admin credentials*

Please notice that we added a logout link to actually log out the user if needed. We will explain more in detail how to use Spring Security login and logout URL later in this chapter.

You will now look in more detail at what is going on in the application and how the configuration you just defined is helping to secure the application. You will follow the request throughout its trip through the framework and look at the different steps that it takes.

When you make the HTTP request to the configured URL, and after your Servlet container deals with it, the request lands in the DelegatingFilterProxy, which in turn delegates the processing to the security FilterChainProxy.

In general, Spring Security utilizes a lot of filters. In the case of HTTP request filter, it will be used to

- Intercept the request.

- Detect authentication (or absence of).

- Redirect to authentication entry point.

- Pass the request to authorization service.

- Send the request to the servlet or throw security exception.

In Spring Security v5, the most important filters are the following:
Security Filter Chain:

- `DelegatingFilterProxy`

- `FilterChainProxy`

Core Security Filters:

- `FilterSecurityInterceptor`

- `ExceptionTranslationFilter`

- `SecurityContextPersistenceFilter`

- `UsernamePasswordAuthenticationFilter`

- `AnonymousAuthenticationFilter`

Basic and Digest Authentication Filters:

- `BasicAuthenticationFilter`

- `DigestAuthenticationFilter`

Session Management:

- `SessionManagementFilter`

CSRF Caveats:

- `HiddenHttpMethodFilter`

Preauthentication Scenarios:

- `AbstractPreAuthenticatedProcessingFilter`

LogoutSuccessHandler:

- LogoutFilter

Spring Security-Aware HttpServletRequestWrapper:

- SecurityContextHolderAwareRequestFilter

RequestCache:

- RequestCacheFilter

The HTTP request and authentication processes and filters are explained in Chapter 4.

Let's see what happen when incorrect or correct credentials are provided when logging in. When the browser is redirecting and asks for the URL /login, the following occurs:

- The process is the same as for the first request until it reaches the DefaultLoginPageGeneratingFilter. At this point, the filter detects that the request is for the URL /login and writes the login form's HTML data directly in the response object. Then the response is rendered.

Now try to log in with incorrect credentials. Let's follow the request through the framework to see what happens:

1. In the login form, type the username **user** and the password **uspass**.

2. When the form is submitted, the filters are activated again in the same order as before. This time, however, when the request arrives at the UsernamePasswordAuthenticationFilter, the filter checks whether the request is for the URL /login and sees that this is indeed the case. The filter extracts the username and password authentication information from the HTTP request parameters username and password, respectively. With this information, it creates the UsernamePasswordAuthenticationToken Authentication object, which then sends it to the AuthenticationManager (or more exactly, its default implementation, ProviderManager) for authentication.

3.   The DaoAuthenticationProvider gets called from the
     ProviderManager with the Authentication object. The
     DaoAuthentication provider is an implementation
     of AuthenticationProvider, which uses a strategy of
     UserDetailsService to retrieve the users from whichever
     storage they live in. With the configuration you currently have,
     it will try to find a user with the username of user using the
     configured InMemoryUserDetailsManager (the implementation of
     UserDetailsService that maintains an in-memory user storage
     in a java.util.Map). Because there is no user with this username,
     the provider throws a UsernameNotFoundException exception.

4.   The provider itself catches this exception and converts it into a
     BadCredentialsException to hide the fact that there is no such
     user in the application; instead, it treats the error as a common
     username-password combination error.

5.   The exception is caught by the
     UsernamePasswordAuthenticationFilter. This filter
     delegates to an instance of an implementation of
     AuthenticationFailureHandler, which in turn decides to
     redirect the response to the URL /login?error. This way, the
     login form is shown again in the browser with an error message
     displayed. You can see this interaction in Figure 5-6.

Figure 5-6. *Authentication filter when authentication details are incorrect*

Let's now log in with the correct credentials.

First, create a new endpoint in the controller to retrieve some simple text. In the
controller UserController, create the method from Listing 5-6 called /showmovie.

Listing 5-6. A Simple Endpoint Method That Returns a Simple String

```
@GetMapping("/showmovie")
@ResponseBody
    public String showMovie() {
        return "movie x";
    }
```

Restart the application, go back to the URL `http:/localhost:8080/` `favoritesmovies/showmovie`, and type **admin** as the username and **admin123** as the password in the form. Then click the Login button.

- The request follows the same filter journey as before. This time, `InMemoryUserDetailsManager` finds a user with the requested username and returns that to `DaoAuthenticationProvider`, which creates a successful `Authentication` object.

- After successful authentication, the `UsernamePasswordAuthenticationFilter` delegates to an instance of `SavedRequestAwareAuthenticationSuccessHandler`, which looks for the original requested URL (`/showmovie`) in the session and redirects the response to that URL.

When `http://localhost:8080/favoritesmovies/showmovie` is requested, the request works its way through the filter chain as in the previous cases. This time, though, you already have a fully authenticated entity in the system. The request arrives in the `FilterSecurityInterceptor`.

- The `FilterSecurityInterceptor` receives an access request to the URL `/showmovie`. Then it recovers the necessary credentials to access that URL (`ROLE_ADMIN`).

- The `AffirmativeBased` access-decision manager gets called and in turn calls the `RoleVoter` voter. The voter evaluates the list of authorities of the authenticated entity and compares them with the required credentials to access the resource. Because the voter finds a match (`ROLE_ADMIN` is in both the `Authentication` authorities and the resource's `config` attributes), it votes with an `ACCESS_GRANTED` vote.

- The `FilterSecurityInterceptor` forwards the request to the next element in the request-handling chain, which in this case is Spring's `DispatcherServlet`.

- The request gets to the `AdminController`, which simply returns the String `movie x`, which then gets rendered to the browser. Figure 5-7 shows this result.

My favorite movie: il postino

Figure 5-7. *The showmovie page is returned when accessing with correct credentials*

- This is the complete flow of the Authentication and Authorization process. Figure 5-8 shows this full interaction in a pseudo flow chart.

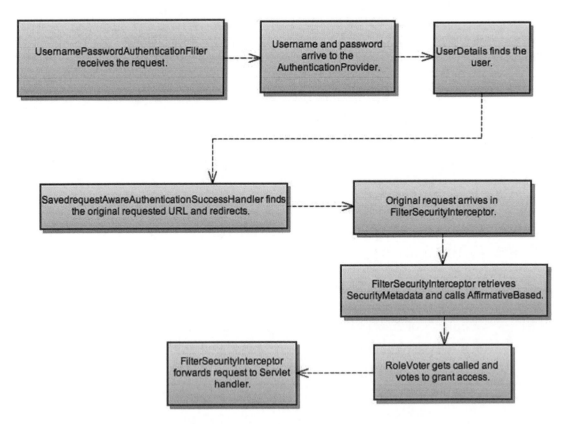

Figure 5-8. *Overall flow of a successful authentication and authorization process*

The Special URLs

From the preceding explanation, you can see that Spring Security's support for web security defines a few preconfigured URLs for you to use in your application. These URLs get special treatment in the framework. The main ones are the following:

- /login: This is the URL that Spring Security uses to show the login form for the application. The framework will redirect to this URL when an authentication is needed but doesn't exist yet.

- /logout: This URL is used by the framework to log out the currently logged-in user, invalidating the corresponding session and SecurityContext.

From the previous URLs, the first thing that comes to mind is how to configure your own login form in the application and, in general, how to customize the login process instead of using the default one. That is what we'll do next.

Note   As of Spring Security v5, /login replaced /j_spring_security_ check, which was in use until Spring Security 4.

Custom Login Form

When you use Spring security v5, the user authentication request to your application is done via the http.authorizeRequests() method.

When you configure the http element, via the http.authorizeRequests() method, as you did before, Spring Security takes care of setting up a default login and logout process for you, including a login URL, login form, default URL after login, and some other options. Basically, when Spring Security's context starts to load up, it will find that there is no custom login page URL configured, so it will assume the default one and create a new instance of DefaultLoginPageGeneratingFilter that will be added to the filter chain. As you saw before, this filter is the one that generates the login form for you.

If you want to configure your own form, you need to do the following tasks. The first thing is to tell the framework to replace the default handling with your own. You define the following element as a child of the `http.authorizeRequests()` method in the `SecurityConfiguration` Java file:

```
formLogin().loginPage("/name of the login page")
```

This element tells Spring Security to change its default login-handling mechanism on startup. First, the `DefaultLoginPageGeneratingFilter` will no longer be instantiated. Let's try this first configuration out. With the new configuration in place, restart the application and try to access the URL `http://localhost:8080/favoritesmovies/movies`.

You get redirected to the URL `/login` and get a 404 HTTP error because you haven't defined any handler for this URL yet. This 404 page is shown in Figure 5-9.

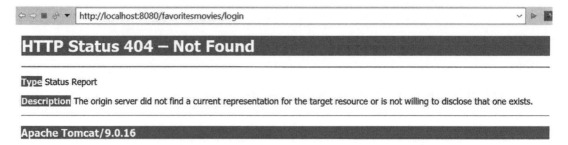

Figure 5-9. *Error 404 that appears when defining a new login handler page*

Let's add a login controller in the `UserController` as shown in Listing 5-7.

Listing 5-7. Login Controller Added to the UserController

```java
@GetMapping("/login")
  public String loginPage() {
      return "login";
  }
}
```

Next add the following line to the SecurityConfiguration file:

```
.and().formLogin().loginPage("/login").permitAll()
```

Now create the `login.jsp` page from Listing 5-8 in the folder `WEB-INF/views` in your application.

Listing 5-8. custom login.jsp

```jsp
<%@ page contentType="text/html;charset=UTF-8" language="java" %>
<%@ taglib prefix="c" uri="http://java.sun.com/jsp/jstl/core"%>
<html>
<head>
    <title>Spring Security Custom Login Form</title>
</head>
<body onload='document.loginForm.username.focus();'>

<h1>Spring Security Custom Login Form:</h1>

<div id="login-box">

    <h2>Login with Username and Password</h2>

    <% if(request.getParameter("error") != null){
        out.println("ERROR LOGIN");
    }
    %>

    <c:url value="/login" var="loginUrl"/>
    <form action="${loginUrl}" method="post">
        <table>
            <tr>
                <td>User:</td>
                <td><input type='text' name='username' value=""></td>
            </tr>
            <tr>
                <td>Password:</td>
                <td><input type='password' name='password' /></td>
            </tr>
            <tr>
                <td>Remember Me:</td>
                <td><input type="checkbox" name="remember-me" /></td>
            </tr>
```

```
        <tr>
            <td colspan='2'><input name="submit" type="submit"
                                    value="submit" /></td>
        </tr>
    </table>

  </form>

</div>

</body>
</html>
```

If you restart the application and again go to `http://localhost:8080/` `favoritesmovies/movies`, you should see your new login form when you get redirected to the `/login` URL The form is shown in Figure 5-10. If you type **admin** as username and **admin123** as password, you get access to the `movie x` page, as you did before with the default login form.

Figure 5-10. *Custom login form*

If you take a look at the `login.jsp`, you can see certain names for the username field, password field, the remember me checkbox, and the action attribute of the form element. These are not random names. Spring Security expects the use of these particular names in order to treat the authentication process correctly. Also, the form should use POST for sending the information to the server because this is required by the framework.

The "Remember Me" checkbox shown in the figure will be explained later.

The element `<form-login>` supports many more configuration options, including changing the default `username` and `password` names for the authentication request parameters.

The `<form-login>` attributes might include

- `always-use-default-target`
- `authentication-details-source-ref`
- `authentication-failure-handler-ref`
- `authentication-failure-url`
- `authentication-success-handler-ref`
- `default-target-url`
- `login-page`
- `login-processing-url`
- `password-parameter`
- `username-parameter`
- `authentication-success-forward-url`
- `authentication-failure-forward-url`

Restart the application, go to the URL /movies, and log in with **admin/admin123**. You should be able to access the application without any problem.

Give this attribute the value /login. Then, in your `login.jsp`, add the content from Listing 5-9 just after the `<body>` tag.

Listing 5-9. Snippet Showing an Error in the login.jsp

```
<% if(request.getParameter("error") != null){
       out.println("ERROR LOGIN");
   }
%>
```

If you now restart the application and try to access the URL `http://localhost:8080/favoritesmovies/movies` and use an incorrect username and password, you will get the login page again, but with the error message shown at the top. Look at Figure 5-11 for the page you should be getting.

Figure 5-11. *A custom error shown in the custom form*

Note that this URL could be a different URL altogether, not related to the login URL at all. But the common pattern is to allow the user another attempt at logging in, showing her any errors.

- `authentication-success-handler-ref`: Reference to an AuthenticationSuccessHandler bean in the Spring application context. This bean is called upon successful authentication and should handle the next step after authentication, usually deciding the redirect destination in the application. A current implementation in the form of SavedRequestAwareAuthenticationSuccessHandler takes care of redirecting the logged-in user to the original requested URL after successful authentication.

- `authentication-failure-handler-ref`: Reference to an AuthenticationFailureHandler bean in the Spring application context. It is used to handle failed authentication requests. When an authentication fails, this handler gets called. A standard behavior for this handler is to present the login screen again or return a 401 HTTP status error. This behavior is provided by the concrete class SimpleUrlAuthenticationFailureHandler.

Let's develop a simple example implementation of the AuthenticationFailureHandler interface. It will simply return a 500 status code when failing to authenticate. Create the class CustomAuthenticationFailureHandler from Listing 5-10.

Listing 5-10. AuthenticationFailureHandler Implementation for ServerErrorFailureHandler

```
package com.apress.pss.springsecurity.configuration;

import org.springframework.security.web.authentication.
AuthenticationFailureHandler;
import org.springframework.security.core.AuthenticationException;
import javax.servlet.http.HttpServletRequest;
import javax.servlet.http.HttpServletResponse;
import java.io.IOException;

public class CustomAuthenticationFailureHandler implements
AuthenticationFailureHandler {
    @Override
    public void onAuthenticationFailure(HttpServletRequest request,
    HttpServletResponse response, AuthenticationException e) throws
            IOException {
        response.sendError(500);
    }
}
```

Then, add to the SecurityConfiguration class file the following:

```
.and().formLogin().loginPage("/login").permitAll().failureHandler(new
CustomAuthenticationFailureHandler())
```

And the new bean:

```
@Bean
public AuthenticationFailureHandler customAuthenticationFailureHandler() {
    return new CustomAuthenticationFailureHandler();
}
```

Restart the application, go to http://localhost:8080/favoritesmovies/movies, use a random username and password, and click the Submit button. You should get a 500 error in the browser.

Listing 5-11 shows the fully updated SecurityConfiguration file so far.

141

Listing 5-11. SecurityConfiguration

```
package com.apress.pss.springsecurity.configuration;

import org.springframework.beans.factory.annotation.Autowired;
import org.springframework.context.annotation.Bean;
import org.springframework.context.annotation.Configuration;
import org.springframework.security.config.annotation.authentication.
builders.AuthenticationManagerBuilder;
import org.springframework.security.config.annotation.web.builders.
HttpSecurity;
import org.springframework.security.config.annotation.web.configuration.
EnableWebSecurity;
import org.springframework.security.config.annotation.web.configuration.
WebSecurityConfigurerAdapter;
import org.springframework.security.crypto.bcrypt.BCryptPasswordEncoder;
import org.springframework.security.crypto.password.PasswordEncoder;
import org.springframework.security.web.authentication.
AuthenticationFailureHandler;

@Configuration
@EnableWebSecurity
public class SecurityConfiguration extends WebSecurityConfigurerAdapter {

    @Autowired
    PasswordEncoder passwordEncoder;

    @Override
    protected void configure(AuthenticationManagerBuilder auth) throws
    Exception {
        auth.inMemoryAuthentication()
                .passwordEncoder(passwordEncoder)
                .withUser("admin").password(passwordEncoder.
                encode("admin123")).roles("ADMIN");
    }
```

```
@Bean
public PasswordEncoder passwordEncoder() {
    return new BCryptPasswordEncoder();
}

@Override
protected void configure(HttpSecurity http) throws Exception {

    http.authorizeRequests()
            .antMatchers("/", "/login").permitAll()
            .antMatchers("/**").hasRole("ADMIN")
            .and().formLogin().loginPage("/login").permitAll().
            failureHandler(new CustomAuthenticationFailureHandler())
            .and().csrf().disable();
}

@Bean
public AuthenticationFailureHandler customAuthenticationFailureHandler() {
    return new CustomAuthenticationFailureHandler();
}

}
```

Basic HTTP Authentication

Sometimes, you can't really use a login form for authenticating users. For instance, if your application is meant to be called by other systems instead of a human user, it doesn't make sense to show a login form to the other application. This is a pretty common use case. Web services talk to each other without user interaction, ESB systems integrate systems with one another, and JMS clients produce and consume messages from other systems.

In the context of HTTP-exposed interfaces that require no human user to access them, a common approach is to use HTTP basic authentication headers. HTTP authentication headers allow you to embed the security information (username and password) in the header of the request that you send to the server, instead of sending it in the body of the request, as is the case for the login form authentication.

HTTP uses a standard header for carrying this information. The header is appropriately named `Authorization`. When using this header, the client that is sending the request (for example, a browser) concatenates the username and the password with a colon between them and then Base64 encodes the resulting string, sending the result of this in the header. For example, if you use the username **neve** and the password **nardone**, the client creates the string `neve:nardone` and encodes it prior to sending it in the header.

Let's use basic HTTP authentication in your application. The first and only thing you need to do is remove the `.formlogin()` element in your configuration file `SecurityConfiguration` and add instead

`.httpBasic()`

After replacing it, restart the application and go to the URL `http://localhost:8080/favoritesmovies/movies` in the browser. A standard HTTP authentication box will pop up asking you for your authentication details, as Figure 5-12 shows. Type **admin/admin123** as the username and password, and send the request. You will successfully arrive on the movies page that you already saw a couple of times before (Figure 5-5).

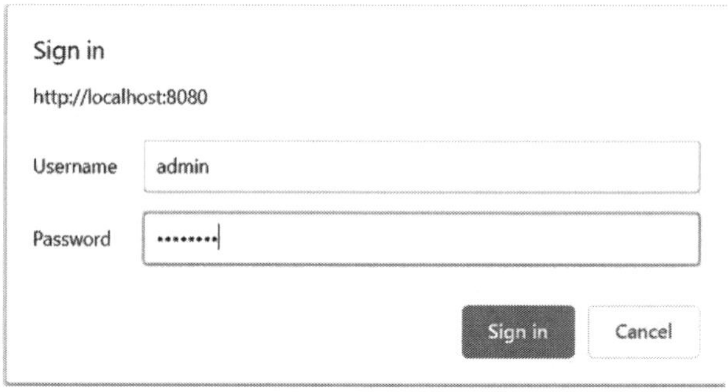

Figure 5-12. *Standard HTTP authentication form, basic authentication configuration*

When you use the `httpBasic` configuration element, `Spring Security's` `BasicAuthenticationFilter` comes into action. A `BasicAuthenticationEntryPoint` strategy will be configured into the `ExceptionTranslationFilter` on startup. When you make the first request to the URL /movies, the framework behaves as before, throwing an access-denied exception that is handled by the `ExceptionTranslationFilter`. This filter delegates to a particular implementation strategy of `AuthenticationEntryPoint`— in this case, `BasicAuthenticationEntryPoint`. `BasicAuthenticationEntryPoint` adds the header `WWW-Authenticate: Basic realm="Spring Security Application"` to the response and then sends an HTTP status of 401 (Unauthorized) to the client. The client should know how to handle this code and work accordingly. (In the case of a browser, it simply shows the authentication pop-up.)

When you introduce the username and password, and submit the request, the request again follows the filter chain until it reaches the `BasicAuthenticationFilter`. This filter checks the request headers, looking for the `Authorization` header starting with `Basic`. The filter extracts the content of the header and uses `Base64.decode` to decode the string, and then it extracts the username and password. The filter creates a `UsernamePasswordAuthenticationToken` object and sends it to the authentication manager for authentication in the standard way. The authentication manager will ask the authentication provider to retrieve the user and then create an `Authentication` object with it. This process is standard and independent of using basic authentication or form authentication.

Digest Authentication

Digest authentication is a very close sibling of basic HTTP authentication. Its main purpose is to avoid sending clear text passwords on the wire, as basic authentication does, by hashing the password prior to sending it to the server. This makes digest authentication more complex than basic authentication.

Digest authentication works with HTTP headers the same way that basic authentication does.

Digest authentication is based on the use of a nonce for hashing the passwords. A *nonce* is an arbitrary server-generated number that is used in the authentication process and is used only once. It is passed through the digest computation together with the username, password, nonce, URI being requested, and so on.

In the authentication process, both the server and client do the digest computation and they should match.

The main processing lies in two classes: `DigestAuthenticationFilter` and `DigestAuthenticationEntryPoint`.

`DigestAuthenticationFilter` queries the request's headers looking for the Authorization header, and then it checks that the header's value starts with `Digest`. If this is the case, the request is carrying the security credentials that will be used for authentication.

DigestAuthenticationEntryPoint is the class that is invoked to generate a response that demands that a digest security authentication process begin. This class sets the header WWW-Authenticate with the correct values (including the nonce) so that the client agent (the browser) knows it has to start the digest authentication process.

To configure the digest authentication, update the SecurityConfiguration file with the following lines:

```
http.addFilter(digestAuthenticationFilter())
.exceptionHandling().authenticationEntryPoint(digestEntryPoint())
```

Next, add the following bean to add the Sigestauthentication filter:

```
private DigestAuthenticationFilter digestAuthenticationFilter() throws
Exception {

    DigestAuthenticationFilter digestAuthenticationFilter = new
    DigestAuthenticationFilter();
    digestAuthenticationFilter.setUserDetailsService(userDetailsService
    Bean());
    digestAuthenticationFilter.setAuthenticationEntryPoint(digestEntry
    Point());
    return digestAuthenticationFilter;
}
```

Then, define the username and password using inMemoryUserDetailsManager:

```
@Override
@Bean
public UserDetailsService userDetailsServiceBean() {
    InMemoryUserDetailsManager inMemoryUserDetailsManager = new
    InMemoryUserDetailsManager();
    inMemoryUserDetailsManager.createUser(User.withUsername("admin").
    password(passwordEncoder.encode("admin123")).roles( "ADMIN").
    build());
    return inMemoryUserDetailsManager;

}
```

Finally, define the `digestEntryPoint`:

```
@Bean
DigestAuthenticationEntryPoint digestEntryPoint() {
    DigestAuthenticationEntryPoint bauth = new
    DigestAuthenticationEntryPoint();
    bauth.setRealmName("Security Digest Authentication");
    bauth.setKey("SecurityKey");

return bauth;
```

If you restart the application and go to `http://localhost:8080/favoritesmovies/movies`, you will be presented with a browser dialog box asking for a username and password exactly like the one that was shown for basic authentication. This is the `DigestAuthenticationEntryPoint`'s work. As explained, the entry point will fill the response object with the required headers so that the browser knows it needs to show the login form. Log in with username **admin** and password **admin123**, and you should be able to access the requested URL.

The browser will create its own digested message with the password input included and put it in the header. It will also put the rest of the information—namely, nonce, cnonce, realm, and so on—in the `Digest` header. An example `Digest` header that is sent to the server with your current request is the following:

```
'Digest username="admin", realm=" Security Digest Authentication",
nonce="MTM1NTY3NDc3NDIy....==", uri=" /movies",
response="225ea6fbad618cfdf1da7d4f7efe53b8", qop=auth,
nc=00000002, cnonce="376a9b27621880bd"'
```

When the request reaches `DigestAuthenticationFilter`, the headers of the request contain the required digest authentication header. The information in this header arrives as a CSV string containing all the required information shown in the last paragraph, including the nonce and the client nonce (`cnonce`). (A nonce is an arbitrary number used only once in a cryptographic communication. See `http://en.wikipedia.org/wiki/Cryptographic_nonce`.). The filter extracts the information from the header, retrieves the user from the `UserDetailsService`, and then computes the digest with the password from the retrieved user to see if the digest matches the one sent in the header by the client. If they match, access is granted.

Remember-Me Authentication

The remember-me authentication functionality is used to allow returning users of the application to use it without needing to log in every time. Basically, the application remembers certain visitors, allowing them to just open the application and be greeted with their personalized version of the application, as if they were logged in.

Remember-me functionality is very convenient for users; however, it is also very dangerous and recommended for private (from home) use only.

The problem should be obvious. If you use an application from a public computer and this application remembers your profile information, the next person who accesses that application from that computer will be able to impersonate you with minimum effort.

It is also common practice to offer just a limited amount of functionality in the remember-me session. This means that even if you are logged in automatically thanks to the remember-me functionality, you won't have access to the whole functionality of the application. More sensitive parts of the application might require you to formally log in to use them.

This is the case, for example, with Amazon.com. When you visit Amazon. com and log in, the next time you visit Amazon, the site will remember you, your recommendations, your name, and other information about you. But if you want to buy something, it will ask you to log in fully to access that functionality.

Remember-me authentication is typically supported by sending a cookie to the browser, which then, on subsequent sessions in the application, is sent back to the server for auto login.

How does remember-me functionality work in Spring Security?

Remember-me functionality in Spring Security is supported mainly by two components: the `RememberMeServices` interface and the `RememberMeAuthenticationFilter` class. Let's see how they work in the context of a request.

When the application starts up, the `RememberMeAuthenticationFilter` is in the filter chain of the server. Also, a `TokenBasedRememberMeServices` is instantiated and injected into the `AbstractAuthenticationProcessingFilter` replacing the no-op `NullRememberMeServices`.

Go to `http://localhost:8080/favoritesmovies/movies`, and log in with **admin** as the username and **admin123** as password.

When the request gets into the application, UsernamePasswordAuthenticationFilter (a subclass of AbstractAuthenticationProcessingFilter) handles the authentication process in the standard way already explained.

After the authentication is successful, UsernamePasswordAuthenticationFilter invokes the configured TokenBasedRememberMeServices's loginSuccess method. This method looks to see if the request contains the parameter remember-me in order to apply the remember-me functionality. (If the property alwaysRemember is set to true in the service, it will also apply the remember-me functionality.) Because you didn't send this request, nothing will happen.

So let's add the parameter to the login form you have. Open the file login.jsp and somewhere inside the <form> paste the following element:

```
<td>Remember Me:</td><td><input type="checkbox" name="remember-me" /></td>
```

Then in the SecurityConfiguration configuration file add the following:

```
.rememberMe() .key("remember-me").rememberMeParameter("remember-me")
.rememberMeCookieName("rememberloginnardone").tokenValiditySeconds(100)
```

These lines will define the key name, the parameter name, the cookie name, and validity time in seconds.

Restart the application and visit http://localhost:8080/favoritesmovies/movies. You should now see a check box along with the username and password fields. Select the check box, and log in with **admin/admin123**.

This time, the request carries the required parameter and TokenBasedRememberMeServices does its work. It extracts the username and password from the Authentication object and creates a token with this information and a time to expire. It basically concatenates these three values and the remember-me key specified in the XML element (favoritesmovies_key). And it creates an MD5 encoding out of the resulting string. This value will then be Base65-encoded again, together with the username, and added to the response as a cookie with the name rememberloginnardone that will be returned to the browser. You can see this cookie in Figure 5-13.

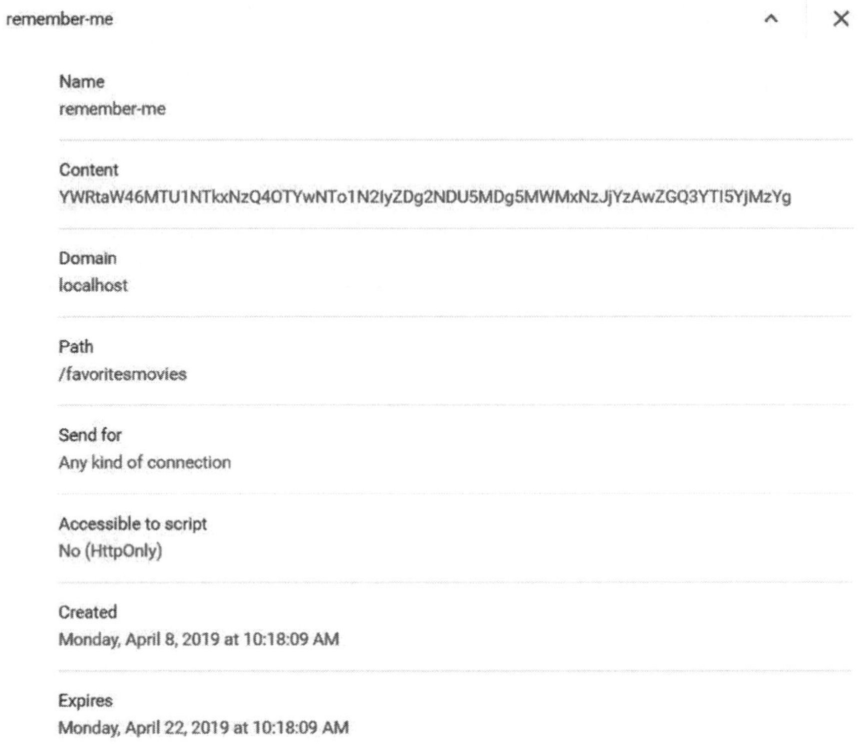

remember-me   ∧   ✕

Name
remember-me

Content
YWRtaW46MTU1NTkxNzQ4OTYwNTo1N2IyZDg2NDU5MDg5MWMxNzJjYzAwZGQ3YTI5YjMzYg

Domain
localhost

Path
/favoritesmovies

Send for
Any kind of connection

Accessible to script
No (HttpOnly)

Created
Monday, April 8, 2019 at 10:18:09 AM

Expires
Monday, April 22, 2019 at 10:18:09 AM

Figure 5-13. *Remember-me cookie example*

Restart the application. Visit `http://localhost:8080/favoritesmovies/movies`. You should be able to access the page without logging in.

When this request gets in the system, it is intercepted by the `RememberMeAuthenticationFilter`, which gets into action. The first thing the filter does is check that there is no current `Authentication` in the `SecurityContext`. Because this means there is no user logged in, the filter calls the `RememberMeServices`'s `autoLogin` method.

In the standard configuration, `TokenBasedRememberMeServices` is the concrete class that implements `RememberMeServices`. This implementation's `autoLogin` method tries to parse the incoming cookie into its composing elements, which are the username, the hashed value of the combined elements (username + ":" + tokenExpiryTime + ":" + password + ":" + key), and the expiry time of the token. Then it retrieves the `UserDetails` from the `UserDetailsService` with the username, recomputes the hashed value with the retrieved user, and compares it with the arriving one. If they don't match, an `InvalidCookieException` is thrown. If they do match, `UserDetails` is checked and an `Authentication` object is created and returned to the caller.

The autoLogin method extracts the remember-me cookie out of the request, decodes it, does some validation, and then calls the configured UserDetailsService's loadUserByUsername method with the username extracted from the cookie. It then creates a RememberMeAuthenticationToken object (an implementation of Authentication).

The RememberMeAuthenticationFilter then tries to authenticate this new Authentication object against the AuthenticationProvider's implementation of RememberMeAuthenticationProvider, which simply returns the same Authentication object after making sure that the hash from the incoming request matches the stored one for the remember-me key.

This Authentication object will be used by the Security Interceptor to allow access to the requested URL.

Logging Out

Logging out is pretty simple. When you log out of an application, you want the application to end your current session, but also to remove any information it might have stored on the client for you.

As mentioned, in Spring Security v5, the URL /logout replaced the URL /j_spring_security_logout. which was used until Spring Security v4.

In Spring Security, logging out is very easy. The only thing you need to do by default is to visit the URL /logout. Let's try that.

Add the following lines to the UserController file:

```
@GetMapping ("/logout")
public String logoutPage (HttpServletRequest request,
HttpServletResponse response) {
    Authentication auth = SecurityContextHolder.getContext().
    getAuthentication();
    if (auth != null){
        new SecurityContextLogoutHandler().logout(request, response,
        auth);
    }
    return "index";
}
```

Update the Security Configuration file with the following lines:

```
.and().logout().deleteCookies("JSESSIONID")
.and().logout().invalidateHttpSession(true)
.and().logout().logoutSuccessUrl("/index").permitAll()
```

These lines tell the application to delete the JSESSIONID cookie, invalidate the HTTP session, and redirect to the index web page once logged out.

Next, add an HTML line to the movies.jsp page linking to logout:

```
<a href="<c:url value="/logout" />">Logout</a>
```

Finally, add a simple HMTL link to the index.jsp page to link back to movies if needed:

```
<a href="<c:url value="/movies" />">My movies</a>
```

Now go to http://localhost:8080/favoritesmovies/movies and log in with **admin**/**admin123** again. Select the check box for activating remember-me functionality. You should be able to log in without problems.

If you look at the cookies stored in your browser, you should see two cookies for the localhost domain: JSESSIONID and rememberloginnardone. Figure 5-13 shows the two cookies. You would expect that if you log out, these two cookies would disappear from the browser, basically removing any trace of the application from your browser. Let's do it.

Click the logout link on the movies.jsp page. You should be logged out of the application. If you open the cookies of your browser, you will see that the cookie rememberloginnardone is gone. The JSESSIONID cookie exists, but the session was already invalidated by the framework. Figure 5-14 shows Remember-me and session cookies.

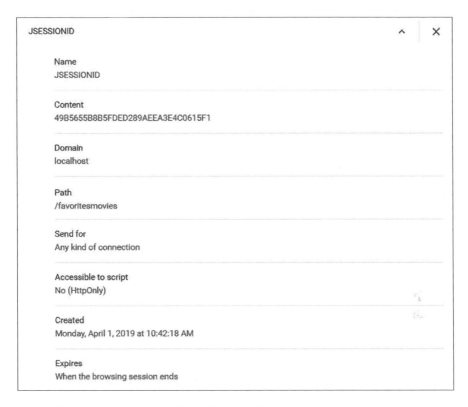

Figure 5-14. *Remember-me and session cookies*

The flow of the logout request is as follows: When the request arrives, it follows the filter chain until it arrives at the LogoutFilter. This filter notices that the URL that is being requested is for logout. The filter calls the configured LogoutHandler(s), which in the running application are SecurityContextLogoutHandler and TokenBasedRememberMeServices. (They implement the LogoutHandler interface.)

The SecurityContextLogoutHandler invalidates the servlet session, in the standard servlet way, calling the invalidate method on the HttpSession object and also clearing the SecurityContext from Spring Security as shown using .logout(). invalidateHttpSession(true).

TokenBasedRememberMeServices simply removes the remember-me cookie by setting its age to 0.

Session Management

Another area of Spring Security's web support is the management of user sessions. One very important thing to do regarding sessions is to make sure you create a new session ID when a user authenticates successfully. Doing this reduces the likelihood of session fixation attacks, in which one user sets another user's session identifier to impersonate him in the application. Spring Security also offers a feature you can use to specify the number of concurrent sessions that the same user can have open at any given time.

These two features are controlled by the class named `SessionFixation ProtectionStrategy`, which implements `SessionAuthenticationStrategy`. This strategy is invoked from `AbstractAuthenticationProcessingFilter` and `SessionManagementFilter`. Let's see how they work.

`SessionFixationProtectionStrategy` is already configured by default in the `UsernamePasswordAuthenticationFilter` that is configured in the application. So when you log in, this strategy is invoked. When the strategy is invoked, it retrieves the current session (which is normally the anonymous session) and invalidates it. Then it immediately creates a new one. It also tries to migrate certain attributes—normally, the ones used by Spring Security itself, but a list can also be specified.

To summarize this strategy, when you log in, it invalidates the current session, creates a new one, and copies certain attributes from the old one to the new one.

Since Spring Session 2.0, it contains the Spring Session Core module and several other modules like Spring Session Data MongoDB module, Spring Session Data Geode modules, etc.

Let's see how you can configure it in your application.

1. Add the following line to the `SecurityConfiguration` file:

    ```
    .sessionManagement().sessionCreationPolicy(Session
    CreationPolicy.ALWAYS)
    ```

2. Restart the application.

3. Open Chrome and go to `http://127.0.0.1:8080/favoritesmovies/movies`. Log in with username **admin** and password **admin123**. You should be able to access the page without a problem.

4. Open another browser, for instance Firefox, and visit
    http://127.0.0.1:8080/favoritesmovies/movies. Log in with
    username **admin** and password **admin123**. You should be able to
    access the page without a problem.

5. Go to Chrome, and refresh the page. You will get the following
    message: "This session has been expired (possibly due to multiple
    concurrent logins being attempted as the same user)." This message
    explicitly indicates the problem. Figure 5-15 shows this page.

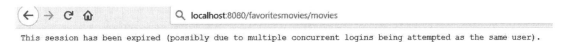

This session has been expired (possibly due to multiple concurrent logins being attempted as the same user).

Figure 5-15. *Error related to concurrent sessions*

Now let's allow two sessions at the same time by adding the following line to the
SecurityConfiguration file:

.sessionManagement().maximumSessions(2)

Restart the application and follow the same flow as before. This time, you should
have both sessions active at the same time.

Forcing the Request to HTTPS

By default, the Spring Security–enabled application serves all content through the
normal HTTP channel. However, you can configure them so that they automatically
ensure a particular web request is delivered over the HTTPS channel.

Note   We're assuming that, in general, you know the advantages of using HTTPS
over HTTP. However, here's a brief reminder. HTTPS (or Hypertext Transfer Protocol
Secure) is a communication protocol that combines the standard HTTP protocol
with Secure Sockets Layer (SSL) or TLS for security purposes. HTTPS achieves
security in two forms. First, it allows a connecting client to authenticate the web
server that it is connecting to, ensuring that it is connecting to the proper certified
website. This is done with the use of server-side certificates. The other security
concern addressed by HTTPS is the encryption of the information that is exchanged

between client and server. HTTPS ensures that the information cannot be read by a third party while it is being exchanged. You can find more extensive information on this topic on Wikipedia (`http://en.wikipedia.org/wiki/HTTP_Secure`) and many other places. Please check the official HTTPS/SSL Apache Tomcat web page for information about how to configure HTTPS at `https://tomcat.apache.org/tomcat-9.0-doc/ssl-howto.html`.

We will assume that you have configured HTTPS for your Apache Tomcat v9.

Setting up HTTPS is really straightforward; you simply add a new configuration element to your Spring Security configuration file.

Suppose you want to configure HTTPS for your login page. Just add the following line to the `SecurityConfiguration` file:

```
http.requiresChannel().antMatchers("/login*").requiresSecure();
```

Go to `http://localhost:8080/favoritesmovies/movies`, as you have always done in this chapter. This time, the application will automatically redirect to the URL `https://localhost:8443/favoritesmovies/login`. (The browser will probably show the typical "insecure certificate" warning, which you can see in Figure 5-16, but you can safely proceed by clicking the "Proceed anyway" option, or a similar option in other browsers.)

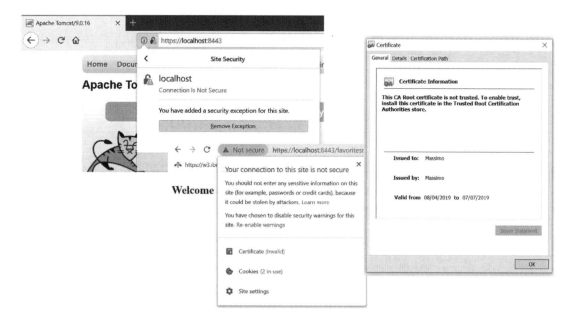

Figure 5-16. *Application with HTTPS channel security and a self-signed certificate*

The channel functionality works in the following way. When the application starts up, the namespace parsing mechanism notes the presence of the attribute `requires-channel` in the `requiresChannel` elements. The class `HttpConfigurationBuilder` finds this attribute and then creates a map of `RequestMatcher`, `ChannelAttributeFactory`. `ChannelAttributeFactory` creates `ConfigAttribute` instances based on the value of the `requires-channel` attribute. For example, if the required channel is HTTPS, it creates an instance of an implementation of `ConfigAttribute` with the value `REQUIRES_SECURE_CHANNEL` associated with the appropriate URL pattern. After the parser finds the `antMatchers-url` with the `requires-channel` attribute configured, it instantiates a new `ChannelProcessingFilter` bean configured with a `ChannelDecisionManager` implementation for deciding which channel to use for each request.

When a request is made, it will, as normal, travel through the filter chain. There is a filter in the filter chain called `ChannelProcessingFilter`, as explained in the previous paragraph. This filter delegates to its configured `ChannelDecisionManager` implementation the responsibility of deciding what to do with the request. The decision manager, with the aid of certain helper classes, decides if the request can proceed or if, on the contrary, the requested channel is not admitted by the requested URL. In the latter case, it delegates to a `ChannelProcessor` and a redirection strategy to send a redirect response to the proper channel URL.

Basically, in this example, this filter looks at the URL `http://localhost:8080/favoritesmovies/login`, finds that this URL matches the `antMatchers-url` pattern that has the `config` requirement `REQUIRES_SECURE_CHANNEL`, and then calls the `RetryWithHttpsEntryPoint` that, in turn, invokes the `RedirectStrategy` implementation's `sendRedirect` method, which tries to redirect to `https://localhost:8443/favoritesmovies/login`.

Summary

In this chapter, we covered one of the biggest concerns of the framework: web support in Spring Security. You saw that the main functionality comes in the form of servlet filters. This is a good thing from a standards point of view, because it means you can leverage Spring Security web support in other frameworks that use the standard Java servlet model.

You should now know a lot of details about the main filters that build the framework, how they work internally, and how they fit within each other and with the rest of the framework. We explained all this in a practical way, trying to solve real-life scenarios.

In the next chapter, we will cover the second major concern of Spring Security—namely, method-level security. We will show how it compares to web-level security, and you will see that you can leverage a lot of your current knowledge to apply it to the method-level security layer.

CHAPTER 6

Configuring Alternative Authentication Providers

One of Spring Security's strongest points is that you can plug different authentication mechanisms into the framework. Spring Security was built to create, as much as possible, a pluggable architecture model, where different things can be plugged into the framework in an easy and unobtrusive way. In the authentication layer, this means that an abstraction exists that takes care of this part of the security process. This abstraction comes in the form, mainly, of the `AuthenticationProvider` interface, but it is also supported by specific security servlet filters and user details services.

Spring Security v5 supports many different authentication mechanisms including:

- Database

- LDAP

- X.509

- OAuth 2/OpenID

- WebSockets

- JSON Web Token (JWT)

- JAAS

- CAS

Most of this chapter deals with explaining how each of these authentication systems work, independently of Spring Security. Although it will give you certain key details, it won't be an in-depth explanation. Of course, you will see how Spring Security implements each of these authentication mechanisms, and you will see that they have

© Carlo Scarioni and Massimo Nardone 2019
C. Scarioni and M. Nardone, *Pro Spring Security*, https://doi.org/10.1007/978-1-4842-5052-5_6

many things in common when it comes to the parts of Spring Security they use. In this chapter, only examples about database, LDAP and X.509 authentication will be provided while OAuth2, JAAS, and CAS will just be introduced.

Database-Provided Authentication

Database-provided authentication works almost exactly the same way as with the memory-provided authentication users. The only difference is that the users are stored in the database and not in memory. This happens at runtime when you define them in the application context configuration file.

When you use database-authentication mechanisms, the AuthenticationProvider implementation doesn't need to change at all; it's still the DaoAuthenticationProvider you used for the in-memory user authentication. As you may remember, this AuthenticationProvider implementation is based on using a UserDetailsService abstraction to retrieve the users, so the difference here is the UserDetailsService implementation you will use.

Configuring the provisioning of users from the database is pretty simple, as you will see.

Start by downloading and unzipping the HyperSQL Database Engine (HSQLDB) .zip file from https://sourceforge.net/projects/hsqldb/postdownload. In your case, you will install the file hsqldb-2.4.1.zip to c:\hsqldb-2.4.1.

In this chapter, you will use IntelliJ IDEA 2019 as an IDE tool. You can download it form https://blog.jetbrains.com/idea/tag/intellij-idea-2019-1/.

You can configure the HSQLDB as shown in Figure 6-1.

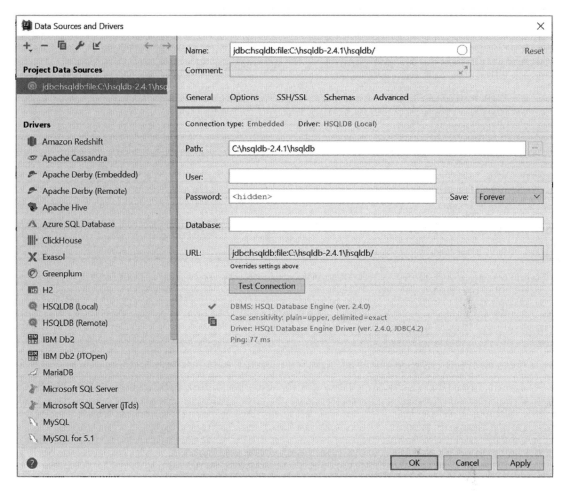

Figure 6-1. *Configuring hsqldb-2.4.1*

Later, when running the HSQLDB SQL page, the result will look like Figure 6-2.

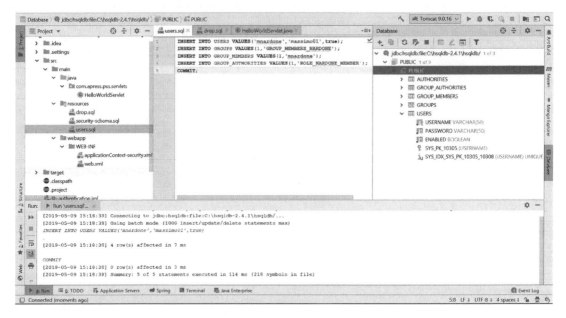

Figure 6-2. Running HSQLDB SQL scripts

Ok now HSQLDB is ready to be used.

The first thing you do is define the database schema you need in order to make the authentication mechanism work. The tables you need to make the authentication work are shown in Figure 6-3.

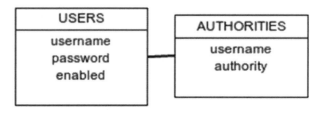

Figure 6-3. Simple DB schema needed to support database authentication

Figure 6-3 shows a simple schema model for supporting authentication backed by a database. Just by looking at the tables, you should be able to see how they work. It is basically a one-to-one mapping from the in-memory implementation you have been using so far. In the USER table, you store the user details—mainly, the username and the password. In the AUTHORITIES table, you store the relationship between the usernames and the granted authorities for that member—for example, ROLE_MEMBER.

Figure 6-4 shows an extended default option you can use to define groups and establish authorities related to those groups instead of to individual users.

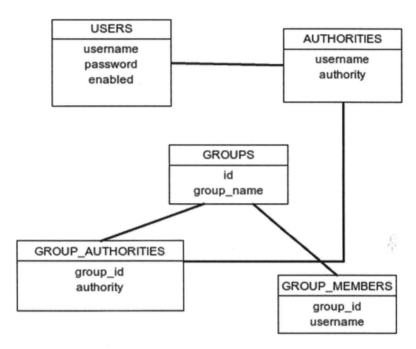

Figure 6-4. *Database-backed authentication scheme with groups*

Figure 6-4 is a bit more complex than Figure 6-3; however, it is still very straightforward. This time, the schema allows you to create named groups and establish authorities belonging to these groups. At the same time, users now can belong to groups as well, meaning that users can inherit the authorities defined for the groups to which they belong. For example, if there is a group named Administrators in the GROUPS table and there are two authorities (ROLE_ADMIN and ROLE_USER) defined in the GROUP_ AUTHORITIES table that map to the group Administrators, then a member belonging to group Administrators (which exists in the table GROUP_MEMBERS) will have the authorities ROLE_ADMIN and ROLE_USER inherited from the group.

By default, the group mechanism is not activated in UserDetailsService. To activate it, you need to configure a groupAuthoritiesByUsernameQuery attribute in the corresponding <jdbc-user-service> in the configuration file, as you will see later in the example.

Note   For this example project and the rest of the examples in this chapter, unless otherwise noted, you will start with an application configured as follows.

1. Use the example you created in Chapter 3.

2. Updated the web.xml file with the one in Listing 6-1.

3. Update spring-security.xml with the contents of Listing 6-2 in the generated WEB-INF folder.

4. Update the servlet in the package com.apress.pss.servlets with the contents from Listing 6-3.

5. Update pom.xml as shown in Listing 6-4.

Listing 6-1. web.xml to Be Used in All Applications in This Chapter

```
<web-app id="WebApp_ID" version="2.4"
        xmlns="http://java.sun.com/xml/ns/j2ee"
        xmlns:xsi="http://www.w3.org/2001/XMLSchema-instance"
        xsi:schemaLocation="http://java.sun.com/xml/ns/j2ee
        http://java.sun.com/xml/ns/j2ee/web-app_2_4.xsd">
  <display-name>Spring MVC Application</display-name>
  <!-- Spring MVC -->
  <servlet>
    <servlet-name>spring</servlet-name>
    <servlet-class>org.springframework.web.servlet.DispatcherServlet
    </servlet-class>
    <load-on-startup>1</load-on-startup>
  </servlet>
  <servlet-mapping>
    <servlet-name>spring</servlet-name>
    <url-pattern>/</url-pattern>
  </servlet-mapping>
```

```
<listener>
  <listener-class>org.springframework.web.context.ContextLoaderListener
  </listener-class>
</listener>

<context-param>
  <param-name>contextConfigLocation</param-name>
  <param-value>
    /WEB-INF/spring-security.xml
  </param-value>
</context-param>

<!-- Spring Security -->
<filter>
  <filter-name>springSecurityFilterChain</filter-name>
  <filter-class>org.springframework.web.filter.DelegatingFilterProxy
  </filter-class>
</filter>

<filter-mapping>
  <filter-name>springSecurityFilterChain</filter-name>
  <url-pattern>/*</url-pattern>
</filter-mapping>

</web-app>
```

Listing 6-2. Starting spring-security.xml to Be Used in All Examples in This Chapter

```
<?xml version="1.0" encoding="UTF-8"?>
<beans:beans xmlns="http://www.springframework.org/schema/security"
          xmlns:xsi="http://www.w3.org/2001/XMLSchema-instance"
          xmlns:beans="http://www.springframework.org/schema/beans"
              xsi:schemaLocation="
     http://www.springframework.org/schema/security
     http://www.springframework.org/schema/security/spring-security-.2.xsd
     http://www.springframework.org/schema/beans
     http://www.springframework.org/schema/beans/spring-beans-4.3.xsd">
```

```xml
<http use-expressions="true">
    <intercept-url pattern="/welcome" access="permitAll"/>
     <intercept-url pattern="/**" access="isAuthenticated()"/>
    <form-login authentication-success-handler-ref="awareAuthentication
    SuccessHandler" />
</http>
<beans:bean
class="org.springframework.security.web.authentication.
SavedRequestAwareAuthenticationSuccessHandler"
name="awareAuthenticationSuccessHandler"/>
  <beans:bean id ="passwordEncoder" class = "org.springframework.
  security.crypto.password.NoOpPasswordEncoder" factory-method =
  "getInstance" />

<authentication-manager>
    <authentication-provider>
        <user-service>
            <user name="admin" password="admin123" authorities=
            "ROLE_USER"/>
        </user-service>
    </authentication-provider>
</authentication-manager>
/beans:beans>
```

Listing 6-3. Simple Servlet Definition

```java
package com.apress.pss.springsecurity.controller;

import org.springframework.security.core.context.SecurityContextHolder;
import org.springframework.security.core.userdetails.UserDetails;
import org.springframework.stereotype.Controller;
import org.springframework.ui.ModelMap;
import org.springframework.web.bind.annotation.RequestMapping;
import org.springframework.web.bind.annotation.RequestMethod;

@Controller
public class UserController {
```

```java
@RequestMapping(value = { "/", "/welcome" }, method = RequestMethod.GET)
public String homePage(ModelMap model) {
    return "welcome";
}

@RequestMapping(value = "/admin", method = RequestMethod.GET)
public String adminPage(ModelMap model) {
    model.addAttribute("user", getPrincipal());
    return "admin";
}

private String getPrincipal(){
    String userName = null;
    Object principal = SecurityContextHolder.getContext().
    getAuthentication().getPrincipal();

    if (principal instanceof UserDetails) {
        userName = ((UserDetails)principal).getUsername();
    } else {
        userName = principal.toString();
    }
    return userName;
}
}
```

Listing 6-4. pom.xml with Configurations

```xml
<?xml version="1.0" encoding="UTF-8"?>
<project xmlns="http://maven.apache.org/POM/4.0.0"
xmlns:xsi="http://www.w3.org/2001/XMLSchema-instance"
xsi:schemaLocation="http://maven.apache.org/POM/4.0.0
http://maven.apache.org/maven-v4_0_0.xsd">

  <modelVersion>4.0.0</modelVersion>
  <packaging>war</packaging>

  <name>pss01_Security</name>
  <groupId>com.apress.pss</groupId>
  <artifactId>pss01_Security</artifactId>
  <version>1.0-SNAPSHOT</version>
```

```xml
<properties>
  <springframework.version>5.1.5.RELEASE</springframework.version>
  <springsecurity.version>5.1.5.RELEASE</springsecurity.version>
</properties>

<dependencies>
  <!-- Spring -->
  <dependency>
    <groupId>org.springframework</groupId>
    <artifactId>spring-core</artifactId>
    <version>${springframework.version}</version>
  </dependency>
  <dependency>
    <groupId>org.springframework</groupId>
    <artifactId>spring-web</artifactId>
    <version>${springframework.version}</version>
  </dependency>
  <dependency>
    <groupId>org.springframework</groupId>
    <artifactId>spring-webmvc</artifactId>
    <version>${springframework.version}</version>
  </dependency>

  <!-- Spring Security -->
  <dependency>
    <groupId>org.springframework.security</groupId>
    <artifactId>spring-security-web</artifactId>
    <version>${springsecurity.version}</version>
  </dependency>
  <dependency>
    <groupId>org.springframework.security</groupId>
    <artifactId>spring-security-config</artifactId>
    <version>${springsecurity.version}</version>
  </dependency>
```

```xml
    <dependency>
      <groupId>javax.servlet</groupId>
      <artifactId>javax.servlet-api</artifactId>
      <version>3.1.0</version>
    </dependency>
    <dependency>
      <groupId>javax.servlet.jsp</groupId>
      <artifactId>javax.servlet.jsp-api</artifactId>
      <version>2.3.1</version>
    </dependency>
    <dependency>
      <groupId>javax.servlet</groupId>
      <artifactId>jstl</artifactId>
      <version>1.2</version>
    </dependency>
    <dependency>
      <groupId>taglibs</groupId>
      <artifactId>standard</artifactId>
      <version>1.1.2</version>
    </dependency>

    <dependency>
      <groupId>org.springframework</groupId>
      <artifactId>spring-jdbc</artifactId>
      <version>3.0.0.RELEASE</version>
    </dependency>
    <dependency>
      <groupId>org.hsqldb</groupId>
      <artifactId>hsqldb</artifactId>
      <version>2.4.1</version>
    </dependency>
  </dependencies>
<!-- Build -->
```

```xml
<build>
  <pluginManagement>
    <plugins>

<!-- Added for JAVA 11 Support START-->
<plugin>
    <groupId>org.apache.maven.plugins</groupId>
    <artifactId>maven-compiler-plugin</artifactId>
    <version>3.8.0</version>
    <configuration>
        <release>11</release>
    </configuration>
</plugin>

    </plugins>
  </pluginManagement>
  <finalName>pss01_Security</finalName>
</build>
</project>
```

Let's get the example going. You'll use an HSQL database, so you need to configure its JDBC dependencies in the pom.xml file, as Listing 6-5 shows.

Listing 6-5. HSQLDB and JDBC Maven Dependencies

```xml
<dependency>
    <groupId>org.hsqldb</groupId>
    <artifactId>hsqldb</artifactId>
    <version>2.4.1</version>
</dependency>
<dependency>
  <groupId>org.springframework</groupId>
  <artifactId>spring-jdbc</artifactId>
  <version>3.0.0.RELEASE</version>
</dependency>
```

Next, let's modify the configuration file `security-security.xml` to include the configuration changes needed to support database-driven user authentication. Listing 6-6 shows the `spring-security.xml` file.

Listing 6-6. spring-security.xml That Uses a Database-Driven UserDetailsService

```xml
<?xml version="1.0" encoding="UTF-8"?>
<beans:beans xmlns="http://www.springframework.org/schema/security"
      xmlns:xsi="http://www.w3.org/2001/XMLSchema-instance"
      xmlns:beans="http://www.springframework.org/schema/beans"
      xmlns:jdbc="http://www.springframework.org/schema/jdbc"
      xsi:schemaLocation="
    http://www.springframework.org/schema/security
    http://www.springframework.org/schema/security/spring-security-4.2.xsd
    http://www.springframework.org/schema/beans
    http://www.springframework.org/schema/beans/spring-beans-4.3.xsd
    http://www.springframework.org/schema/jdbc
    http://www.springframework.org/schema/jdbc/spring-jdbc-3.0.xsd">
  <http use-expressions="true">
    <intercept-url pattern="/welcome" access="permitAll"/>
    <intercept-url pattern="/**" access="ROLE_NARDONE_MEMBER"/>
    <form-login authentication-success-handler-ref="awareAuthentication
    SuccessHandler" />
  </http>
  <beans:bean
  class="org.springframework.security.web.authentication.
  SavedRequestAwareAuthenticationSuccessHandler" name="aware
  AuthenticationSuccessHandler"/>
  <beans:bean id ="passwordEncoder" class = "org.springframework.
  security.crypto.password.NoOpPasswordEncoder" factory-method =
  "getInstance" />

  <authentication-manager>
      <authentication-provider>
          <jdbc-user-service data-source-ref="dataSource" />
      </authentication-provider>
  </authentication-manager>
```

```
    <jdbc:embedded-database id="dataSource">
        <jdbc:script location="classpath:security-schema.sql"/>
        <jdbc:script location="classpath:users.sql"/>
    </jdbc:embedded-database>
</beans:beans>
```

In Listing 6-6, you can see that you are using the namespace `<jdbc:>` to define a new embedded datasource through the element `<embedded-database>`. Embedded datasources are a new feature introduced in Spring 3.0. You can use them to define different kinds of embedded datasources (basically, in-memory datasources that run within the Java process where they are used), such as HSQL and Derby. HSQL is the default. You can also see here that in the tag you are also allowed to specify SQL script locations you want to execute when the datasource is started up. The scripts execute in sequential order from the top down; in this example, `security-schema.sql` is executed first, and then `users.sql` is executed. The SQL files specified here allow you to create a simple database schema to support the configuration of users and authorities the way we defined them in the previous section.

Using this embedded datasource is very convenient for examples of this type and for unit testing your application, but most likely you won't use them in production environments. For production environments, you will use full database solutions, such as MySQL, PostgreSQL, Oracle, and others.

Listing 6-7 shows the `spring-servlet.xml` file, which did not change.

Listing 6-7. spring-servlet.xml That Uses a Database-Driven UserDetailsService

```
<beans xmlns="http://www.springframework.org/schema/beans"
       xmlns:context="http://www.springframework.org/schema/context"
       xmlns:xsi="http://www.w3.org/2001/XMLSchema-instance"
       xsi:schemaLocation="
        http://www.springframework.org/schema/beans
        http://www.springframework.org/schema/beans/spring-beans-3.0.xsd
        http://www.springframework.org/schema/context
        http://www.springframework.org/schema/context/spring-context-
        3.0.xsd">
```

```
    <context:component-scan base-package="com.apress.*" />

    <bean

class="org.springframework.web.servlet.view.InternalResourceViewResolver">
        <property name="prefix">
            <value>/WEB-INF/pages/</value>
        </property>
        <property name="suffix">
            <value>.jsp</value>
        </property>
    </bean>

</beans>
```

Creating the Basic Tables

Next, you create the two SQL files you are referencing in the configuration file and put them in the root of the classpath. Listing 6-8 shows the file security-schema.sql, and Listing 6-9 shows the file users.sql. Later, you will see groups coming into the picture as well.

Listing 6-8. security-schema.sql Defines the Needed Security Database Schema for Storing Users and Authorities

```
CREATE TABLE USERS(USERNAME VARCHAR_IGNORECASE(50) NOT NULL PRIMARY KEY,
                   PASSWORD VARCHAR_IGNORECASE(50) NOT NULL,
                   ENABLED BOOLEAN NOT NULL);

CREATE TABLE AUTHORITIES(
           USERNAME VARCHAR_IGNORECASE(50) NOT NULL PRIMARY KEY,
           AUTHORITY VARCHAR_IGNORECASE(50) NOT NULL,
           CONSTRAINT FK_AUTHORITIES_USERS
               FOREIGN KEY(USERNAME) REFERENCES USERS(USERNAME));
```

```
CREATE TABLE GROUPS(
        id BIGINT NOT NULL PRIMARY KEY,
        GROUP_NAME VARCHAR_IGNORECASE(50) NOT NULL);

CREATE TABLE GROUP_MEMBERS(
        group_id BIGINT NOT NULL,
        username VARCHAR_IGNORECASE(50) NOT NULL);

CREATE TABLE GROUP_AUTHORITIES(
        group_id BIGINT NOT NULL,
        authority VARCHAR_IGNORECASE(50) NOT NULL);
```

Listing 6-9. users.sql Users That Can Be Used in the Application with Their Authorities

```
INSERT INTO USERS VALUES('mnardone','nardone',true);
INSERT INTO AUTHORITIES VALUES('mnardone','ROLE_NARDONE_MEMBER');
COMMIT;
```

Everything should be set up now, so let's run the application on a Server Tomcat 9 stand-alone server and log in and access the URL http://localhost:8080/pss01_Security/login with the username **mnardone** and the password **nardone**. Figures 6-5 and 6-6 show the login page and the admin.jsp page we got in our execution of the example.

What is happening here is pretty simple and similar to what you have been working with up until now. When you define the element <security:jdbc-user-service> in the configuration file security-security.xml, Spring Security instantiates a different kind of UserDetailsService at startup than the one used for in-memory user details.

The instantiated UserDetailsService is an org.springframework.security. provisioning.JdbcUserDetailsManager. This instance gets injected into the DaoAuthenticationProvider for retrieving users from a JDBC datastore.

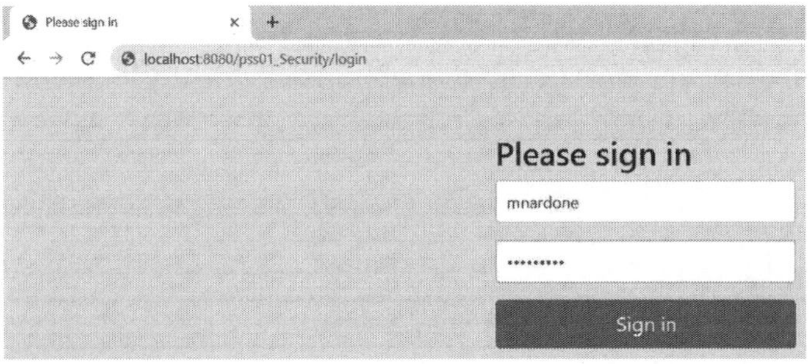

Figure 6-5. *Login screen*

It gets redirected to `http://localhost:8080/pss01_Security/admin`, as shown in Figure 6-6.

Welcome to Admin Page: **mnardone**

Figure 6-6. *The Admin page shown after a successful authentication*

Using Groups

To use groups now, let's modify the `users.sql` file a little bit and add the lines from Listing 6-10 to it. These lines effectively create a group and put the user mnardone into that group. You should also remove the SQL where you insert into the `AUTHORITIES` table the role for user mnardone.

Listing 6-10. The users.sql Lines Used to Create a Group and Put Members into the Group

```
INSERT INTO GROUPS VALUES(1,'GROUP_MEMBERS_NARDONE');
INSERT INTO GROUP_MEMBERS VALUES(1,mnardone);
INSERT INTO GROUP_AUTHORITIES VALUES(1,'ROLE_NARDONE_MEMBER');
```

Now, to activate the use of groups in the `UserDetailsService` you need to set the property `enableGroups` to `true` in the `JdbcDaoImpl` implementation; however, for some reason, the `<jdbc-user-service>` namespace element currently doesn't support the setting of this simple property directly. What it does support is the setting of the attribute `group-authorities-by-username-query`, which allows you to specify the query to retrieve the groups from the database schema. Setting this attribute automatically sets the property enableGroups to true. The other option, of course, is not to use the XML namespace and instead use the standard bean definition and set the property. You are going to use the first option and make the `<jdbc-user-service>` in the security-security.xml look like Listing 6-11.

Listing 6-11. `<jdbc-user-service>` in the Configuration File That Specifies the group-authorities-by-username-query Attribute

```
<security:jdbc-user-service data-source-ref="dataSource"
      group-authorities-by-username-query="select g.id, g.group_name,
      ga.authority
            from groups g, group_members gm, group_authorities ga
            where gm.username = ? and g.id = ga.group_id and g.id = gm.group_id"/>
```

Consider the query you specified in Listing 6-11; the group-authorities-by-username-query attribute is extracted directly from the class file JdbcDaoImpl (the query string, that is). It is configured in the DEF_GROUP_AUTHORITIES_BY_USERNAME_QUERY constant in that file (JdbcDaoImpl), and it is the default query used by the class to retrieve the groups and authorities.

If you restart the application now, you should see the same behavior as before. This time, however, the behavior internally is different because the group query is the one being executed to retrieve the authorities for the user. The code that makes this choice in the JdbcDaoImpl is very simple, and you can see it in Listing 6-12. The property that is used in the second if condition is set automatically by Spring Security when starting up, particularly in the class JdbcUserServiceBeanDefinitionParser when you set the group-authorities-by-username-query attribute, as we explained before. The enableAuthorities property in the first if is automatically set to true in the JdbcDaoImpl class itself.

Listing 6-12. Code Inside JdbcDaoImpl That Queries by Group or Username

```
if (enableAuthorities) {
   dbAuthsSet.addAll(loadUserAuthorities(user.getUsername()));
}

if (enableGroups) {
   dbAuthsSet.addAll(loadGroupAuthorities(user.getUsername()));
}
```

The advantage of using groups is that it offers a new level of organizing users into the same category and does not relate them directly to particular authorities. Instead, it relates the whole group to the authorities. For example, you would normally say that all administrators belong to the Administrator group, and this group has many authorities related to it, like ROLE_ADMIN, ROLE_USER, ROLE_OPERATOR, and others. All these authorities can be grouped into the same conceptual group, and at the same time, all users can be grouped into their respective groups. This means that not all users need to reference all these authorities. They simply need to be made part of the group. Of course, a user can belong to more than one group at the same time.

Using Existing Schemas

JdbcDaoImpl, by default, is configured to use the database schema and queries you have looked at already. However, the schema configuration is flexible, and you can adapt your existing database user schema (if any) to be used by Spring Security JDBC UserDetails support instead of writing a custom schema just for Spring Security. Of course, certain concepts need to exist in your current schema, like a "user" abstraction, an "authorities" or "role" definition, and a "group" abstraction if you will also be using groups. If you have these abstractions in place in your database, accessing the information from Spring Security's JDBC support is straightforward. The two attributes (authorities-by-username-query and group-authorities-by-username-query) in the element <jdbc-user-service> allow you to specify the exact SQL that will be used to retrieve the authorities for a particular username when not using groups or when indeed using groups.

You saw the example in the previous section of how to use the group-authorities-by-username-query attribute. The authorities-by-username-query is configured similarly, and it should be a query that returns a pair of columns in its resultset. The first one represents the username, and the second one represents a particular authority. For example, the default query looks like this:

```
select username,authority from authorities where username = ?
```

The other attribute you need to change in the <jdbc-user-service> element is users-by-username-query. Here you use the query needed to retrieve users using their username. The query needs to return three columns in a record: username, password, and enabled.

Let's try this out with a quick example. You will change some files from the example you are currently working on. First, change the `security-schema.sql` and `users.sql` files to something that doesn't really match the default values Spring Security expects. So replace the contents of these files with the contents of Listing 6-13 and Listing 6-14, respectively.

Listing 6-13. A security-schema.sql That Doesn't Match Spring Security Defaults

```
CREATE TABLE PEOPLE(
        NAME VARCHAR_IGNORECASE(50) NOT NULL PRIMARY KEY,
        KEY VARCHAR_IGNORECASE(50));

CREATE TABLE ROLES(
        NAME VARCHAR_IGNORECASE(50) NOT NULL PRIMARY KEY,
        ROLE VARCHAR_IGNORECASE(50) NOT NULL,
        CONSTRAINT FK_AUTHORITIES_USERS FOREIGN KEY(NAME)
        REFERENCES PEOPLE(NAME));
COMMIT;
```

Listing 6-14. A users.sql That Doesn't Match Spring Security Defaults

```
INSERT INTO PEOPLE VALUES(mnardone,nardone);
INSERT INTO ROLES VALUES('mnardone','ROLE_NARDONE_MEMBER');
COMMIT;
```

Next, replace the `<security:jdbc-user-service>` element from the file `security-security.xml` with the one from Listing 6-15.

Listing 6-15. JDBC User Service with Custom Queries

```
<security:jdbc-user-service
    data-source-ref="dataSource"
    authorities-by-username-query="select name, role from roles where
    name = ?"
    users-by-username-query="select name,key,1 from people where
    name = ?" />
```

Now restart the application, log in with the username **mnardone** and the password **nardone**, and access the URL `http://localhost:8080/pss01_Security/admin`. You should be able to reach the page in exactly the same way as before.

LDAP Authentication

The Lightweight Directory Access Protocol (LDAP) is an application-level, message-oriented protocol used for storing and accessing information in the way of an accessible tree-like directory. A directory, in general, is simply an organized datastore that allows for easy queries in its particular domain. For example, a TV Guide is a directory that allows you to find TV shows easily, and a phone book is a directory that provides easy access to phone numbers.

LDAP allows the storage of very different kinds of information in a directory. Probably the most widely known use of LDAP-like structures is the Microsoft Windows Active Directory system. Other LDAP systems are widely used to store the corporate user databases of many companies that serve as the centralized user store.

LDAP is not an easy system to understand, and we will try to explain it along with the example that we develop in this section. We will use the same code as in the previous section, but modify it as needed to work with LDAP instead of database authentication. Remember that in the previous section, we offered a bootstrap application to start working in all the examples in this chapter, including this one.

The first thing to do is configure your users in the LDAP directory. To do this, you need to understand the LDAP Information Model, which defines the type of data you can store in your directory.

The data in LDAP is defined by entries, attributes, and values. An *entry* is the basic unit of information in the directory and commonly represents an entity from the real world, like a user. Entries are normally defined by a particular object class. Each entry in the directory has an identification known as a Distinguished Name (or, more commonly, DN). Each entry in the directory also has a set of *attributes* that describe different things about the entry. Each attribute has a type and one or more *values*.

You must define the data you will need. You will use users, groups, and credentials, as you have been doing so far. Commonly in LDAP, the user entry definition is known as *People*, so you will use that name to define the user entries. Your user will also use the standard LDAP object class `person` to define its attributes.

Installing and Configuring LDAP

For your LDAP implementation you will download and install Apache Directory Server (ApacheDS) at `https://directory.apache.org/apacheds/downloads.html` and Apache Directory Studio at `https://directory.apache.org/studio/downloads.html`. The installation process of both tools is straightforward and shouldn't give you any issues. Consult the official web page for directions.

Apache Directory Studio allows you to access and query the server. It is an Eclipse application built of plugins adapted to access LDAP servers. Regarding the ApacheDS server, when it is installed (at least on a Mac), it will be started up automatically; however, you also have the option of running the ApacheDS server as an embedded server within the application process instead of having a standalone, independent LDAP server. We will be using the standalone server in the example.

First of all, you want to start ApacheDS as shown in the services list in Figure 6-7.

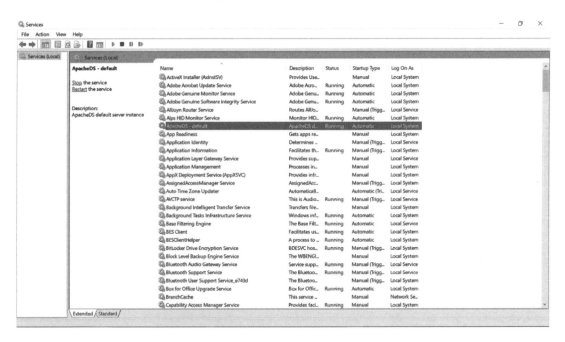

Figure 6-7. *Starting ApacheDS*

After installing Apache Server and Studio, you need to connect to Server from Studio.

Once the ApacheDS service is running, open Apache Studio and start the LDAP Server, as shown in Figure 6-8.

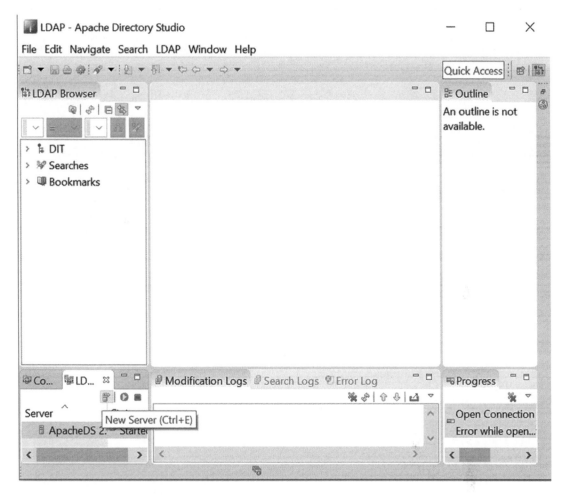

Figure 6-8. *Starting the LDAP server*

Now you can connect Apache Studio to ApacheDS. Go to the File menu in the Studio, select New, and then select LDAP Connection, as shown in Figure 6-9. In the LDAP connection form, enter the values to connect to the local ApacheDS server as shown in Figure 6-10, using **uid=admin,ou=system** as the DN and **secret** as the password. You can see the host is localhost and the port is 10389. Click Next to finish the connection configuration.

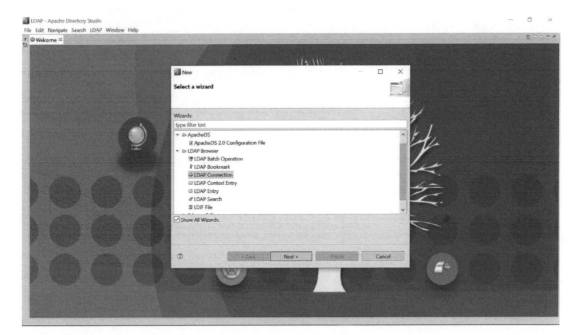

Figure 6-9. *Apache Directory Studio connecting to the LDAP server*

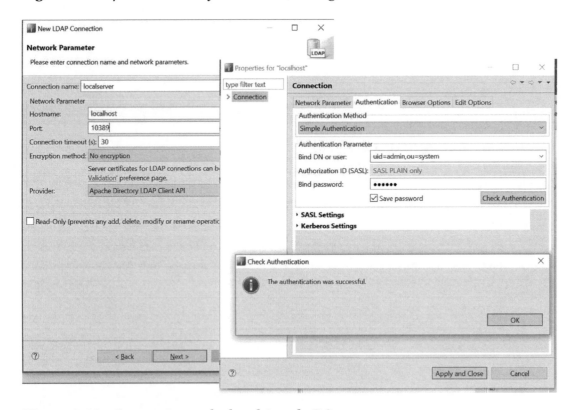

Figure 6-10. *Connecting to the local ApacheDS server*

Once the connection to the ApacheDS server is established, you need to create a context entry representing the top-level entry in the local directory. To do so, right-click the left panel's Root DSE element and then select New ➤ New Context Entry in the contextual menu, as shown in Figure 6-11.

Figure 6-11. *Creating a new context entry top-level entry*

In the first form in New Context Entry, choose to create an entry from scratch. Then, from the list of available object classes in the left panel, select dNSDomain and click Add. The idea here is that you are creating the top-level entry from which all other entries derive. You end up with something like Figure 6-12. Then click Next. In the next input form, use dc=example,dc=com as the DN name of the context entry, and click Next. These values (example and com) are the default values for the partition and the top-level context entry included in the ApacheDS server. These values also partially identify every entry you create in the directory because, as mentioned, LDAP follows a hierarchical structure that builds names for entries on top of its parent entries.

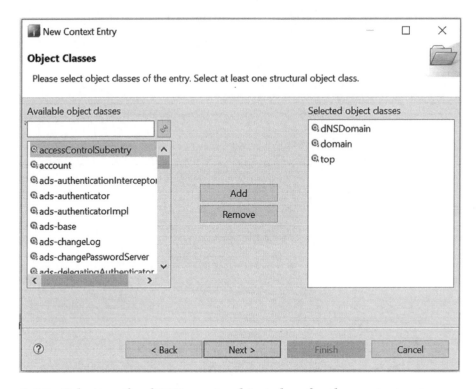

Figure 6-12. *Selecting the dNSDomain object class for the context entry*

The next step is to import your users, for the example, into the LDAP server. You will be importing a couple of users using an LDIF file. An LDIF file is a text file that uses LDIF formatting, a standard format for describing directory entries in LDAP. It allows you to import and export your directory data into or from another LDAP directory in a standard way or just to create new data or modify existing data. You use it here to import the data with your users. Listing 6-16 shows the LDIF file you will import. You can name this file whatever you like, but we call it users.ldif in this example.

Listing 6-16. LDIF File with the Two Users You Want to Import into the LDAP Directory

```
version: 1

dn: dc=example,dc=com
objectclass: top
objectclass: domain
dc: example
```

```
dn: ou=groups,dc=example,dc=com
objectclass: organizationalUnit
objectclass: top
ou: groups

dn: cn=administrators,ou=groups,dc=example,dc=com
objectclass: groupOfUniqueNames
objectclass: top
cn: administrators
uniqueMember: uid=mnardone,ou=people,dc=example,dc=com
ou: admin

dn: cn=users,ou=groups,dc=example,dc=com
objectclass: groupOfNames
objectclass: top
cn: users
member: uid=lnardone,ou=people,dc=example,dc=com
ou: user

dn: ou=people,dc=example,dc=com
objectclass: organizationalUnit
objectclass: top
ou: people

dn: uid=lnardone,ou=people,dc=example,dc=com
objectclass: inetOrgPerson
objectclass: organizationalPerson
objectclass: person
objectclass: top
cn: Leo Nardone
sn: Leo
uid: lnardone
userPassword: {SHA}F1OkcxtiioPmVX3tJlIHzZsXkDQ=

dn: uid=mnardone,ou=people,dc=example,dc=com
objectclass: inetOrgPerson
objectclass: organizationalPerson
objectclass: person
```

```
objectclass: top
cn: Massimo Nardone
sn: Nardone
uid: mnardone
userPassword: {SHA}xcS5y9T0kjBXDpYijejbhmILFwY=
```

As you can see, this code generated two users, mnarodne, part of the administrators group, and lnardone, who is not included in that group.

Notice that we generated the SHA password via this web page: `http://aspirine.org/htpasswd_en.html`. The passwords are

$$nardone01 = \{SHA\}xcS5y9T0kjBXDpYijejbhmILFwY=$$

$$nardone02 = \{SHA\}F1OkcxtiioPmVX3tJlIHzZsXkDQ=$$

To import the file from Listing 6-16, from Apache Directory Studio, right-click the left panel in the newly created context entry. Then select Import ➤ LDIF Import. In the input form, shown in Figure 6-13, select and find the file where you stored the content from Listing 6-16 (`users.ldif`, in our case), and click Finish.

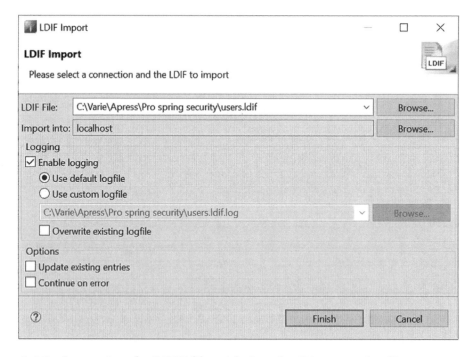

Figure 6-13. *Importing the LDIF file with Apache Directory Studio*

You can see in Listing 6-16 the hierarchical nature of the directory and how everything inherits the DN dc=example,dc=com. As we just said, you can also see how the different entries use different standard object classes. You have created two groups: administrators and users. You also established that *lnardone* is a member of the users group and *mnardone* is a member of the administrators group, and the two SHA passwords. Graphically, the hierarchy is simple enough and looks like Figure 6-14.

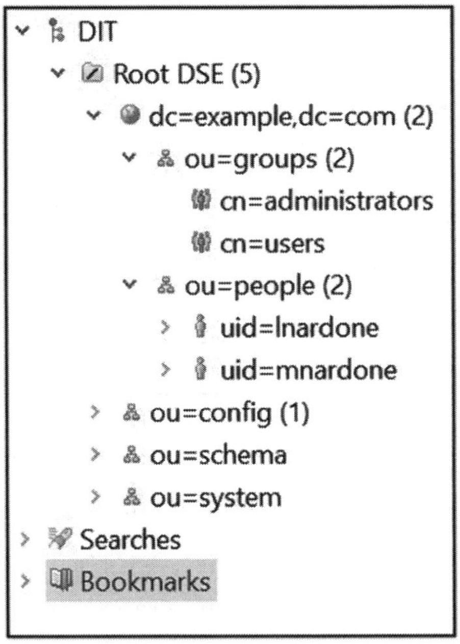

Figure 6-14. *LDAP hierarchy showing the structure you created with the LDIF file*

The next thing you need to do is configure the example application to be able to connect to the LDAP server and query the information stored on it. You have a clean application at the moment, with only the bootstrap components. You will start to add the required functionality now.

First, you add the Spring Security LDAP dependency to the pom.xml file. The dependency is shown in Listing 6-17.

Listing 6-17. Spring Security LDAP Dependency

```
<dependency>
        <groupId>org.springframework.ldap</groupId>
        <artifactId>spring-ldap-core</artifactId>
</dependency>
```

```
<dependency>
        <groupId>org.springframework.security</groupId>
        <artifactId>spring-security-ldap</artifactId>
</dependency>
```

Create a new Spring Security Boot project with Web, Security, LDAP and Thymeleaf as shown in Figure 6-15.

Figure 6-15. *New Spring Boot LDAP project*

Next, update the POM.xml file as shown in Listing 6-18.

Listing 6-18. Pom.xml File

```xml
<?xml version="1.0" encoding="UTF-8"?>
<project xmlns="http://maven.apache.org/POM/4.0.0"
xmlns:xsi="http://www.w3.org/2001/XMLSchema-instance"
        xsi:schemaLocation="http://maven.apache.org/POM/4.0.0
        http://maven.apache.org/xsd/maven-4.0.0.xsd">
        <modelVersion>4.0.0</modelVersion>
        <groupId>com.apress</groupId>
        <artifactId>SpringSecurityldapAuthentication</artifactId>
        <version>0.0.1-SNAPSHOT</version>
        <name>SpringSecurityldapAuthentication</name>
        <description>Demo project for Spring Boot</description>

        <properties>
                <java.version>11</java.version>
        </properties>

        <parent>
                <groupId>org.springframework.boot</groupId>
                <artifactId>spring-boot-starter-parent</artifactId>
                <version>1.5.7.RELEASE</version>
        </parent>

        <dependencies>
                <dependency>
                        <groupId>org.springframework.boot</groupId>
                        <artifactId>spring-boot-starter-web</artifactId>
                </dependency>
                <dependency>
                        <groupId>org.springframework.boot</groupId>
                        <artifactId>spring-boot-starter-security</artifactId>
                </dependency>
```

```
<dependency>
        <groupId>org.springframework.ldap</groupId>
        <artifactId>spring-ldap-core</artifactId>
</dependency>
<dependency>
        <groupId>org.springframework.security</groupId>
        <artifactId>spring-security-ldap</artifactId>
</dependency>

<dependency>
        <groupId>com.unboundid</groupId>
        <artifactId>unboundid-ldapsdk</artifactId>
</dependency>
<dependency>
        <groupId>org.springframework.boot</groupId>
        <artifactId>spring-boot-starter-thymeleaf
        </artifactId>
</dependency>
<dependency>
        <groupId>org.thymeleaf.extras</groupId>
        <artifactId>thymeleaf-extras-springsecurity5
        </artifactId>
</dependency>

<!-- testing -->
<dependency>
        <groupId>org.springframework.boot</groupId>
        <artifactId>spring-boot-starter-test</artifactId>
        <scope>test</scope>
</dependency>
<dependency>
        <groupId>org.springframework.security</groupId>
        <artifactId>spring-security-test</artifactId>
        <scope>test</scope>
</dependency>
    </dependencies>
```

```xml
    <build>
        <plugins>
            <plugin>
                <groupId>org.springframework.boot</groupId>
                <artifactId>spring-boot-maven-plugin
                </artifactId>
            </plugin>
            <plugin>
                <artifactId>maven-compiler-plugin
                </artifactId>
                <version>3.8.0</version>
                <configuration>
                    <source>11</source>
                    <target>11</target>
                </configuration>
            </plugin>
        </plugins>
    </build>

</project>
```

As with the previous project in this book, you create two HTML files under templates, welcome.html and admin.html as shown in Listings 6-19 and 6-20, respectively.

Listing 6-19. welcome.html

```html
<!DOCTYPE html>
    <html>
    <head>
        <title>Spring Boot Security 5 and LDAP Example</title>
    </head>
    <body>
    <h1>Welcome to Spring Boot Security 5 and LDAP Example!</h1>
    <p>Please <a href="/login">login.</a></p>
    </body>
</html>
```

Listing 6-20. admin.html

```html
<!DOCTYPE html>
<html xmlns:th="http://www.thymeleaf.org"
      xmlns:sec="http://www.thymeleaf.org/extras/spring-security">

<head>
    <title>Spring Security 5 and LDAP.</title>
</head>
<body>
<h2>Welcome: <br/> <div th:text="${currentUser}"></div></h2>
<h2>You are succesfully logged as an Admin!</h2>

<div sec:authorize="isAuthenticated()">
    N1: This content is only shown to authenticated users.
</div>
<div sec:authorize="hasAnyAuthority('ADMIN')">
    N2: This content is only shown to administrators.
</div>
<br/>
<form action="/logout" method="post">
    <input type="submit" value="Sign Out"/>
</form>

</body>
</html>
```

Next, create some Java classes. Start with `LoginController`, shown in Listing 6-21, which is similar to one used in other projects in this book.

Listing 6-21. LoginController Java Class

```java
package com.apress.SpringSecurityldapAuthentication.controller;

import org.springframework.security.authentication.
UsernamePasswordAuthenticationToken;
import org.springframework.security.config.annotation.web.builders.
WebSecurity;
import org.springframework.security.core.context.SecurityContextHolder;
```

```java
import org.springframework.security.ldap.userdetails.LdapUserDetailsImpl;
import org.springframework.web.bind.annotation.GetMapping;
import org.springframework.web.bind.annotation.RequestMapping;
import org.springframework.web.bind.annotation.RequestMethod;
import org.springframework.web.bind.annotation.RestController;
import org.springframework.web.servlet.ModelAndView;

@RestController
public class LoginController {

    @GetMapping("/")
    public ModelAndView home() {
        ModelAndView modelAndView = new ModelAndView();
        modelAndView.setViewName("welcome");
        return modelAndView;
    }

    @GetMapping("/welcome")
    public ModelAndView welcome() {
        ModelAndView modelAndView = new ModelAndView();
        modelAndView.setViewName("welcome");
        return modelAndView;
    }

    @GetMapping("/admin")
    public ModelAndView admin() {
        ModelAndView modelAndView = new ModelAndView();
        UsernamePasswordAuthenticationToken authentication =
                (UsernamePasswordAuthenticationToken)
                        SecurityContextHolder.getContext().
                        getAuthentication();
        LdapUserDetailsImpl principal = (LdapUserDetailsImpl)
        authentication.getPrincipal();

        modelAndView.addObject("currentUser", principal.getDn());
        modelAndView.addObject("role", principal.getAuthorities());
        modelAndView.addObject("adminMessage", "Content Available only for
        Authenticated Admins!");
```

```
        modelAndView.setViewName("admin");
        return modelAndView;
    }

    public void configure(WebSecurity web) throws Exception {
        web
                .ignoring()
                .antMatchers("/resources/**");
    }

}
```

Listing 6-21 works as you saw previously, such as using @GetMapping to redirect the application to a certain HTML page like welcome, admin, etc.

So how does the LDAP authentication works? Let's start by writing a simple application.yml file to tell Spring the LDAP Server and entry to utilize; see Listing 6-22.

Listing 6-22. application.yml File

```
spring:
  ldap:

    urls: ldap://localhost:10389
    base: dc=example,dc=com
    username: uid=admin,ou=system
    password: secret
```

Next, create another Java class named SpringSecurityConfiguration, shown in Listing 6-23, to take care of the LDAP authentication.

Listing 6-23. SpringSecurityConfiguration Java Class

```
package com.apress.SpringSecurityldapAuthentication.Configuration;

import org.springframework.context.annotation.Bean;
import org.springframework.context.annotation.Configuration;
import org.springframework.security.authentication.encoding.
LdapShaPasswordEncoder;
import org.springframework.security.config.annotation.authentication.
builders.AuthenticationManagerBuilder;
```

```java
import org.springframework.security.config.annotation.web.builders.
HttpSecurity;
import org.springframework.security.config.annotation.web.configuration.
EnableWebSecurity;
import org.springframework.security.config.annotation.web.configuration.
WebSecurityConfigurerAdapter;
import org.springframework.security.ldap.
DefaultSpringSecurityContextSource;
import org.springframework.security.web.util.matcher.AntPathRequestMatcher;
import org.springframework.security.web.authentication.logout.
LogoutSuccessHandler;

import java.util.Collections;

    @Configuration
    @EnableWebSecurity
    public class SpringSecurityConfiguration extends
    WebSecurityConfigurerAdapter {

        @Override
        protected void configure(HttpSecurity http) throws Exception {
            http
                    .authorizeRequests()
                    .antMatchers("/").permitAll()
                    .antMatchers("/login").permitAll()
                    .antMatchers("/logout").permitAll()
                    .antMatchers("/welcome").permitAll()
                    .antMatchers("/admin").hasRole("ADMINISTRATORS")
                    .anyRequest().fullyAuthenticated()
                    .and()
                    .formLogin()
                    .defaultSuccessUrl("/admin", true)
                    .and().logout()
                    .logoutUrl("/perform_logout")
                    .logoutRequestMatcher(new AntPathRequestMatcher
                    ("/logout"))
                    .logoutSuccessUrl("/welcome.html")
```

```
                .deleteCookies("JSESSIONID")
                .invalidateHttpSession(true)
                .logoutRequestMatcher(new AntPathRequestMatcher
                ("/logout"));

        ;
    }

    @Override
    public void configure(AuthenticationManagerBuilder auth) throws
    Exception {
        auth
                .ldapAuthentication()
                .userDnPatterns("uid={0},ou=people")
                .groupSearchBase("ou=groups")
                .contextSource(contextSource())
                .passwordCompare()
                .passwordEncoder(new LdapShaPasswordEncoder())
                .passwordAttribute("userPassword");
    }

    @Bean
    public DefaultSpringSecurityContextSource contextSource() {
        return  new DefaultSpringSecurityContextSource(
                Collections.singletonList("ldap://localhost:10389"),
                "dc=example,dc=com");
    }

}
```

Start the application now with this configuration. You should be able to see the welcome page via the URL http://localhost:8080/, as shown in Figure 6-16.

Welcome to Spring Boot Security 5 and LDAP Example!

Please login.

Figure 6-16. *Application welcome page*

Log in and access the Spring Security v5 login page, as shown in Figure 6-17.

Login with Username and Password

User: mnardone

Password: •••••••••

Login

Figure 6-17. *Application login page*

In the LDAP, there are two users: mnardone and lnardone. The difference is that mnardone is part of the administrators group so he can access the admin.html page.

So log in with the username **mnardone** and the password **nardone01** and you will be able to access the admin page, as shown in Figure 6-18.

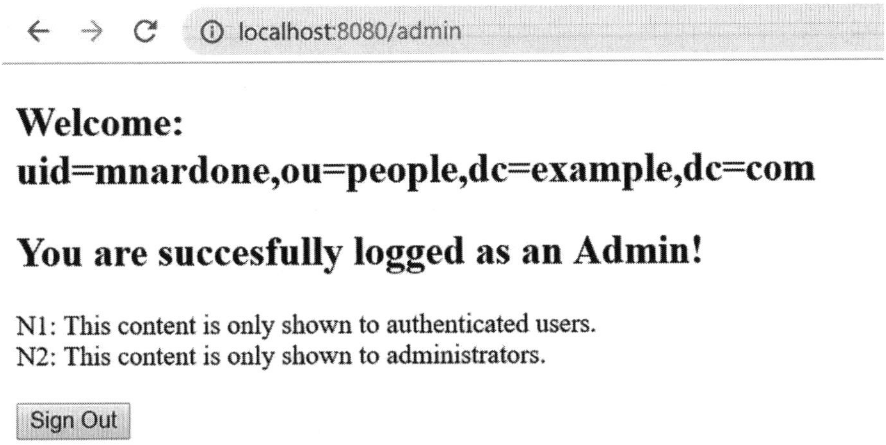

Welcome:
uid=mnardone,ou=people,dc=example,dc=com

You are succesfully logged as an Admin!

N1: This content is only shown to authenticated users.
N2: This content is only shown to administrators.

Sign Out

Figure 6-18. *Admin-credentialed user accessing the admin page*

If you try now with the **lnardone** user and the password **nardone02,** you will not be able to access the admin page since that user is not part of the administrators group; you'll receive the "access denied" message shown in Figure 6-19.

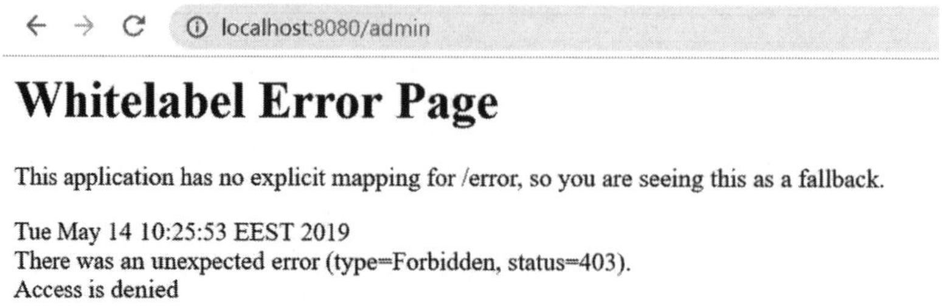

Whitelabel Error Page

This application has no explicit mapping for /error, so you are seeing this as a fallback.

Tue May 14 10:25:53 EEST 2019
There was an unexpected error (type=Forbidden, status=403).
Access is denied

Figure 6-19. *A non-authorized user receiving the "access denied" message*

The configuration is not that difficult to understand. The login configuration is within the SpringSecurityConfiguration Java class.

The configure(HttpSecurity http) will configure the HTTP with things like login, logout, etc. The most important configuration value is .antMatchers("/admin"). hasRole("ADMINISTRATORS") which tells you that the /admin URL can only be accessed by users in the LDAP as part of the administrators group, as you saw before:

```
dn: cn=administrators,ou=groups,dc=example,dc=com
objectclass: groupOfUniqueNames
objectclass: top
cn: administrators
uniqueMember: uid=mnardone,ou=people,dc=example,dc=com
ou: admin
```

In your case, mnardone is part of the administrators LDAP group so he can access the /admin page.

Remember that all your entries will be relative to the domain name dc=example,dc=com.

Next, the configure(AuthenticationManagerBuilder auth) will take care of the authentication builder checking the user and SHA password via the following:

```
                .ldapAuthentication()
                .userDnPatterns("uid={0},ou=people")
                .groupSearchBase("ou=groups")
                .contextSource(contextSource())
```

```
.passwordCompare()
.passwordEncoder(new LdapShaPasswordEncoder())
.passwordAttribute("userPassword");
```

So you defined the LDAP DN patter to look for a user as part of the ou=people group.

Finally, DefaultSpringSecurityContextSource contextSource() specifies the LDAP URL to connect to.

As you can see from the example, configuring LDAP's basic support as the authentication solution for your application with Spring Security is not that complex. In fact, it is very straightforward thanks to the modular architecture and the well-thought-out XML namespace. For us, the complexity with LDAP is LDAP itself. Although it is a simple hierarchical system (very much like the file system in your standard Unix box), some of the nomenclature and functionality seems a bit complex and very different from the database-based solution you explored in the previous section.

As we said before, using LDAP as your authentication solution makes great sense in the context of corporate intranets, where the company user base is already stored in LDAP-like directories in a centralized manner. Plugins into this already existing user-management infrastructure are a good way to reuse the user information within the company instead of writing a parallel authentication datastore that then needs to be kept in sync with the main repository.

X.509 Authentication

X.509 authentication is an authentication scheme that uses client-side certificates instead of username-password combinations to identify the user. Using this approach, a scheme known as *mutual authentication* takes place between the client and the server. In practice, mutual authentication means that, as part of the Secure Sockets Layer (SSL) handshake, the server requests that the client identify himself by providing a certificate. In a production-ready server, the incoming client certificate needs to be issued and signed by a proper certificate-signing authority.

To work with client certificates, the application needs to be configured to use SSL channels in the sections that are expected to deal with the authenticated user, because the X.509 authentication protocol itself is part of the SSL protocol.

As a first thing, let's create a Spring Security Boot project using the Spring Initializr at https://start.spring.io/.

Create the new project with the following dependencies: Web, Security, and Thymeleaf, as shown in Figure 6-20.

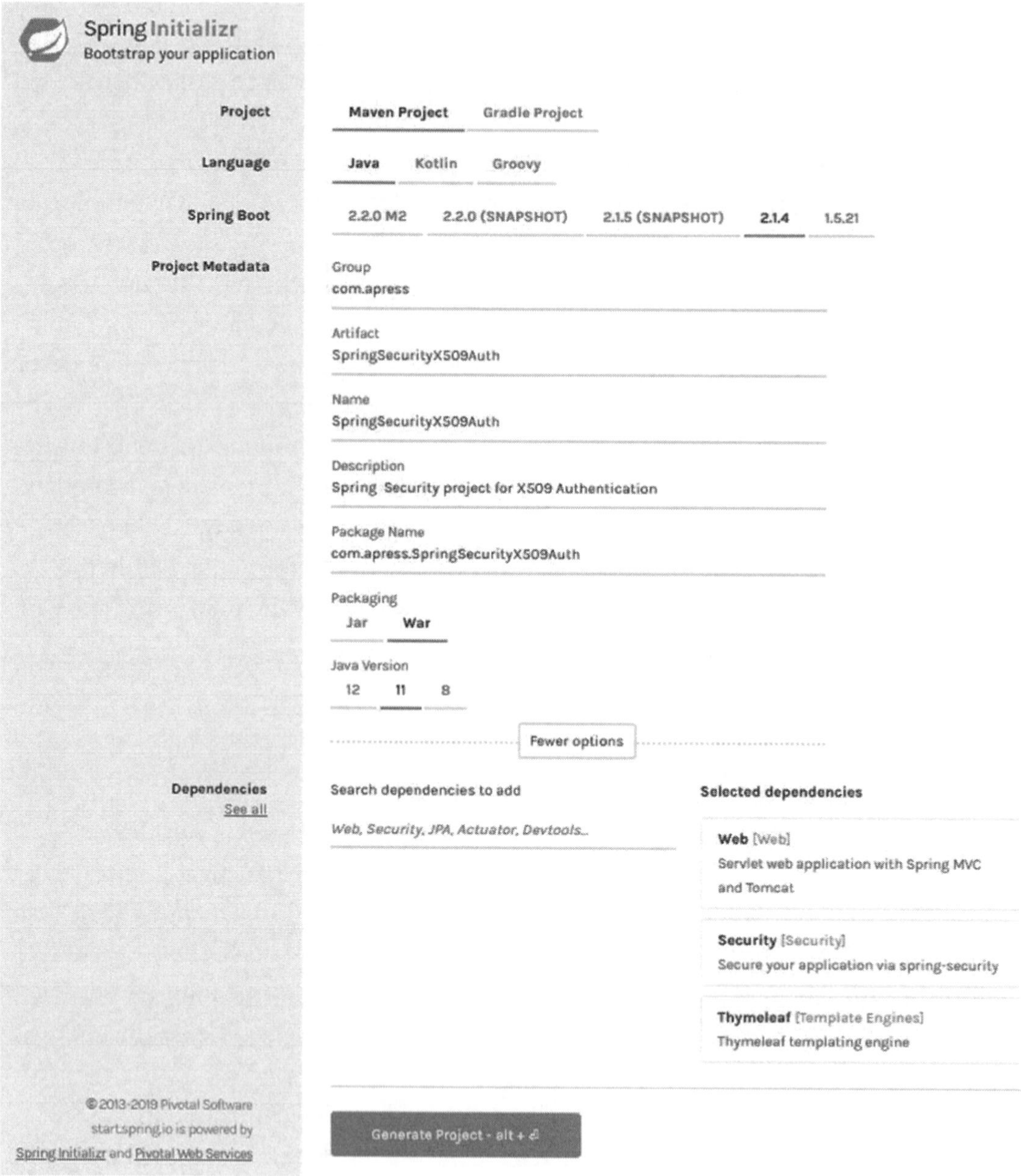

Figure 6-20. *Creating a new Spring Initilizr project*

Open the project and update the pom.xml file as shown Listing 6-24.

Listing 6-24. pom.xml File

```xml
<?xml version="1.0" encoding="UTF-8"?>
<project xmlns="http://maven.apache.org/POM/4.0.0"
xmlns:xsi="http://www.w3.org/2001/XMLSchema-instance"
     xsi:schemaLocation="http://maven.apache.org/POM/4.0.0
     http://maven.apache.org/xsd/maven-4.0.0.xsd">
     <modelVersion>4.0.0</modelVersion>
     <parent>
       <groupId>org.springframework.boot</groupId>
       <artifactId>spring-boot-starter-parent</artifactId>
       <version>2.1.4.RELEASE</version>
       <relativePath/> <!-- lookup parent from repository -->
     </parent>
     <groupId>com.apress</groupId>
     <artifactId>SpringSecurityX509Auth</artifactId>
     <version>0.0.1-SNAPSHOT</version>
     <packaging>war</packaging>
     <name>SpringSecurityX509Auth</name>
     <description>Spring  Security project for X509 Authentication
     </description>

     <properties>
       <java.version>11</java.version>
     </properties>

     <dependencies>
       <dependency>
               <groupId>org.springframework.boot</groupId>
               <artifactId>spring-boot-starter-security</artifactId>
       </dependency>
       <dependency>
               <groupId>org.springframework.boot</groupId>
               <artifactId>spring-boot-starter-thymeleaf</artifactId>
       </dependency>
```

```xml
        <dependency>
                <groupId>org.springframework.boot</groupId>
                <artifactId>spring-boot-starter-web</artifactId>
        </dependency>

        <dependency>
                <groupId>org.springframework.boot</groupId>
                <artifactId>spring-boot-starter-tomcat</artifactId>
                <scope>provided</scope>
        </dependency>
        <dependency>
                <groupId>org.springframework.boot</groupId>
                <artifactId>spring-boot-starter-test</artifactId>
                <scope>test</scope>
        </dependency>
        <dependency>
                <groupId>org.springframework.security</groupId>
                <artifactId>spring-security-test</artifactId>
                <scope>test</scope>
        </dependency>
    </dependencies>

    <build>
      <plugins>
                <plugin>
                    <groupId>org.springframework.boot</groupId>
                    <artifactId>spring-boot-maven-plugin</artifactId>
                </plugin>
      </plugins>
    </build>

</project>
```

As with the previous LDAP project in this chapter, create one HTML file under templates named admin.html, as shown in Listing 6-25.

Listing 6-25. admin.html

```html
<!DOCTYPE html>
<html xmlns:th="http://www.thymeleaf.org"
      xmlns:sec="http://www.thymeleaf.org/extras/spring-security">

<head>
    <title>Spring Security 5 and LDAP.</title>
</head>
<body>
<h2>Welcome: <br/> <div th:text="${currentUser}"></div></h2>
<h2>You are succesfully logged as an Admin!</h2>

<div sec:authorize="isAuthenticated()">
    This content is only shown to authenticated users.
</div>
<div sec:authorize="hasAnyAuthority('ROLE_USER')">
    This content is only shown to administrators.
</div>
<br/>
<form action="/logout" method="post">
    <input type="submit" value="Sign Out"/>
</form>

</body>
</html>
```

Now create three packages under Java in your project.

- Configuration: Contains the SpringSecurityConfiguration
  Java class

- Controller: Contains the UserController Java class

- Domain: Contains the User Java class

Now create three Java classes: SpringSecurityConfiguration, UserController, and User.

Let's start by create the SpringSecurityConfiguration Java class shown in Listing 6-26.

Listing 6-26. SpringSecurityConfiguration Java Class

```
package com.apress.SpringSecurityX509Auth.Configuration;

import org.springframework.context.annotation.Bean;
import org.springframework.context.annotation.Configuration;
import org.springframework.security.config.annotation.method.configuration.
EnableGlobalMethodSecurity;
import org.springframework.security.config.annotation.web.builders.
HttpSecurity;
import org.springframework.security.config.annotation.web.configuration.
EnableWebSecurity;
import org.springframework.security.config.annotation.web.configuration.
WebSecurityConfigurerAdapter;
import org.springframework.security.core.authority.AuthorityUtils;
import org.springframework.security.core.userdetails.User;
import org.springframework.security.core.userdetails.UserDetails;
import org.springframework.security.core.userdetails.UserDetailsService;
import org.springframework.security.core.userdetails.
UsernameNotFoundException;
import org.springframework.security.web.util.matcher.AntPathRequestMatcher;

@Configuration
@EnableWebSecurity
@EnableGlobalMethodSecurity(securedEnabled = true)
public class SpringSecurityConfiguration extends
WebSecurityConfigurerAdapter {

    @Override
    protected void configure(HttpSecurity http) throws Exception {
        http
                .authorizeRequests()
                .anyRequest().authenticated().and()
                .x509()
                .subjectPrincipalRegex("CN=(.*?)(?:,|$)")
                .userDetailsService(userDetailsService())
                .and().logout()
                .logoutUrl("/perform_logout")
```

```java
                .logoutRequestMatcher(new AntPathRequestMatcher("/logout"))
                .logoutSuccessUrl("/admin")
                .deleteCookies("JSESSIONID")
                .invalidateHttpSession(true)
                .logoutRequestMatcher(new AntPathRequestMatcher("/logout"));
    }

    @Bean
    public UserDetailsService userDetailsService() {
        return (UserDetailsService) username -> {
            if (username.equals("nardone")) {
                return new User(username, "",
                        AuthorityUtils
                                .commaSeparatedStringToAuthorityList
                                ("ROLE_USER"));
            } else {
                throw new UsernameNotFoundException(String.format("User %s
                not found", username));
            }
        };
    }
}
```

This Java class is very simple to understand. Once you provide a valid client certificate, it will get the value "CN" from it via the following lines:

```java
                .anyRequest().authenticated().and()
                .x509()
                .subjectPrincipalRegex("CN=(.*?)(?:,|$)")
                .userDetailsService(userDetailsService());
```

Then it will check if the value "CN" is equal to "**nardone**". If so, it will return the username "**nardone**" with the authority as ROLE_USER and authorize the user to proceed:

```java
            if (username.equals("nardone")) {
                return new User(username, "",
                        AuthorityUtils
                                .commaSeparatedStringToAuthorityList
                                ("ROLE_USER"));
```

Now create the UserController Java class shown in Listing 6-27.

Listing 6-27. UserController Java Class

```
package com.apress.SpringSecurityX509Auth.Controller;

import org.springframework.security.access.annotation.Secured;
import org.springframework.security.authentication.UsernamePassword
AuthenticationToken;
import org.springframework.security.config.annotation.web.builders.WebSecurity;
import org.springframework.security.core.Authentication;
import org.springframework.security.core.context.SecurityContextHolder;
import org.springframework.web.bind.annotation.*;

import com.apress.SpringSecurityX509Auth.Domain.User;
import org.springframework.web.servlet.ModelAndView;

@RestController
public class UserController {

    @Secured("ROLE_USER")

    @RequestMapping(value = {"/","/admin"}, method = RequestMethod.GET)
    public ModelAndView admin() {
        ModelAndView modelAndView = new ModelAndView();
        modelAndView.setViewName("admin");
        Authentication auth = SecurityContextHolder.getContext().
        getAuthentication();
        modelAndView.addObject("currentUser", auth.getName());
        User user = new User();
        return modelAndView;
    }

    public void configure(WebSecurity web) throws Exception {
        web
                .ignoring()
                .antMatchers("/resources/**");
    }
}
```

This is a simple User controller Java class which will redirect URLs as requested. Now create the User Java class shown in Listing 6-28.

Listing 6-28. User Java Class

```
package com.apress.SpringSecurityX509Auth.Domain;

public class User {

    private String name;

    public User() {
        this.name = name;
    }

    public String getName() {
        return name;
    }

    public void setName(String name) {
        this.name = name;
    }
}
```

This class will fetch data from the X.509 client certificate provided for the authentication.

This is all the configuration Spring needs to handle client certificates.

Of course, things are not that simple and the job is not yet done. In reality, Spring Security X.509 support doesn't authenticate the user. The user is assumed to be already authenticated, and Spring Security simply creates a successful Authentication object with information extracted from the certificate and stores it in the SecurityContext in the standard way.

So the entity that is actually in charge of authenticating the user (or more exactly, accepting the user as a properly identified one) is the web server, which does this by accepting the provided client certificate. Basically, if the server decides that the certificate sent by the user is a valid one, the user is who she claims to be and gets authenticated.

In a production system, the web server makes sure that the certificate provided by the client is signed by an authorized trusted authority.

However, you will use a test environment with your common Maven-configured Tomcat installation, and for that you will configure a self-signed certificate and make sure that Tomcat accepts it.

Before you start, make sure you installed the openssl tool on your machine. Download it from `https://wiki.openssl.org/index.php/Binaries`.

Let's create the server and client certificates needed. It is pretty straightforward to do, and you will use the `openssl` tool to do it:

For the server:

1. Generate a server private key (PEM) and a server self-signed certificate (CRT):

   ```
   openssl req -x509 -newkey rsa:4096 -keyout serverPrivateKey.pem
   -out server.crt -days 3650 -nodes
   ```

2. Create a PKCS12 keystore containing a private key (P12) and a related self-signed certificate (CRT) (password used: changeit):

   ```
   openssl pkcs12 -export -out keyStore.p12 -inkey serverPrivateKey.
   pem -in server.crt
   ```

3. Generate a server trust store (JKS) from the server certificate (CRT):

   ```
   keytool -import -trustcacerts -alias root -file server.crt
   -keystore trustStore.jks
   ```

For the client:

4. Generate the client's private key (PEM) and a certificate signing request (CSR):

   ```
   openssl req -new -newkey rsa:4096 -out request.csr -keyout
   myPrivateKey.pem -nodes
   ```

For the client and server:

5. Sign a client's certificate signing request (CSR) with a server private key (PEM) and a related certificate (CRT):

   ```
   openssl x509 -req -days 360 -in request.csr -CA server.crt -CAkey
   serverPrivateKey.pem -CAcreateserial -out nardone.crt -sha256
   ```

For the client:

6. Verify the client's certificate (CRT):

   ```
   openssl x509 -text -noout -in nardone.crt
   ```

7. Create a PKCS12 keystore (P12) containing the client's private key
   (PEM) and related self-sign certificate (CRT):

   ```
   openssl pkcs12 -export -out client_nardone.p12 -inkey
   myPrivateKey.pem -in nardone.crt -certfile myCertificate.crt
   ```

Figures 6-21 and 6-22 show some of the client commands you just executed.

Figure 6-21. *Client certificate commands*

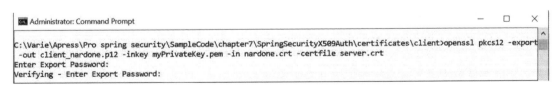

Figure 6-22. *Generating a client certificate*

When executing that last step, it is important that when asked to introduce your name by the command-line prompt, you use the name nardone because it is the username you configured in the application configuration file. The command line will show you the following prompt: *Common Name (e.g. server FQDN or YOUR name) []:**nardone***

That's it! That process created a self-signed X509 certificate with 365 days of duration signed with the private key.

Note   A truststore is a repository of certificates that are trusted by the JRE that uses such a truststore. By default the JRE truststore trusts any certificates signed by a recognized Certificate Authority (CA). If you have a certificate not signed by a CA (like the self-signed certificates), you will need to add it manually to the truststore so that it can be trusted.

The execution of that file is shown in Figure 6-23. That simple line created the file trustStore.jks, which you will use as the trust store for the Tomcat server to accept the client certificate.

```
C:\Varie\Apress\Pro spring security\SampleCode\chapter7\SpringSecurityX509Auth\certificates\server>keytool -import -trustcacerts -alias r
Enter keystore password:
Re-enter new password:
Owner: EMAILADDRESS=massimonardone@gmail.com, CN=DevServer, OU=Apress Dev, O=Apress, L=Naples, ST=Naples, C=IT
Issuer: EMAILADDRESS=massimonardone@gmail.com, CN=DevServer, OU=Apress Dev, O=Apress, L=Naples, ST=Naples, C=IT
Serial number: 3b00eaff943320f795b2e01b620f2caad110a936
Valid from: Wed May 15 12:28:25 EEST 2019 until: Sat May 12 12:28:25 EEST 2029
Certificate fingerprints:
        SHA1: 33:A4:54:23:A4:CF:DB:DE:D1:5C:C8:62:56:19:B2:40:8D:86:F7:54
        SHA256: 5F:F6:2B:DE:7A:BD:C6:59:CB:DF:73:21:BB:D2:FF:E6:1C:14:06:03:55:06:4A:A8:A4:6D:76:E1:2A:0F:42:AF
Signature algorithm name: SHA256withRSA
Subject Public Key Algorithm: 4096-bit RSA key
Version: 3

Extensions:

#1: ObjectId: 2.5.29.35 Criticality=false
AuthorityKeyIdentifier [
KeyIdentifier [
0000: 61 52 F4 69 77 70 10 B3   7E EF DD 23 A2 3F 59 66  aR.iwp.....#.?Yf
0010: 8B 81 F6 49                                        ...I
]
]
```

Figure 6-23. *A truststore created with an imported certificate*

Next, you need to add the certificate to the browser you will use to connect to the application. Let's use Chrome in this example. Earlier you created the .p12 file that contains information about the client and server certificates and the private keys associated with both certificates.

To import that file into the client certificates of Chrome, do the following:

1. Click Chrome ➤ Settings.

2. Click the Advanced tab.

3. Click View Certificates.

4. Click Import.

5. Locate `client_nardone.p12` in the directory where it is stored, and double-click it.

6. Use **changeit** as the password when requested.

The result can be seen in Figure 6-24.

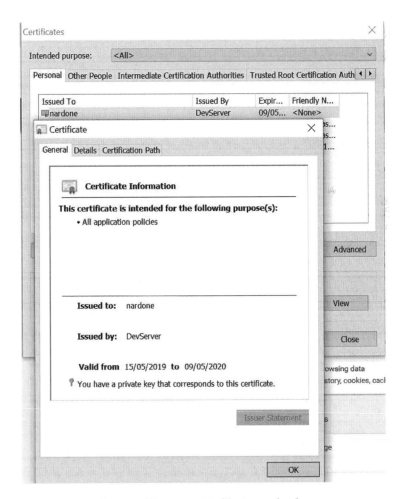

Figure 6-24. *Importing the certificate .p12 file into the browser*

The next step is to add the server certificate to the Trusted Root Certificate Authorities list in the web browser, shown in Figure 6-25.

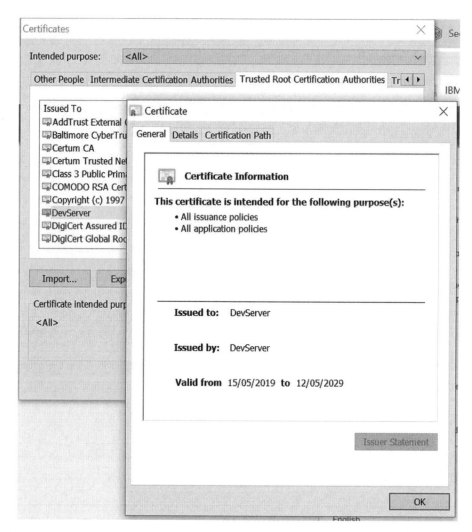

Figure 6-25. *Importing the server certificate .crt file into the browser*

The next step is to update the `application.properties` with the following lines:

```
server.port=8443
server.ssl.key-store-type=PKCS12
server.ssl.key-store=classpath:keyStore.p12
server.ssl.key-store-password=changeit
```

```
server.ssl.trust-store=classpath:trustStore.jks
server.ssl.trust-store-password=changeit
server.ssl.trust-store-type=JKS
server.ssl.client-auth=need
```

All these lines will tell the application to use the ssl port 8443, the file type for the server key store used, where the keys are located, and that the client certificate is "needed."

Make sure you add all the certificates and that the keys are stored in the project as shown in Figure 6-26.

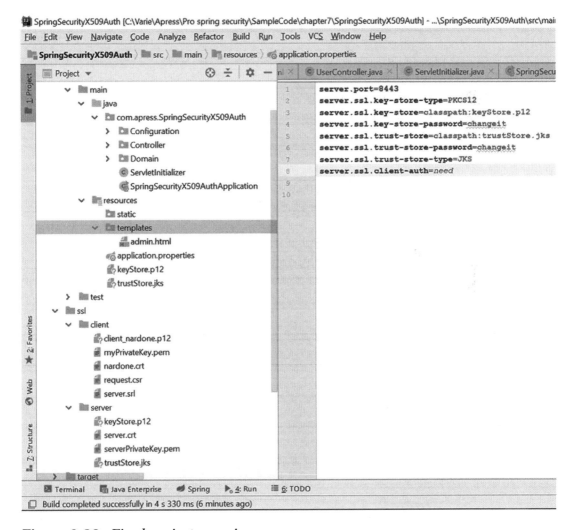

Figure 6-26. *Final project overview*

Now the configuration is complete and the application is ready. The browser is also ready for the mutual authentication process to get underway.

To try it out, start the application. Then visit the URL `https://localhost:8443/admin`. You need to accept the self-signed certificate from the server to continue. After you accept it, you will be presented with a screen that asks you to select the client certificate to use to authenticate. You might have some different client certificates to choose from; for this case, select the nardone certificate you just imported, as shown in Figure 6-27.

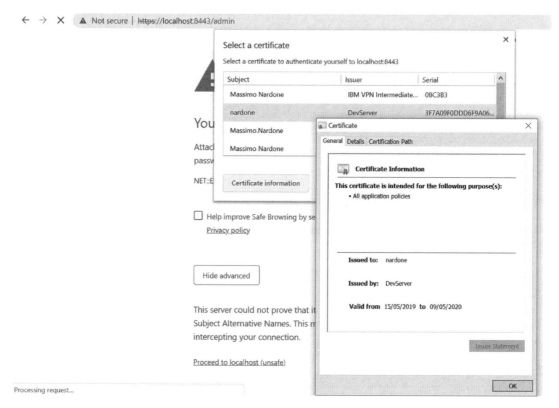

Figure 6-27. *Selecting a client certificate to use*

After clicking OK, you get the admin page, meaning that the authentication was successful; see Figure 6-28.

Figure 6-28. *A succesfull client certificate authentication admin page*

That is the whole flow that is followed by a request using client-certificate authentication. As you can see, Spring Security support for it is pretty straightforward.

OAuth 2

OAuth 2.0 is the industry-standard protocol for authorization. You can get more information at `https://oauth.net/2/`.

Spring Security 5.0 now supports the OAuth 2.0 Authorization Framework and OpenID Connect 1.0. with Spring Security 5.1. It introduced new Resource Server support as well as additional Client support.

The OAuth 2.0 implementation for authentication, which conforms to the OpenID Connect specification and is OpenID Certified, can be used for both authentication and authorization via Google's OAuth 2.0 APIs. For more information, please go to `https://developers.google.com/identity/protocols/OAuth2`.

OAuth 2 supports

- Client

- Resource Server

- Authorization Server

The OAuth 2.0 Client features provide support for the Client role as defined in the OAuth 2.0 Authorization Framework. You can get more information at `https://tools.ietf.org/html/rfc6749#section-1.1`.

When developing an OAuth 2.0 Client, the following main features are available:

- Authorization Code Grant

- Client Credentials Grant

- WebClient extension for servlet environments (for making protected resource requests)

Notice that Spring Security 5 introduces a new `OAuth2LoginConfigurer` class that you can use for configuring an external Authorization Server.

JSON Web Token

Spring Security 5 supports JSON Web Token (JWT) Authentication.

Basically you need to

- Configure Spring Security for JWT

- Expose the REST POST API with mapping/authenticate

- Configure a valid JSON Web Token

Specifically, to configure Spring Security and JWT, you need to perform two operations:

1. Generate JWT by

    - Exposing a POST API with mapping/authenticating

    - Passing the correct username and password

    - Generating a JSON Web Token

2. Validate a JWT by

    - When trying to access the GET API with a certain mapping like `/Testing`

    - Allowing access only if a request has a valid JSON Web Token

Spring Security and JWT dependencies include the following:

```
<dependency>
<groupId>io.jsonwebtoken</groupId>
<artifactId>jjwt</artifactId>
<version>0.9.1</version>
</dependency>
```

Spring WebSockets

Spring Security 5 MVC supports Spring WebSockets. For WebSocket implementation, you want add the following Maven dependencies such as

```
<dependency>
    <groupId>org.springframework</groupId>
    <artifactId>spring-websocket</artifactId>
    <version>${spring.version}</version>
</dependency>
<dependency>
    <groupId>org.springframework</groupId>
    <artifactId>spring-messaging</artifactId>
    <version>${spring.version}</version>
</dependency>
<dependency>
    <groupId>org.springframework.security</groupId>
    <artifactId>spring-security-messaging</artifactId>
    <version>${spring-security.version}</version>
</dependency>
```

Then you simply define the configuration of WebSocket-specific security using the spring-security-messaging library centers via the AbstractSecurityWebSocketMessageBrokerConfigurer class like this:

```
@Configuration
public class SocketSecurityConfig
  extends AbstractSecurityWebSocketMessageBrokerConfigurer {
    //...//
}
```

JAAS Authentication

The Java Authentication and Authorization Service (JAAS) is the existing standard Java support for managing authentication and authorization. Its functionality clearly overlaps with that of Spring Security.

JAAS is a relatively large standard that involves a lot more than the small amount of information we covered here. However, the main concepts are the ones we showed you, and the goal of the section is to show the building blocks for integrating it with Spring Security.

Check out the Spring Security 5 reference documentation for more info about JAAS.

Central Authentication Service Authentication

Central Authentication Service (CAS) is an enterprise single sign-on solution built in Java and open source. It has a great support community and integrates into many Java projects. CAS provides a centralized place for authentication and access control in an enterprise.

Overview

JA-SIG, at `http://www.ja-sig.org`, produces an enterprise-wide single sign-on system known as CAS. JA-SIG's Central Authentication Service is a simple, open source, independent platform that supports proxy capabilities. Spring Security fully supports CAS for single applications as well as multiple-application deployments secured by an enterprise-wide CAS server. You can learn more about CAS at `www.apereo.org/projects/cas`.

One important characteristic of CAS is that it is designed to serve as a proxy to different authentication storage solutions. This means it can be used in combination with LDAP, JDBC, or a few other user stores that contain real user data. This looks a lot like the way Spring Security leverages these same user data stores.

Check out the Spring Security 5 reference documentation for more info about CAS.

Summary

In this chapter, we showed how you can use Spring Security's modular architecture to integrate different authentication mechanisms with relative ease. We explained some of the authentication mechanisms that come with the framework. In particular, we showed how to authenticate your users against a database, an LDAP server, by using Client X.509 certificates. JAAS, OAuth2/OpenID, WebSockets, JWT, and CAS were only introduced.

This chapter focused on showing how all these different authentication providers relate to each other when they are used inside the framework. The goal was to show you that integrating new providers into the framework is simple enough for you to try. Of course, how easy it is depends on the authentication scheme that you want to plug in.

There are more authentication providers that we haven't covered in this chapter, but the main ideas tend to remain the same: create a connector into Spring Security that deals with the particulars of the integrating protocol, and adapt it to use the Spring Security model of authentication and authorization.

CHAPTER 7

Business Object Security with ACLs

This chapter will introduce access control lists (ACLs) in the context of Spring Security.

Access control lists can be thought of as an extension to the business-level security rules we reviewed in Chapter 6. In this case, however, we'll be looking at more fine-grained rules to secure individual domain objects, instead of the relatively coarse-grained rules used to secure method calls on services.

What this means is that ACLs are in charge of securing instances of domain classes (such as a `Forum` class, a `Cart` class, and so on), while the standard method-level rules secure entry points determined by methods (like a `Service` method or a `DAO` method).

Securing domain objects with ACLs is conceptually simple. The idea is that any user has a certain level of access (read, write, none, and so on) to each domain object. A user's level of access (*permissions*) to a particular domain object depends on the user, or the role or group to which the user belongs.

As in other chapters, we'll explain each concept as we walk through an example. The example will be, as usual, a very simple and not *real-world* application pared down to focus on the concepts relevant to understanding how ACLs work.

The Security Example Application

The example application is a simple forum system with two types of users: standard users and administrator users. Any user can create a forum entry, but only the user who created the entry can edit it; the other standard users can only read it. Administrator users can read or delete an entry, but they cannot edit it. This give us all the combinations we need to show the full power of ACLs. The permission logic is shown in Figure 7-1. The action is shown with a solid line and permissions are shown with a dotted line.

© Carlo Scarioni and Massimo Nardone 2019
C. Scarioni and M. Nardone, *Pro Spring Security*, https://doi.org/10.1007/978-1-4842-5052-5_7

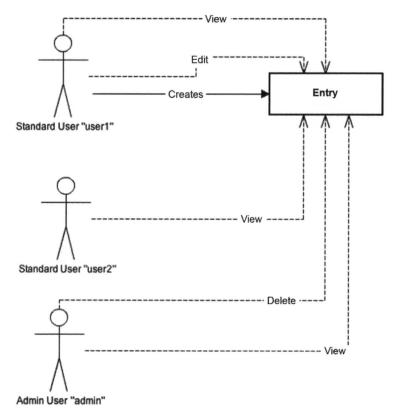

Figure 7-1. *Permission logic for forum entries*

So let's set up the example project.

But first, let's review the required database schema to support ACLs in the application. Currently, this is the only support for ACLs in Spring Security, and it needs to be configured for the whole functionality to work. Spring Security's ACL module comes with the SQL scripts necessary to define its own support in a file named createAclSchema.sql that currently targets the HSQL database. (There is also an alternative file called createAclSchemaPostgres.sql that targets the PostgreSQL database.) You can find this file in the source code of the Spring Security ACL module or inside the .jar file itself: spring-security-acl-3.1.3.RELEASE.jar. It will be in the src/main/resources folder in the source code, which means it will be in the root of the classpath. Listing 7-1 shows the contents of this file.

Listing 7-1. The createAclSchema.sql That Defines the Needed Tables for
Supporting ACL in Spring Security

```
-- ACL schema sql used in HSQLDB

-- drop table acl_entry;
-- drop table acl_object_identity;
-- drop table acl_class;
-- drop table acl_sid;

create table acl_sid(
    id bigint generated by default as identity(start with 100) not null
    primary key,
    principal boolean not null,
    sid varchar_ignorecase(100) not null,
    constraint unique_uk_1 unique(sid,principal));

create table acl_class(
    id bigint generated by default as identity(start with 100) not null
    primary key,
    class varchar_ignorecase(100) not null,
    constraint unique_uk_2 unique(class)
);

create table acl_object_identity(
    id bigint generated by default as identity(start with 100) not null
    primary key,
    object_id_class bigint not null,
    object_id_identity bigint not null,
    parent_object bigint,
    owner_sid bigint,
    entries_inheriting boolean not null,
    constraint unique_uk_3 unique(object_id_class,object_id_identity),
    constraint foreign_fk_1 foreign key(parent_object)references acl_
    object_identity(id),
```

```
    constraint foreign_fk_2 foreign key(object_id_class)references acl_
    class(id),
    constraint foreign_fk_3 foreign key(owner_sid)references acl_sid(id)
);

create table acl_entry(
    id bigint generated by default as identity(start with 100) not null
    primary key,
    acl_object_identity bigint not null,
    ace_order int not null,
    sid bigint not null,
    mask integer not null,
    granting boolean not null,
    audit_success boolean not null,
    audit_failure boolean not null,
    constraint unique_uk_4 unique(acl_object_identity,ace_order),
    constraint foreign_fk_4 foreign key(acl_object_identity) references
    acl_object_identity(id),
    constraint foreign_fk_5 foreign key(sid) references acl_sid(id)
);
```

To understand the meaning of these tables, you need to appreciate the main abstractions in Spring Security's ACL support:

- **SID (security identity)**: An abstraction that represents a security identity in the system to be used by the ACL infrastructure. A security identity can be a user, role, group, and so forth. It maps to the table ACL_SID.

- **Access control entry (ACE)**: Represents an individual permission in the particular ACL making relationships between objects, SIDs, and permissions. It maps to the table ACL_ENTRY.

- **Object identity**: Represents the identity of an individual domain object instance. They are the entities on which the permissions are set. It maps to the table ACL_OBJECT_IDENTITY.

Let's break down the database tables into their main attributes to see their meaning. (We won't explain the ID attributes because they are the surrogate identifiers of each row in the pertinent table, and they serve to, well, identify the particular entry.) Figure 7-2 shows the tables in graphical form followed by the explanation of the attributes.

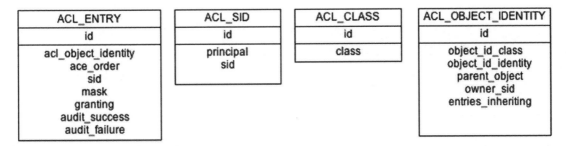

Figure 7-2. *Tables in the ACL schema*

Here are the main attributes (columns) in the tables from Figure 7-2:

- Table ACL_SID

  - principal: A Boolean that indicates if the particular SID is a principal or not. Remember that the SID can represent a group or role.

  - sid: The name of the SID. It can be a username of a principal, a role name, and so on.

- Table ACL_CLASS

  - class: The name of the class of the domain objects you can have in the ACL system.

- Table ACL_OBJECT_IDENTITY

  - object_id_identity: A number that identifies uniquely (when combined with the object_id_class) the particular instance of the domain object you are representing.

  - object_id_class: A foreign key to the table ACL_CLASS that identifies the class of the domain object you are representing.

  - parent_object: Allows for a hierarchy of domain objects by creating a recursive relation with itself. So permission can be shared between the objects in the hierarchy. It is a foreign key to itself.

- • `owner_sid`: The SID owning this particular domain object.

- • `entries_inheriting`: A Boolean that specifies if, in a hierarchy of domain objects, permissions are inherited between the objects.

- • Table `ACL_ENTRY`

  - • `acl_object_identity`: The identity of the object. It's a reference to a row in table `ACL_OBJECT_IDENTITY`.

  - • `sid`: Identifies the SID in this ACE. It's a reference to a row in table `ACL_SID`.

  - • `mask`: The actual permission. Permissions in ACL support are given as a bitmask represented with an integer value. In code, the default permissions are defined in the class `org.springframework.security.acls.domain.BasePermission`, which is reproduced in Listing 7-2. You can easily create your own class and define extra permissions if you want to do so.

  - • `granting`: A Boolean that determines if the particular ACE is for granting or, if false, for denying access according to the rules defined in the entry.

You can see that there are not a lot of tables defined in the schema, but it is important that you understand them individually and their relationships. Figure 7-3 shows the ER (entity-relationship) diagram for this data model to help you understand them better. The diagram describes the meanings of the relationships between tables in simple terms.

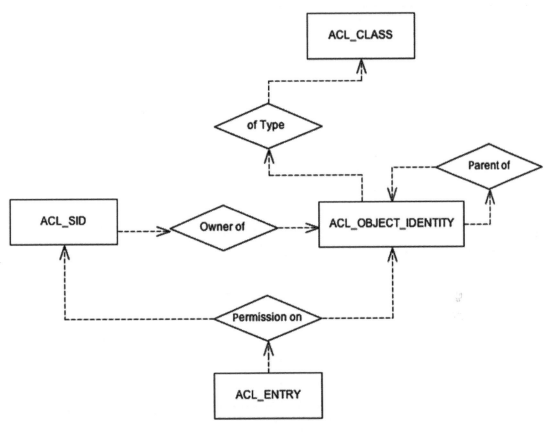

Figure 7-3. *The ER diagram for the ACL security model*

Listing 7-2. The BasePermission Class with the Default Permissions to Use in the ACL System

```
package org.springframework.security.acls.domain;

import org.springframework.security.acls.model.Permission;

public class BasePermission extends AbstractPermission {
    public static final Permission READ = new BasePermission(1 << 0, 'R'); // 1
    public static final Permission WRITE = new BasePermission(1 << 1, 'W'); // 2
    public static final Permission CREATE = new BasePermission(1 << 2, 'C'); // 4
    public static final Permission DELETE = new BasePermission(1 << 3, 'D'); // 8
    public static final Permission ADMINISTRATION = new BasePermission(1 << 4,
    'A'); // 16
```

```
protected BasePermission(int mask) {
    super(mask);
}

protected BasePermission(int mask, char code) {
    super(mask, code);
}
}
```

Listing 7-2 shows the existing permissions with bitmasks represented as the integers 1, 2, 4, 8, and 16 for Read, Write, Create, Delete, and Administration, respectively. There are 32 bits available for permissions, and the default permissions set bit 0, bit 1, bit 2, bit 3, and bit 4, respectively, to each integer value mentioned before. This class can be replaced with a custom Permission implementation class that includes different permissions, or it can be extended to include more permissions.

In theory, working this way allows for the permissions to be easily combined to create composed permissions by adding two of them together. For example, you could combine READ and WRITE permissions by summing their respective values (1 + 2 = 3) to grant both READ and WRITE permissions. However, in practice, it doesn't really work like this. The class org.springframework.security.acls.domain. DefaultPermissionGrantingStrategy, which is the one in charge of evaluating the permissions required for an object against the permissions stored in the list of access control entries, will do comparisons for exact matches. So you normally have to include an ACE for READ and another one for WRITE.

You should now have an understanding of the main concepts used in ACLs and how they map to the database schema that the framework itself provides. Next, let's set up the application itself. Again, you'll be using Maven for this. From some directory in your shell, execute the command mvn archetype:create -DarchetypeGroupId=org. apache.maven.archetypes -DarchetypeArtifactId=maven-archetype-webapp -DarchetypeVersion=1.0 -DgroupId=com.apress.pss -DartifactId=acl-example -Dversion=1.0-SNAPSHOT. Then, in the generated pom.xml file, add all the required dependencies shown in Listing 7-3, including the new ACL dependency.

Listing 7-3. Maven Dependencies in the Spring Security ACL Project

```xml
<properties>
        <!-- JDK version -->
        <java.version>11</java.version>

        <!-- Spring versions -->
        <springframework.version>5.1.5.RELEASE</springframework.version>
        <springsecurity.version>5.1.5.RELEASE</springsecurity.version>

</properties>

<dependencies>
        <dependency>
                <groupId>javax.servlet</groupId>
                <artifactId>javax.servlet-api</artifactId>
                <version>4.0.1</version>
        </dependency>

        <dependency>
                <groupId>junit</groupId>
                <artifactId>junit</artifactId>
                <version>4.5</version>
                <scope>test</scope>
        </dependency>

        <!-- Spring Security -->
        <dependency>
                <groupId>org.springframework.security</groupId>
                <artifactId>spring-security-core</artifactId>
                <version>${springsecurity.version}</version>
        </dependency>
        <dependency>
                <groupId>org.springframework.security</groupId>
                <artifactId>spring-security-config</artifactId>
                <version>${springsecurity.version}</version>
        </dependency>
```

```
<dependency>
        <groupId>org.springframework.security</groupId>
        <artifactId>spring-security-web</artifactId>
        <version>${springsecurity.version}</version>
</dependency>
<dependency>
        <groupId>org.springframework.security</groupId>
        <artifactId>spring-security-taglibs</artifactId>
        <version>${springsecurity.version}</version>
</dependency>
<dependency>
        <groupId>org.springframework.security</groupId>
        <artifactId>spring-security-acl</artifactId>
        <version>3.1.2.RELEASE</version>
</dependency>

<!-- Spring -->
<dependency>
        <groupId>org.springframework</groupId>
        <artifactId>spring-core</artifactId>
        <version>${springframework.version}</version>
</dependency>
<dependency>
        <groupId>org.springframework</groupId>
        <artifactId>spring-web</artifactId>
        <version>${springframework.version}</version>
</dependency>
<dependency>
        <groupId>org.springframework</groupId>
        <artifactId>spring-webmvc</artifactId>
        <version>${springframework.version}</version>
</dependency>
```

```xml
<dependency>
        <groupId>org.springframework</groupId>
        <artifactId>spring-context-support</artifactId>
        <version>${springframework.version}</version>
</dependency>

<dependency>
        <groupId>org.aspectj</groupId>
        <artifactId>aspectjweaver</artifactId>
        <version>1.7.0</version>
</dependency>

<dependency>
        <groupId>commons-logging</groupId>
        <artifactId>commons-logging</artifactId>
        <version>1.1.1</version>
</dependency>
<dependency>
        <groupId>commons-codec</groupId>
        <artifactId>commons-codec</artifactId>
        <version>1.3</version>
</dependency>
<dependency>
        <groupId>javax.servlet.jsp</groupId>
        <artifactId>javax.servlet.jsp-api</artifactId>
        <version>2.3.1</version>
</dependency>
<dependency>
        <groupId>javax.servlet</groupId>
        <artifactId>jstl</artifactId>
        <version>1.2</version>
</dependency>
<dependency>
        <groupId>javax.annotation</groupId>
        <artifactId>jsr250-api</artifactId>
        <version>1.0</version>
</dependency>
```

```xml
<dependency>
        <groupId>org.hsqldb</groupId>
        <artifactId>hsqldb</artifactId>
        <version>2.4.1</version>
</dependency>
<dependency>
        <groupId>net.sf.ehcache</groupId>
        <artifactId>ehcache-core</artifactId>
        <version>2.6.0</version>
</dependency>
<dependency>
        <groupId>org.thymeleaf.extras</groupId>
        <artifactId>thymeleaf-extras-springsecurity3</artifactId>
</dependency>
<dependency>
        <groupId>taglibs</groupId>
        <artifactId>standard</artifactId>
        <version>1.1.2</version>
</dependency>
<dependency>
        <groupId>org.slf4j</groupId>
        <artifactId>slf4j-jdk14</artifactId>
        <version>1.7.25</version>
</dependency>
</dependencies>
```

Next, let's create your first configuration file, the web.xml. Copy the one from Listing 7-4.

Listing 7-4. web.xml

```xml
<?xml version="1.0" encoding="UTF-8"?>
<web-app xmlns="http://java.sun.com/xml/ns/javaee"
     xmlns:xsi="http://www.w3.org/2001/XMLSchema-instance"
     xsi:schemaLocation="http://java.sun.com/xml/ns/javaee
     http://java.sun.com/xml/ns/javaee/web-app_3_0.xsd" version="3.0">
   <listener>
```

```
    <listener-class>
        org.springframework.web.context.ContextLoaderListener
    </listener-class>
</listener>
<context-param>
    <param-name>contextConfigLocation</param-name>
    <param-value>
        /WEB-INF/applicationContext-acl.xml
        /WEB-INF/applicationContext-security.xml
    </param-value>
</context-param>

<servlet>
    <servlet-name>acl-example</servlet-name>
    <servlet-class> org.springframework.web.servlet.DispatcherServlet
    </servlet-class>
    <load-on-startup>1</load-on-startup>
</servlet>
<servlet-mapping>
    <servlet-name>acl-example</servlet-name>
    <url-pattern>/</url-pattern>
</servlet-mapping>
<filter>
    <filter-name>springSecurityFilterChain</filter-name>
    <filter-class>
        org.springframework.web.filter.DelegatingFilterProxy
    </filter-class>
</filter>
<filter-mapping>
    <filter-name>springSecurityFilterChain</filter-name>
    <url-pattern>/*</url-pattern>
</filter-mapping>
</web-app>
```

The next file to create is the ACL configuration file, so let's do that. This is a very standard default ACL file. Later, we'll show you some things that can be changed to adapt to different needs. In the WEB-INF folder, create a file named applicationContext-acl.xml with the contents from Listing 7-5. After the listing, you will read a description of the relevant parts.

Listing 7-5. The applicationContext-acl.xml with the ACL Configuration Needed

```xml
<?xml version="1.0" encoding="UTF-8"?>

<beans xmlns="http://www.springframework.org/schema/beans"
    xmlns:tx="http://www.springframework.org/schema/tx"
    xmlns:util="http://www.springframework.org/schema/util"
    xmlns:xsi="http://www.w3.org/2001/XMLSchema-instance"
    xsi:schemaLocation="http://www.springframework.org/schema/beans
    http://www.springframework.org/schema/beans/spring-beans-4.3.xsd
   http://www.springframework.org/schema/tx
   http://www.springframework.org/schema/tx/spring-tx-3.0.xsd
   http://www.springframework.org/schema/util
   http://www.springframework.org/schema/util/spring-util-3.0.xsd">
    <bean id="dataSource"
            class="org.springframework.jdbc.datasource.
             DriverManagerDataSource">
            <property name="driverClassName" value="org.hsqldb.jdbcDriver" />
            <property name="url" value="jdbc:hsqldb:file:aclexample" />
            <property name="username" value="sa" />
            <property name="password" value="" />
    </bean>

    <bean id="jdbcTemplate" class="org.springframework.jdbc.core.JdbcTemplate">
            <property name="dataSource" ref="dataSource" />
    </bean>

    <bean id="transactionManager"
            class="org.springframework.jdbc.datasource.
            DataSourceTransactionManager">
            <property name="dataSource" ref="dataSource" />
    </bean>
```

```xml
<tx:annotation-driven transaction-manager="transactionManager" />

<bean id="aclCache"
        class="org.springframework.security.acls.domain.
        EhCacheBasedAclCache">
        <constructor-arg>
                <bean class="org.springframework.cache.ehcache.
                EhCacheFactoryBean">
                        <property name="cacheManager">
                                <bean class="org.springframework.cache.
                                ehcache.EhCacheManagerFactoryBean" />
                        </property>
                        <property name="cacheName" value="aclCache" />
                </bean>
        </constructor-arg>
</bean>

<bean id="lookupStrategy"
        class="org.springframework.security.acls.jdbc.
        BasicLookupStrategy">
        <constructor-arg ref="dataSource" />
        <constructor-arg ref="aclCache" />
        <constructor-arg ref="aclAuthorizationStrategy" />
        <constructor-arg>
                <bean class="org.springframework.security.acls.domain.
                ConsoleAuditLogger" />
        </constructor-arg>
</bean>

<bean id="aclAuthorizationStrategy"
        class="org.springframework.security.acls.domain.
        AclAuthorizationStrategyImpl">
        <constructor-arg>
```

```xml
                    <list>
                        <bean
class="org.springframework.security.core.authority.
SimpleGrantedAuthority">
<constructor-arg value="ROLE_ADMINISTRATOR" />
                        </bean>
                        <bean
class="org.springframework.security.core.authority.
SimpleGrantedAuthority">
<constructor-arg value="ROLE_ADMINISTRATOR" />
                        </bean>
                        <bean
class="org.springframework.security.core.authority.
SimpleGrantedAuthority">
<constructor-arg value="ROLE_ADMINISTRATOR" />
                        </bean>
                    </list>
        </constructor-arg>
</bean>

<bean id="aclService"
        class="org.springframework.security.acls.jdbc.
        JdbcMutableAclService">
        <constructor-arg ref="dataSource" />
        <constructor-arg ref="lookupStrategy" />
        <constructor-arg ref="aclCache" />
</bean>
<bean id="setupDb" class="com.apress.pss.acl.DatabaseSeeder">
        <constructor-arg ref="jdbcTemplate" />
</bean>

<bean id="aclDeletePostVoter" class="org.springframework.security.acls.
AclEntryVoter">
        <constructor-arg ref="aclService" />
        <constructor-arg value="ACL_POST_DELETE" />
        <constructor-arg>
```

```xml
            <list>
                    <util:constant
                            static-field="org.springframework.
                            security.acls.domain.BasePermission.
                            DELETE" />
            </list>
      </constructor-arg>
      <property name="processDomainObjectClass"
            value="com.apress.pss.acl.domain.Post" />
</bean>
<bean id="aclUpdatePostVoter" class="org.springframework.security.acls.
AclEntryVoter">
      <constructor-arg ref="aclService" />
      <constructor-arg value="ACL_POST_UPDATE" />
      <constructor-arg>
            <list>
                    <util:constant
                            static-field="org.springframework.
                            security.acls.domain.BasePermission.
                            ADMINISTRATION" />
            </list>
      </constructor-arg>
      <property name="processDomainObjectClass"
            value="com.apress.pss.acl.domain.Post" />
</bean>
<bean id="aclReadPostVoter" class="org.springframework.security.acls.
AclEntryVoter">
      <constructor-arg ref="aclService" />
      <constructor-arg value="ACL_POST_READ" />
      <constructor-arg>
            <list>
                    <util:constant
                            static-field="org.springframework.
                            security.acls.domain.BasePermission.
                            READ" />
```

```
        </list>
      </constructor-arg>
      <property name="processDomainObjectClass"
            value="com.apress.pss.acl.domain.Post" />
  </bean>
```

```
</beans>
```

We'll give an overview of each of the beans defined in Listing 7-5. Later, when using the application, we'll offer a more in-depth explanation of the inner works of the framework and exactly what is going on both at startup and at execution time.

The first three beans are not ACL specific because they simply define a data source, a JDBC template, and a transaction manager. These beans will be used by the ACL infrastructure to access the ACL-specific tables and data in the schema.

Note   The support beans for working with databases that we defined use classes from the Spring Framework core libraries. If you have worked with Spring before, you most likely have encountered and used these classes. You can find information about Spring database support on the official site at `https://docs.spring.io/spring/docs/3.0.x/reference/jdbc.html`.

The next bean is the one with the ID `aclCache`. You need to have a cache implementation for the ACL system to work. Its function is to make ACL accesses faster by caching the ACLs and not accessing the database for every single query. The implementation we are using in the bean definition (`EhCacheBasedAclCache`) is the only one defined currently in the ACL module, and it is a very simple implementation that delegates to EhCache (`http://ehcache.org/`).

The next bean is the one with the ID `lookupStrategy`. A lookup strategy is in charge of retrieving the object identities (as explained before) and the ACLs that apply to each of those object identities. The implementation we are using (`BasicLookupStrategy`) is again the only one defined in the framework. It will try to load the ACLs from the cache, and if they are not there, it will look them up on the database and cache the results. The lookup to the database is done in batches so that many items can be loaded to the cache at the same time to improve performance.

The next bean, with the ID aclAuthorizationStrategy, defines an org.springframework.security.acls.domain.AclAuthorizationStrategy. The goal of an AclAuthorizationStrategy is to determine if a particular principal is able to execute administrative activities in the ACL infrastructure itself. For example, the currently defined permissions are CHANGE_OWNERSHIP, CHANGE_AUDITING, and CHANGE_GENERAL. The default implementation we are using in the bean definition file receives in the constructor three instances of GrantedAuthority, which determine the entities that will have the permissions mentioned before. In this example—and, in general, this is the most common approach—we are setting the ROLE_ADMIN to be the one that will have the mentioned permissions. In the default implementation, note that the owner of a particular ACL is also allowed the permissions CHANGE_OWNERSHIP and CHANGE_GENERAL in the particular ACL.

The last bean, with the ID aclService, is the main component of the whole framework. The interfaces AclService and MutableAclService allow access to all the ACL-related operations, such as reading ACLs by ID, creating ACLs, deleting ACLs, and updating ACLs.

These are all the beans needed in the application to work with ACLs. Let's continue configuring the application. As always, you need to make the file from Listing 7-6 load up with the application. You already know how to do this by modifying the contextConfigLocation context-param in the web.xml. In case it is needed, the web.xml provided already has the appropriate configuration.

Now let's make a bean to create the database schema for ACL. You normally will not do this in a standard application, but we'll do it here just for convenience. You define the bean from Listing 7-6 in the file applicationContext-acl.xml and create the class from Listing 7-7 in the corresponding package. This class (which is named DatabaseSeeder) uses a copy of the provided createAclSchema.sql file with uncommented drop tables to create the required tables in the database. (The file is provided in the source code of the book. It is named customCreateAclSchema.sql and is located in the src/main/resources folder.) If you want to create it yourself, simply take the one that comes with the framework and uncomment the beginning lines that have the commented drop table statements. (Remember that the database is an in-memory HSQL database named aclexample that is defined in the dataSource bean.) This bean will be instantiated by the context as normal when starting up, and the constructor will take care of setting up the schema.

Listing 7-6. *The Bean That Creates the Database Tables Needed for Working with ACLs*

```
<bean id="databaseSeeder" class="com.apress.pss.acl.DatabaseSeeder" >
        <constructor-arg ref="jdbcTemplate" />
</bean>
```

Listing 7-7. *The DatabaseSeeder Class That Executes the Schema Creation*

```
package com.apress.pss.acl;

import java.io.IOException;

import org.springframework.core.io.ClassPathResource;
import org.springframework.jdbc.core.JdbcTemplate;
import org.springframework.util.FileCopyUtils;

public class DatabaseSeeder {
    public DatabaseSeeder(JdbcTemplate jdbcTemplate) throws IOException{
            String sql = new String(FileCopyUtils.copyToByteArray(new Class
            PathResource("customCreateAclSchema.sql").getInputStream()));
            jdbcTemplate.execute(sql);
    }
}
```

Now you can create ACLs for domain objects, so let's create the classes to set up the whole process. This will involve a bit of coding because you'll need a controller, service, domain object, and JSP file. You can see these files in Listings 7-8, 7-9, 7-10, 7-11, 7-12 and 7-13, respectively.

Listing 7-8. *The ForumController Entry Point into Post Creation*

```
package com.apress.pss.acl.controllers;

import java.util.HashMap;
import java.util.Map;

import org.springframework.beans.factory.annotation.Autowired;
import org.springframework.security.core.context.SecurityContextHolder;
import org.springframework.stereotype.Controller;
import org.springframework.ui.ModelMap;
```

```java
import org.springframework.web.bind.annotation.RequestBody;
import org.springframework.web.bind.annotation.RequestMapping;
import org.springframework.web.bind.annotation.RequestMethod;
import org.springframework.web.bind.annotation.RequestParam;
import org.springframework.web.servlet.ModelAndView;
import org.springframework.security.core.userdetails.UserDetails;

import com.apress.pss.acl.domain.Post;
import com.apress.pss.acl.services.ForumService;

@Controller
@RequestMapping("/forum")
public class ForumController {
        @Autowired
        private ForumService forumService;
        @RequestMapping(method = RequestMethod.POST, value = "/post")
        public ModelAndView createPost(@RequestBody String postContent){
                forumService.createPost(new Post(postContent));
                return showForm();
        }

        @RequestMapping(method = RequestMethod.POST, value = "/post/delete")
        public ModelAndView deletePost(@RequestParam Integer postId){
                Post post = new Post("non-relevant");
                post.setId(postId);
                forumService.deletePost(post);
                return showForm();
        }

        private ModelAndView showForm(){
                Map<String, Object> model = new HashMap<String, Object>();
                model.put("posts", forumService.getPosts());
                return new ModelAndView("posts",model);
        }
```

```
    @RequestMapping(value = {"/posts" }, method = RequestMethod.GET)
    public String posts(ModelMap model) {
            return "posts";
    }

@RequestMapping(value = { "/", "/welcome" }, method = RequestMethod.GET)
public String homePage(ModelMap model) {
    return "welcome";
}

@RequestMapping(value = "/admin", method = RequestMethod.GET)
public String adminPage(ModelMap model) {
    model.addAttribute("user", getPrincipal());
    return "admin";
}

private String getPrincipal(){
    String userName = null;
    Object principal = SecurityContextHolder.getContext().
    getAuthentication().getPrincipal();

    if (principal instanceof UserDetails) {
        userName = ((UserDetails)principal).getUsername();
    } else {
        userName = principal.toString();
    }
    return userName;
}

}
```

The first version of the controller shown in Listing 7-8 allows you to show the form to create new posts and has the action to actually post these new posts for them to be saved. Later, you'll add to this controller to support more functionality.

Listing 7-9. *ForumServiceImp, Which Currently Just Allows for Creating Posts in an In-Memory Map and Creating the ACL in the Database*

```java
package com.apress.pss.acl.services;

import java.util.ArrayList;
import java.util.Collection;
import java.util.HashMap;
import java.util.Map;

import org.springframework.beans.factory.annotation.Autowired;
import org.springframework.security.access.annotation.Secured;
import org.springframework.security.access.prepost.PostFilter;
import org.springframework.security.acls.domain.BasePermission;
import org.springframework.security.acls.domain.GrantedAuthoritySid;
import org.springframework.security.acls.domain.ObjectIdentityImpl;
import org.springframework.security.acls.domain.PrincipalSid;
import org.springframework.security.acls.model.MutableAcl;
import org.springframework.security.acls.model.MutableAclService;
import org.springframework.security.acls.model.ObjectIdentity;
import org.springframework.security.core.GrantedAuthority;
import org.springframework.security.core.context.SecurityContextHolder;
import org.springframework.security.core.userdetails.User;
import org.springframework.stereotype.Service;
import org.springframework.transaction.annotation.Transactional;
import org.springframework.web.servlet.ModelAndView;

import com.apress.pss.acl.domain.Post;

@Service
public class ForumServiceImpl implements ForumService {
    @Autowired
    private MutableAclService mutableAclService;
    private Map<Integer, Post> postStore = new HashMap<Integer, Post>();

    @Transactional
    public void createPost(Post post) {
            Integer id = new Integer(Math.abs(post.hashCode()));
            ObjectIdentity oid = new ObjectIdentityImpl(Post.class, id);
```

```
        MutableAcl acl = mutableAclService.createAcl(oid);
        User user = (User)SecurityContextHolder.getContext().
        getAuthentication().getPrincipal();
        acl.insertAce(0, BasePermission.ADMINISTRATION, new
        PrincipalSid(
                        user.getUsername()), true);
        acl.insertAce(1, BasePermission.DELETE, new
        GrantedAuthoritySid(
                        "ROLE_ADMIN"), true);
        if(isAdminUserLogged()){
                acl.insertAce(2, BasePermission.READ, new
                GrantedAuthoritySid(
                                "ROLE_ADMIN"), true);
        }else{
        acl.insertAce(2, BasePermission.READ, new GrantedAuthoritySid(
                        "ROLE_USER"), true);
        }
        mutableAclService.updateAcl(acl);
        post.setId(id);
        postStore.put(id, post);
    }

    @Transactional
    @Secured("ACL_POST_DELETE")
    public void deletePost(Post post){
            ObjectIdentity oid = new ObjectIdentityImpl(Post.class,
            post.getId());
            mutableAclService.deleteAcl(oid, true);
            postStore.remove(postStore.get(post.getId()));
    }

    //@PostFilter("hasPermission(filterObject, 'READ')")
    public Collection<Post> getPosts(){
            return new ArrayList<Post>(postStore.values());
    }
```

```
public void setMutableAclService(MutableAclService mutableAclService) {
        this.mutableAclService = mutableAclService;
}

private boolean isAdminUserLogged() {
        for(GrantedAuthority authority: SecurityContextHolder.
        getContext().getAuthentication().getAuthorities()){
                if(authority.getAuthority().equals("ROLE_ADMIN")){
                        return true;
                }
        }
        return false;
}

}
```

Listing 7-9 has the core functionality for creating an ACL for a domain object instance. In this case, you are creating a new Post object. The Post instance is stored in a memory map (which is not a realistic example, but is enough to show the functionality). The ACL is created using the hash code of the Post instance as the ID of the domain object. Then you create three ACEs for the ACL. In the first one, you specify that the ADMINISTRATION permission is granted to the creator of the Post, given by the SecurityContext's principal. The second one gives DELETE permission to any user with the role ROLE_ADMIN, and the third one gives the READ permission to any authenticated user with the role ROLE_USER. You can also see that the method is marked as @Transactional. This is a requirement of the JdbcMutableAclService so that it can execute all the SQLs in the context of a transaction. The ForumService interface that is implemented by ForumServiceImpl is simply defined as the following:

```
package com.apress.pss.acl.services;

import java.util.Map;

public interface ForumService {
    void createPost(Post post);
    Map<Integer, Post> getPosts();
}
```

Note   Keep in mind that the last code sample of the class `ForumServiceImpl` is just an example of the functionality for populating ACLs for a particular domain object. We're saying this because in a real application, you would probably move the security-related code away from the core business methods and not mix them together the way we are doing here. You could create an aspect to deal with this or simply another helper service you can call to take care of all the ACL functionality.

Listing 7-10. The Post Class. A Simple Domain Model That You'll Use for Trying ACL Rules

```java
package com.apress.pss.acl.domain;

public class Post {

    private String content;
    private Integer id;

    public Post(String postContent) {
        this.content = postContent;
    }

    public String getContent() {
        return content;
    }

    public Integer getId() {
        return id;
    }

    public void setId(Integer id) {
        this.id = id;
    }

    @Override
    public int hashCode() {
        final int prime = 31;
        int result = 1;
```

```java
        result = prime * result + ((content == null) ? 0 : content.
        hashCode());
        result = prime * result + ((id == null) ? 0 : id.hashCode());
        return result;
    }

    @Override
    public boolean equals(Object obj) {
        if (this == obj)
            return true;
        if (obj == null)
            return false;
        if (getClass() != obj.getClass())
            return false;
        Post other = (Post) obj;
        if (content == null) {
            if (other.content != null)
                return false;
        } else if (!content.equals(other.content))
            return false;
        if (id == null) {
            if (other.id != null)
                return false;
        } else if (!id.equals(other.id))
            return false;
        return true;
    }

}
```

Listing 7-11. The welcome.jsp File as the Starting Page

```html
<!DOCTYPE html>
<html>
<head>
    <title>Spring Boot Security 5 and ACL Example</title>
</head>
```

```
<body>
<h1>Welcome to Spring Boot Security 5 and ACL Example!</h1>
<p>Please <a href="/forum/admin">login.</a></p>
</body>
</html>
```

Listing 7-12. The admin.jsp File as the Admin Page

```
<%@ page language="java" contentType="text/html; charset=ISO-8859-1"
        pageEncoding="ISO-8859-1"%>
<%@ taglib prefix="security"
            uri="http://www.springframework.org/security/tags"%>
<%@ taglib prefix="c" uri="http://java.sun.com/jsp/jstl/core"%>

<!DOCTYPE html>
<html xmlns:th="http://www.thymeleaf.org"
      xmlns:sec="http://www.thymeleaf.org/extras/spring-security">

<head>
    <title>Spring Security 5 and ACL.</title>
</head>
<body>

<h1>Welcome to Admin page: <strong>${user}</strong></h1>
<h2>You are succesfully logged as Admin!</h2>

<br/>
<p>Click <a href="/forum/posts">here</a> to manage your posts.</p>

</br>
<form action="/logout" method="post">
    <input type="submit" value="Sign Out"/>
</form>

</body>
</html>
```

Listing 7-13. The posts.jsp File with a Form for a New Post and a List of Existing Posts

```
<%@ page language="java" contentType="text/html; charset=ISO-8859-1"
        pageEncoding="ISO-8859-1"%>
<%@ taglib prefix="security"
           uri="http://www.springframework.org/security/tags"%>
<%@ taglib prefix="c" uri="http://java.sun.com/jsp/jstl/core"%>

<!DOCTYPE html>
<html xmlns:th="http://www.thymeleaf.org"
      xmlns:sec="http://www.thymeleaf.org/extras/spring-security">

<head>
    <title>Spring Security 5 and ACL.</title>
</head>
<body>
<h1>Welcome!</h1>
<h2>You are succesfully logged as Admin!</h2>
<h3>Add or remove your posts here:</h3>

<br/>

<form method="post" action="/forum/post">
    New Post Content: <input type="text" name="postContent"/><br/>
    <input type="submit"/>
</form>
<br/>
<c:forEach items="${posts}" var="post">
    <security:accesscontrollist  domainObject="${post}" hasPermission="READ">
        <form method="post" action="/forum/post/delete">
                ${post.content} <br />
            <input type="hidden" value="${post.id}" name="postId"/>
            <input type="submit" value="delete"/><br/>
        </form>
    </security:accesscontrollist>
</c:forEach>
```

```
</br>
<form action="/logout" method="post">
    <input type="submit" value="Sign Out"/>
</form>

</body>
</html>
```

After you put all the .jsp files in the WEB-INF/views directory, the application is almost ready to run. You just need the files acl-example-servlet.xml and applicationContext-security.xml from Listings 7-14 and 7-15, which should go in the WEB-INF directory.

Listing 7-14. The acl-example-servlet.xml

```
<?xml version="1.0" encoding="UTF-8"?>
<beans xmlns="http://www.springframework.org/schema/beans"
       xmlns:security="http://www.springframework.org/schema/security"
       xmlns:xsi="http://www.w3.org/2001/XMLSchema-instance"
       xmlns:context="http://www.springframework.org/schema/context"
       xmlns:mvc="http://www.springframework.org/schema/mvc"
       xsi:schemaLocation="http://www.springframework.org/schema/mvc
http://www.springframework.org/schema/mvc/spring-mvc-4.2.xsd
http://www.springframework.org/schema/beans
http://www.springframework.org/schema/beans/spring-beans-3.0.xsd
http://www.springframework.org/schema/context
http://www.springframework.org/schema/context/spring-context-3.0.xsd
http://www.springframework.org/schema/security
http://www.springframework.org/schema/security/spring-security-4.2.xsd">

        <context:component-scan base-package="com.apress.pss.acl.controllers" />
        <mvc:annotation-driven />
        <security:global-method-security secured-annotations="enabled" />

        <bean class="org.springframework.web.servlet.view.
        InternalResourceViewResolver">
                <property name = "prefix" value="/WEB-INF/views/" />
                <property name = "suffix" value=".jsp" />
        </bean>

</beans>
```

Listing 7-15. The applicationContext-security.xml

```xml
<?xml version="1.0" encoding="UTF-8"?>
<beans xmlns="http://www.springframework.org/schema/beans"
       xmlns:security="http://www.springframework.org/schema/security"
       xmlns:context="http://www.springframework.org/schema/context"
       xmlns:xsi="http://www.w3.org/2001/XMLSchema-instance"
       xsi:schemaLocation="http://www.springframework.org/schema/beans
       http://www.springframework.org/schema/beans/spring-beans-4.3.xsd
    http://www.springframework.org/schema/security
    http://www.springframework.org/schema/security/spring-security-4.2.xsd
    http://www.springframework.org/schema/context
    http://www.springframework.org/schema/context/spring-context-3.0.xsd">

        <security:http use-expressions="true" auto-config="true">
                <security:intercept-url pattern="/" access="permitAll"/>
                <security:intercept-url pattern="/forum/welcome"
                access="permitAll"/>
                <security:intercept-url pattern="/**"
                access="isAuthenticated()"/>
                <security:form-login authentication-success-handler-ref=
                "awareAuthenticationSuccessHandler"/>
                <security:logout logout-url="/logout" delete-
                cookies="JSESSIONID" />
        </security:http>

        <bean class="org.springframework.security.web.authentication.
        SavedRequestAwareAuthenticationSuccessHandler" name="aware
        AuthenticationSuccessHandler"/>
        <bean id ="passwordEncoder" class = "org.springframework.security.
        crypto.password.NoOpPasswordEncoder" factory-method = "getInstance" />

        <security:authentication-manager>
                <security:authentication-provider>
                        <security:user-service>
                                <security:user authorities="ROLE_USER"
                                name="leo"
```

251

```xml
                                      password="nardone01" />
                     <security:user authorities="ROLE_ADMIN"
                     name="luna"
                                      password="nardone01" />
                     <security:user authorities="ROLE_USER,
                     ROLE_ADMIN"
                                      name="massimo" password="nardone01" />
                </security:user-service>
        </security:authentication-provider>
</security:authentication-manager>
<context:component-scan base-package="com.apress.pss.acl.services" />
<security:global-method-security
        secured-annotations="enabled" access-decision-manager-
        ref="customAccessDecisionManager"
        pre-post-annotations="enabled">
        <security:expression-handler ref="customExpressionHandler" />
</security:global-method-security>

<bean id="customAccessDecisionManager" class="org.springframework.
security.access.vote.AffirmativeBased">
        <property name="allowIfAllAbstainDecisions" value="false" />
        <constructor-arg name="decisionVoters"
        ref="aclUpdatePostVoter" />

</bean>

<bean id="preInvocationAuthorizationAdviceVoter"
        class="org.springframework.security.access.prepost.
        PreInvocationAuthorizationAdviceVoter">
        <constructor-arg>
                <bean
class="org.springframework.security.access.expression.method.
ExpressionBasedPreInvocationAdvice" />
        </constructor-arg>
</bean>
```

```
<bean id="customPermissionEvaluator"
        class="org.springframework.security.acls.
        AclPermissionEvaluator">
        <constructor-arg ref="aclService" />
    </bean>

    <bean id="customExpressionHandler"
        class="org.springframework.security.access.expression.
        method.DefaultMethodSecurityExpressionHandler">
        <property name="permissionEvaluator"
        ref="customPermissionEvaluator" />
    </bean>

</beans>
```

When you start the application, navigate to the URL `http://localhost:8080/` `forum/welcome`, as shown in Figure 7-4.

← → C   ① localhost:8080/forum/welcome

Welcome to Spring Boot Security 5 and ACL Example!

Please login.

Figure 7-4. *The welcome page*

Next, click the login link, which will redirect to the Spring Security login page. Log in with username **leo** and password **nardone01**, as shown in Figure 7-5.

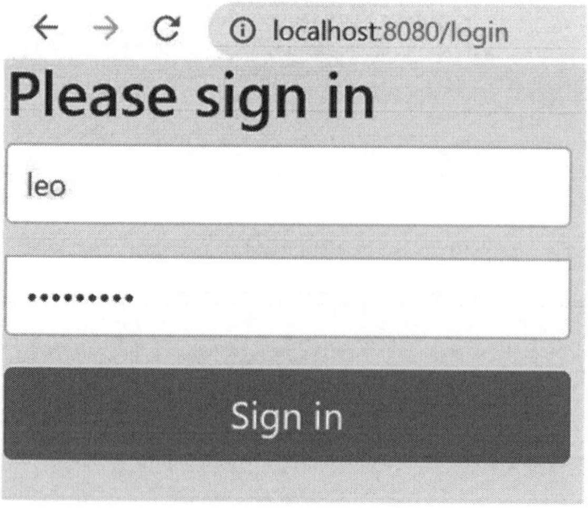

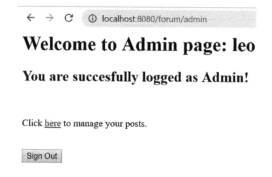

Figure 7-5. *The login page*

Once you're authenticated as leo, it will redirect to the Admin page shown in Figure 7-6.

Figure 7-6. *The admin page*

Next, click the "click here to manage your posts" link, which will open the posts page shown in Figure 7-7.

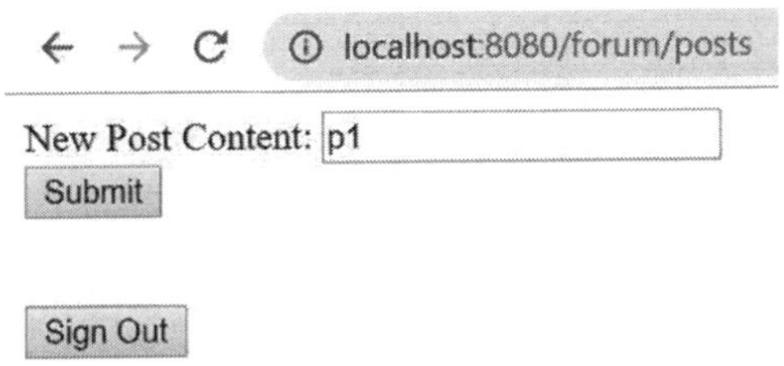

Figure 7-7. *The posts page*

You will be shown a very small form with just a text box. You can create a new form there. When you submit the form, it will be stored on the map and the corresponding ACL will be stored on the database, as shown in Figure 7-8.

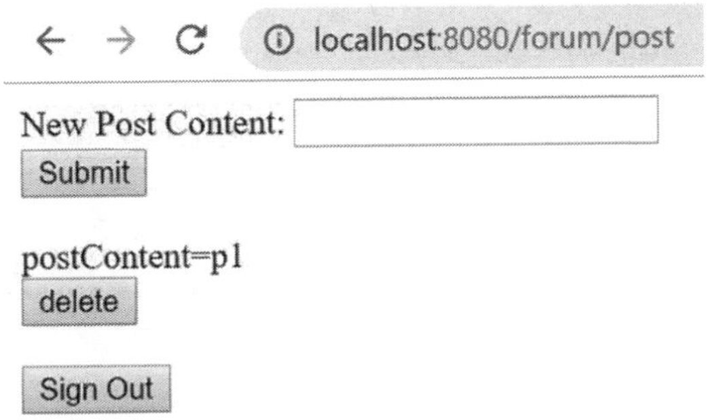

Figure 7-8. *Adding a post*

You can use a SQL client to look at it. What is happening under the covers inside the framework is simply the execution of some SQL scripts that are in charge of populating the tables mentioned before with the corresponding data. The ACL system offers the APIs that can be used to manipulate this data using classes, which you can see in the ForumServiceImpl class. Internally, all the requests are translated to SQL instructions against the configured database. It's also worth mentioning that among the internal workings of the framework is the use of the authentication's principal as the owner of the ACL and the caching of the ACLs after they have been persisted to the database. JdbcMutableAclService internally uses Spring's own JdbcTemplate and batch updates with prepared statements.

Accessing Secured Objects

The next logical step is to make sure the rules are actually working by trying to access the created posts. To do that, you set up a couple more users and finish your service and controller so that they can handle the new options. Remember that you are recreating the database every time you restart the app. (Again, that's not what you want in a production environment.) Also, the posts are in an in-memory map, so they are lost when you shut down the application. So let's make all the code changes now step by step.

The first thing you do is add an org.springframework.security.acls. AclEntryVoter to the configuration of your application. AclEntryVoter is an implementation of AccessDecisionVoter like the ones you studied before (RoleVoter, and so forth), which votes whether to grant or deny access based on the rules given by the ACL configuration of domain objects. You need to create an AclEntryVoter instance for each of the operations you want ACLs to vote on. For example, in your case, you create three voters: one for voting on reading access, one for voting on update permission, and one for voting on delete permission. Add these voters in the file applicationContext-acl.xml. Listing 7-16 shows the definition of these three voters, followed by a more comprehensive explanation of their work.

Listing 7-16. The AclEntryVoter(s) That Correspond to the Delete, Read, and Update Actions

```
<bean id="aclDeletePostVoter" class="org.springframework.security.acls.
AclEntryVoter">
        <constructor-arg ref="aclService" />
        <constructor-arg value="ACL_POST_DELETE" />
        <constructor-arg>
            <list>
                <util:constant
                    static-field="org.springframework.security.acls.domain.
                    BasePermission.DELETE" />
            </list>
        </constructor-arg>
        <property name="processDomainObjectClass"
            value="com.apress.pss.acl.domain.Post" />
    </bean>
```

```xml
<bean id="aclUpdatePostVoter" class="org.springframework.security.acls.
AclEntryVoter">
    <constructor-arg ref="aclService" />
    <constructor-arg value="ACL_POST_UPDATE" />
    <constructor-arg>
        <list>
            <util:constant
                static-field="org.springframework.security.acls.domain.
                BasePermission.ADMINISTRATION" />
        </list>
    </constructor-arg>
    <property name="processDomainObjectClass"
        value="com.apress.pss.acl.domain.Post" />
</bean>

<bean id="aclReadPostVoter" class="org.springframework.security.acls.
AclEntryVoter">
    <constructor-arg ref="aclService" />
    <constructor-arg value="ACL_POST_READ" />
    <constructor-arg>
        <list>
            <util:constant
                static-field="org.springframework.security.acls.domain.
                BasePermission.READ" />
        </list>
    </constructor-arg>
    <property name="processDomainObjectClass"
        value="com.apress.pss.acl.domain.Post" />
</bean>
```

You have three voter beans; however, to analyze one is to analyze them all. When you define an AclEntryVoter, you need to pass three arguments to its constructor. The first argument is a reference to the AclService defined earlier, and the second parameter is mapped to a config attribute name. We talked about config attributes earlier in the book, so here we'll just say that they are the attributes that Spring Security looks for in the @Secured annotation in order to use them when intercepting methods.

The `AccessDecisionManager` has access to this value and as well as to the different voters that decide if they support a particular config attribute. For example, if you have an annotation like `@Secured("ROLE_USER")` and you have `RoleVoter` configured, the voter will do its work because the `RoleVoter` supports, by default, any config attribute that starts with `ROLE_`. In the case of the `AclEntryVoter`, you are specifying exactly which config attribute that particular voter will support. In this example, the first bean will support annotations like `@Secured("ACL_POST_DELETE")`, the second bean will support annotations like `@Secured("ACL_POST_UPDATE")`, and the third will support annotations like `@Secured("ACL_POST_READ")`.

The third parameter that you pass to the `AclEntryVoter` constructor is the permission needed to allow access to the particular operation you are trying to perform on the object. For example, the scenario for the first `AclEntryVoter` bean is as follows: You have a method annotated with `@Secured("ACL_POST_DELETE")` that receives a `Post` instance as a parameter. When the method is called, the `AclEntryVoter` receives the `Post` object and then retrieves the principal from the authentication and evaluates its permissions against the `Post`'s ACL to see if it has the required permission—in this case, `BasePermission.ADMINISTRATION`. If it does, it will vote to grant access; if it doesn't, it will vote to deny access. We'll explain this in more depth a little later when executing the application.

For these voters to work, you need to add them to the `AccessDecisionManager`. Currently, you are using the default `AccessDecisionManager`, so you need to define an explicit one in the application context with the voters injected so that you can use those voters in the application. You do this in the `applicationContext-security.xml` file. It's as simple as adding the two beans shown in Listing 7-17.

Listing 7-17. The Beans for Using a Custom AccessDecisionManager

```xml
<bean id="customAccessDecisionManager" class="org.springframework.security.
access.vote.AffirmativeBased">
            <property name="allowIfAllAbstainDecisions" value="false" />
            <constructor-arg name="decisionVoters"
            ref="aclUpdatePostVoter" />

    </bean>
```

There's nothing special in this listing. You are using an affirmative-based access decision manager, and you are injecting the three voters in the decisionVoters property.

Next, let's create the delete action in the service. The deletePost method in ForumServiceImpl looks like Listing 7-18. Remember to update the ForumService interface as well with the new method.

Listing 7-18. The deletePost Method in ForumServiceImpl

```
@Transactional
    @Secured("ACL_POST_DELETE")
    public void deletePost(Post post){
        ObjectIdentity oid = new ObjectIdentityImpl(Post.class, post.
        getId());
        mutableAclService.deleteAcl(oid, true);
        postStore.remove(postStore.get(post.getId()));
    }
```

It's a very simple method. Worth noting is the @Secured annotation. If you recall the previous definition of the voters, you should be able to see that the invocation of this method will be supported by the first voter bean you defined (aclDeletePostVoter). Let's try this out and see what happens. Before doing so, you need to update the ForumController, adding the method from Listing 7-19.

Listing 7-19. The deletePost in ForumController

```
@RequestMapping(method = RequestMethod.POST, value = "/post/delete")
        public ModelAndView deletePost(@RequestParam Integer postId){
                Post post = new Post("non-relevant");
                post.setId(postId);
                forumService.deletePost(post);
                return showForm();
        }
}
```

If you restart the application now, visit the URL http://localhost:8080/forum/admin, and create a post, it will look like Figure 7-9.

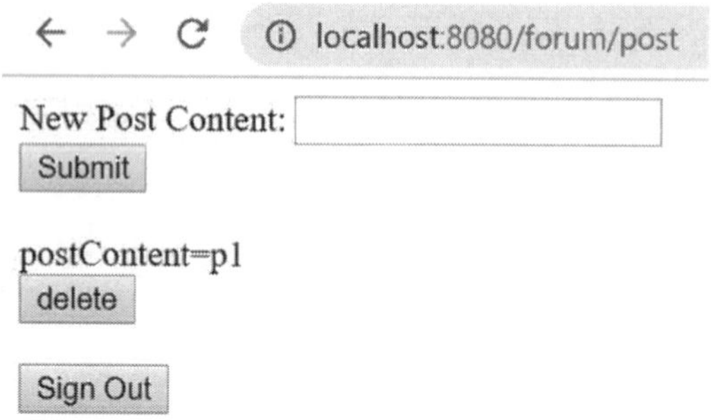

Figure 7-9. *Screen showing a created post*

If you click the delete button, the application will redirect you to the familiar login screen page.

This is what happens: When you click the delete button, the request goes all the way to the `AffirmativeBased` access decision manager, as we explained in previous chapters. The access decision manager iterates through its configured `AccessDecisionVoter(s)`—in this case, the `AclEntryVoter(s)` you injected explicitly. One of the voters gets into action—the one dealing with `ACL_POST_DELETE` config attribute. The voter traverses the `MethodInvocation` object of the method that was just intercepted, and it iterates through its parameters looking for parameters that are of the type configured in the `processDomainObjectClass` property of the `AclEntryVoter`, which in your case is `com.apress.pss.acl.domain.Post`. If an object of this type isn't found on the parameter list of the method, an `AuthorizationServiceException` is thrown, informing you of this. In your case, it is found, and it is actually the only parameter that the `deletePost` method expects. If the object that arrives in this parameter is null, the voter will simply abstain from voting.

The next thing the voter does is try to retrieve an `ObjectIdentity` instance from the domain object. It does this by using an `ObjectIdentityRetrievalStrategy` that is configured by default and whose only implementation is `org.springframework.security.acls.domain.ObjectIdentityRetrievalStrategyImpl`. This strategy simply invokes the constructor of `ObjectIdentityImpl` that receives a domain object as its only parameter. This constructor in `ObjectIdentityImpl` assumes that the domain object provides a `getId` method to be able to retrieve the identifier for it. If the method is not there, a corresponding exception is thrown. Your `Post` class has such a method, so this works fine, invoking that method and setting the return value as the identifier of the `ObjectIdentity`.

After obtaining the `ObjectIdentity`, the voter tries to retrieve the SIDs from the `Authentication` object. For this, the voter uses a `SidRetrievalStrategy`, whose sole implementation (`SidRetrievalStrategyImpl`) retrieves both the authorities (for example, `ROLE_USER`) of the `Authentication` object plus the principal. So it will have an instance of `PrincipalSid` and as many instances of `GrantedAuthoritySid` as the authenticated user has authorities.

The next step for the voter is to retrieve the actual ACL for that particular `ObjectIdentity` and the SIDs. It does this with the help of the configured `AclService`, which we already talked about.

In the next step, the retrieved ACL is consulted by its `isGranted` method to see whether or not access should be granted. This method receives the required permission (as defined by the third constructor argument of the beans of type `AclEntryVoter`, which in the case of `DELETE` has the value `org.springframework.security.acls.domain.BasePermission.DELETE`) and the list of SIDs obtained before. The ACL, in turn, delegates to an instance of `PermissionGrantingStrategy` (actually, to the implementation `DefaultPermissionGrantingStrategy`) to make the final call on whether the SIDs have the required permissions on the domain object. `PermissionGrantingStrategy`'s sole implementation, `DefaultPermissionGrantingStrategy`, simply iterates through the list of permissions, the list of SIDs, and the list of ACEs in the ACL. It compares the permissions one by one against the permissions on the ACE, and it compares the SIDs against the SIDs on the ACE. If it finds a match, it allows access; if it doesn't find any match, it rejects access by throwing an exception, which is caught by the voter to return `ACCESS_DENIED`. In your case, because the current authenticated user is `ANONYMOUS`, this whole flow is what happens.

On the login page, log in now with the username **leo** and the password **nardone01** (which is one of the users defined in the `applicationContext-security.xml` file) and try to delete the post. You'll get an "access denied" page, as shown in Figure 7-10.

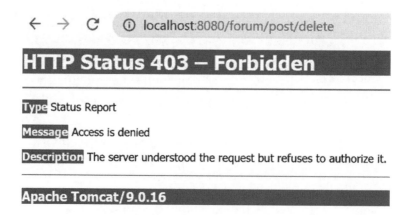

Figure 7-10. *Screen showing the access denied page*

The same thing as before is happening: the logged-in user *leo* and their role of ROLE_ USER don't match the rules required to execute the deletePost action on that particular post. As we said before, only a user with role ROLE_ADMIN can delete the post. So let's try that out.

First, log out by visiting the URL http://localhost:8080/logout. Next, log in with the username **luna** and the password **nardone01** and try to delete the post again. This time, the Acl.isGranted method returns true and the voter returns ACCESS_GRANTED because the match exists between the role of the authenticated user and the authorities required to perform the required action. This means that the code execution will finally reach the deletePost method in the ForumServiceImpl. This is a very simple method that removes the entry from the ACL for that object and, of course, deletes the object from the store. (Remember, you are using a java.util.Map as your in-memory store, which is not the most realistic simulation but works for the purposes of the example.) Figure 7-11 shows the most important aspects of the process just explained.

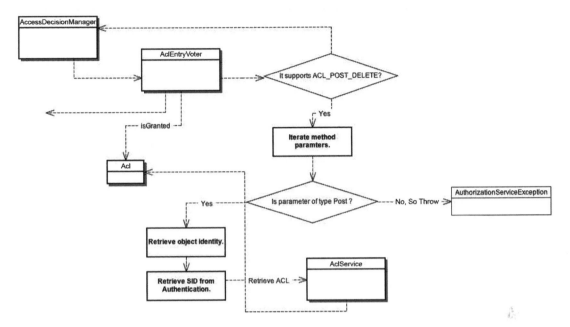

Figure 7-11. *A high-level overview of AclEntryVoter*

Filtering Returned Objects

So you successfully tested the DELETE action with a Post domain instance that should be allowed only to ROLE_ADMIN users. The other two actions follow a similar pattern. Let's secure the READ one so that only users with role ROLE_USER can read them. (Users with ROLE_ADMIN need to have ROLE_USER as well to read the posts. Normally, your users wouldn't need to have both roles defined, but for the sake of the example, it is OK to do it this way.) However, if the post was created by a user with role ROLE_ADMIN, it will be readable only by users with ROLE_ADMIN. First of all, let's create another user with both roles, ROLE_USER and ROLE_ADMIN. In the file applicationContext-security.xml in the <user-service>, add this user: <security:user authorities="ROLE_USER,ROLE_ADMIN" name="massimo" password="nardone01" />.

In this example, you want to secure the method getPosts in the ForumServiceImpl class in such a way that when the posts are returned, they are filtered out by the rules explained in the last paragraph. To do this, use the @PostFilter annotation.

First, you need to add a new voter to the list of voters of your AccessDecisionManager. The new voter is of type org.springframework.security.access.prepost. PreInvocationAuthorizationAdviceVoter and is shown in Listing 7-20. This voter is needed because even if you'll be using only the @PostFilter annotation, Spring Security

will try to evaluate the config attributes when it's doing the voting, and it includes a
PreInvocationAttribute in the list of config attributes that it will evaluate with the value
permitAll, so the PreInvocationAuthorizationAdviceVoter will vote to grant access
all the time. The code in Listing 7-20 should be added in the file applicationContext-
security.xml.

Listing 7-20. PreInvocationAuthorizationAdviceVoter Needed to Vote on the
Automatically Generated permitAll Expression

```
<bean id ="preInvocationAuthorizationAdviceVoter"
      class="org.springframework.security.access.prepost.
      PreInvocationAuthorizationAdviceVoter">
   <constructor-arg>
      <bean class="org.springframework.security.access.expression.method.
            ExpressionBasedPreInvocationAdvice"/>
   </constructor-arg>
</bean>
```

Next, you need to change the return type of your getPosts method because the filter
you're adding works only with instances of java.util.Collection or arrays, and since
you currently are returning a map from that method, the implementation won't work.
You'll now just return a collection of the posts. The new method looks like Listing 7-21.
If you are following along with the code, you should change all the classes and files that
depend on this method, including the form.jsp file.

Listing 7-21. The getPosts Method Now Returns a Collection of Posts and Not
the Map

```
public Collection<Post> getPosts(){
    return new ArrayList<Post>(postStore.values());
}
```

Next, on top of the method from Listing 7-21, add the annotation @PostFilter
("hasPermission(filterObject, 'READ')"), where filterObject is each of
the objects of the returned collection and READ is the permission that matches the
BasePermission.READ that you saw before. This is where the filtering functionality
will get triggered. Next, we'll explain how it works, in the context of an execution

scenario. However, first you need to configure a couple of beans manually in the application context to allow the correct evaluation of permission expressions. This is needed because, by default, the SpEL expression evaluator configured in Spring Security will use an `org.springframework.security.access.expression.` `DenyAllPermissionEvaluator` which, as its name implies, will deny all permission evaluation requests. This configuration is hardcoded in the class `org.springframework.` `security.access.expression.AbstractSecurityExpressionHandler<T>`, and you need to replace it with a proper evaluator.

Fortunately, Spring Security provides us with the proper evaluator in the form of the class `org.springframework.security.acls.AclPermissionEvaluator`. It takes a bit of work to configure it, but it is not that difficult. First, you need to define the bean that will be the new `ExpressionHandler`. You do that in the `applicationContext-security.xml` file by adding the code from Listing 7-22.

Listing 7-22. The ExpressionHandler Bean with the Correct Permission Evaluator Injected

```
<bean id="customPermissionEvaluator"
      class="org.springframework.security.acls.AclPermissionEvaluator">
      <constructor-arg ref="aclService" />
   </bean>

   <bean id="customExpressionHandler"
      class="org.springframework.security.access.expression.method.
         DefaultMethodSecurityExpressionHandler">
      <property name="permissionEvaluator" ref="customPermissionEvaluator" />
   </bean>
```

Then, in the element `<security:global-method-security>`, add as a child the element `<security:expression-handler ref="customExpressionHandler" />` to make a reference to the new expression handler you just defined.

Restart the application now. After the application is restarted, if you visit `http://` `localhost:8080/forum/` and create a post, you will see that the post won't be shown on the page. This is because you created the post as an ANONYMOUS user. Remember that posts now will show only for ROLE_USER users. If you log in to the application with the username **leo** and the password **nardone01** and again go to `http://localhost:8080/`

forum/, you will see the post on the page and the delete button. The following paragraphs explain how it all works under the hood.

As you might recall from previous chapters, the core of Spring Security is the concept of the SecurityInterceptor and its two personifications: FilterSecurityInterceptor and MethodSecurityInterceptor. As you probably recall as well, the interceptors work in a preprocess, process, postprocess flow. The actual business logic happens in the process phase, and both the preprocess and postprocess phases are used for the framework itself to apply all the security concerns, regarding authorization and access control, that are needed to secure the application.

The preprocess phase is taken care of mainly by the access decision managers and the access decision voters that decide whether or not access should be allowed to a particular resource (be it a method, a domain object, or a URL). The postprocess phase is handled by an AfterInvocationManager that is called from the SecurityInterceptor. By default, an instance of AfterInvocationProviderManager is called.

We explained this process before: the AfterInvocationProviderManager iterates through a list of AfterInvocationProvider, which makes the final decision of whether or not access to a particular domain object instance is allowed. The important part in this current example is that the chain of calls ends in an instance of ExpressionBasedPost InvocationAdvice (through the PostInvocationAdviceProvider), which checks to see if there is a postFilter expression that needs to be handled. If there is, it calls the DefaultMethodSecurityExpressionHandler that you defined in Listing 7-22. This handler checks that the returned value from the business method with the @PostFilter annotation was indeed a collection or an array (and throws an exception if it wasn't). Then it iterates through this collection, evaluating the SpEL expression on each object and discarding the object to which the evaluation of the expression gives the value false. The expression you are using is an ACL expression and, like most of the other expressions, its backing method is defined in the class SecurityExpressionRoot. This method (hasPermission) uses the permission evaluator defined in Listing 7-22 to decide if the authentication has the required permissions on the object being passed. This evaluator uses the same suites of classes and helpers that the AclEntryVoter uses to decide whether or not to grant access, such as the AclService and the method isGranted in the ACL interface.

So you know what happened in the example. When you tried to access the list with the anonymous user, the only existing post was discarded from the return elements because the user didn't match the permissions required to read the object. (ACL's isGranted method returned false.) When you logged in as *leo/nardone01,* you acquired the role ROLE_USER. This role is indeed allowed to read post objects, as specified by the ACL rules you created when you first created the post.

Let's see how filtering works in an example with more than one post. This time, you'll create a post with a user with the role ROLE_ADMIN. You'll modify the post creation code so that when an Admin user creates a post, only other ROLE_ADMIN users can read that post. To do that, change the createPost method in the ForumServiceImpl class to look like Listing 7-23. This listing (like many others in the book) takes an approach of preferring convenience over particularly good design. For example, you might argue, and rightly, that the ACL mutation is not part of the core createPost method business functionality, and also that hardcoding role names in the code is not right. Again, we're doing this to illustrate concepts in a convenient way, without too much abstraction and directly to the point that we're trying to show. In a real environment, you should try to achieve a good separation of concerns, giving the security concerns their own space (whether using AOP or other methods) and leaving the business method to handle, well, business concerns.

Listing 7-23. The createPost Method That Creates Different ACLs Depending on the User Creating the Post, Along with a Needed Helper Method to Check Whether the Logged-In User Has the ROLE_ADMIN Role

```
@Transactional
    public void createPost(Post post) {
        Integer id = new Integer(Math.abs(post.hashCode()));
        ObjectIdentity oid = new ObjectIdentityImpl(Post.class, id);
        MutableAcl acl = mutableAclService.createAcl(oid);
        User user = (User)SecurityContextHolder.getContext().
        getAuthentication().getPrincipal();
        acl.insertAce(0, BasePermission.ADMINISTRATION, new PrincipalSid(
                user.getUsername()), true);
        acl.insertAce(1, BasePermission.DELETE, new GrantedAuthoritySid(
                "ROLE_ADMIN"), true);
        if(isAdminUserLogged()){
            acl.insertAce(2, BasePermission.READ, new GrantedAuthoritySid(
                    "ROLE_ADMIN"), true);
```

```
        }else{
            acl.insertAce(2, BasePermission.READ, new GrantedAuthoritySid(
                "ROLE_USER"), true);
        }
        mutableAclService.updateAcl(acl);
        post.setId(id);
        postStore.put(id, post);
    }
private booleanisAdminUserLogged() {
        for(GrantedAuthority authority: SecurityContextHolder.getContext().
        getAuthentication().getAuthorities()){
            if(authority.getAuthority().equals("ROLE_ADMIN")){
                return true;
            }
        }
        return false;
    }
```

Here you added a conditional saying, basically, that if the logged-in user is an Administrator, the READ permission will be available only to other Administrators (users with the role ROLE_ADMIN). If the logged-in user is not an Administrator, the READ permission will be available to any user with the ROLE_USER role.

Let's see an execution of this new configuration step by step.

Test Scenario 7-7

To execute this new configuration, follow these steps:

1. Restart the application, visit `http://localhost:8080/forum/ admin`, and log in with the username **leo** and the password **nardone01**.

2. Visit `http://localhost:8080/forum/posts` and create a new post with the content *p1*. This creates the screen you see in Figure 7-12.

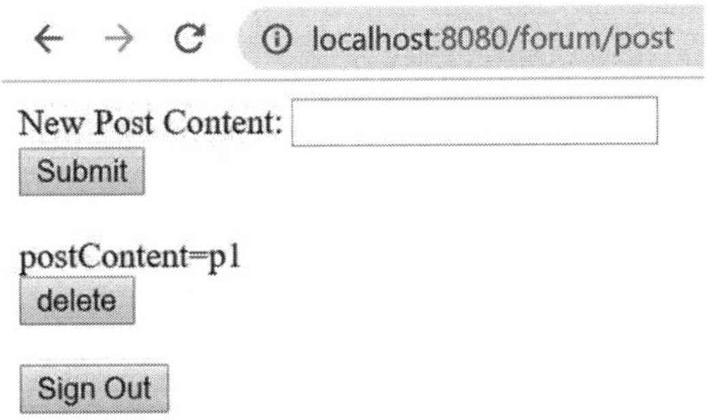

localhost:8080/forum/post
New Post Content:
Submit
postContent=p1
delete
Sign Out

***Figure 7-12.** The screen that is generated after a user with the role ROLE_USER creates a post*

3. Visit `http://localhost:8080/logout` to log out of the application. Then visit `http://localhost:8080/login` and log in with the username **luna** and password **nardone01**.

4. Visit `http://localhost:8080/forum/posts` and create a post with the content *p2*. See Figure 7-13.

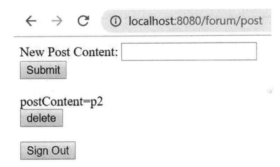

localhost:8080/forum/post
New Post Content:
Submit
postContent=p2
delete
Sign Out

***Figure 7-13.** The sceen that is generated after an admin user creates a post*

5. Visit `http://localhost:8080/logout` to log out of the application. Then visit `http://localhost:8080/login` and log in with the username **massimo** and the password **nardone01**.

6. Visit `http://localhost:8080/forum/posts`, and you should see both posts, as Figure 7-14 shows.

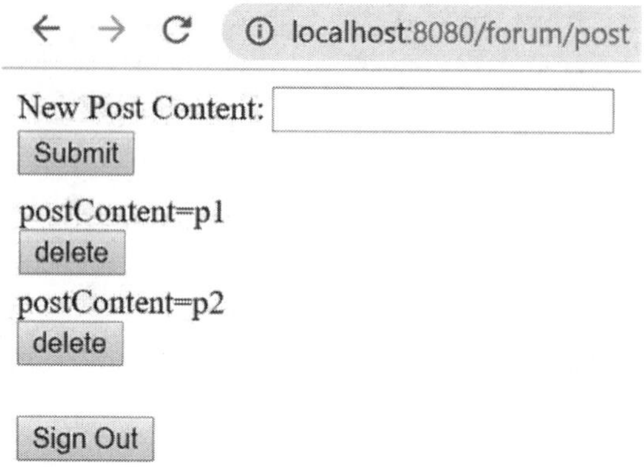

Figure 7-14. *Posts for a user with both ROLE_USER and ROLE_ADMIN roles*

7. Visit http://localhost:8080/logout to log out of the
    application. Then visit http://localhost:8080/login and log in
    with the username **leo** and the password **nardone01**.

8. Visit http://localhost:8080/forum/posts, and you'll only see
    the Post post1 since it is the only one accessible for standard users.
    The view is exactly the same as Figure 7-12.

Spring Security ACL support also offers the @PreFilter annotation which, as you
can imagine, works in the preprocess phase of the method security interception process
rather than the way that the @PostFilter annotation works. As we said before, the
preprocessing activities are taken care of by AccessDecisionVoter implementations. In
the case of the @PreFilter annotation, it is taken care of by the org.springframework.
security.access.prepost.PreInvocationAuthorizationAdviceVoter which, in turn,
uses an instance of DefaultMethodSecurityExpressionHandler as in the previous case.
As in the case of @PostFilter, @PreFilter-annotated methods are expected to receive a
collection. In this case, however, arrays are not supported.

We just showed you a simple walkthrough of how this ACL filtering functionality
works in practice. You can see that by providing only the @PostFilter annotation with
the hasPermission expression (which, as you know, internally calls a method in the
SpEL context), we are instructing the framework what to do with the returned values of
the method. This process that we explained first, and demonstrated later in the small test
case, can be summarized with Figures 7-15, 7-16, and 7-17.

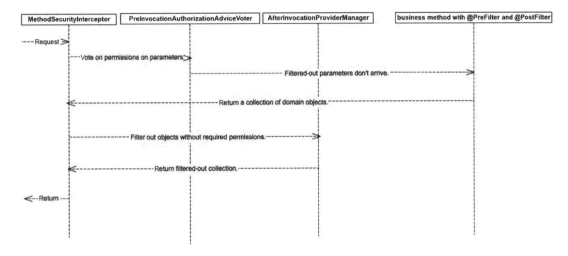

Figure 7-15. *A simplified sequence diagram of what happens when a method with @PreFilter and @PostFilter annotations is invoked. The diagram shows how parameters and return collections of domain objects are filtered out on the way in and out of the method*

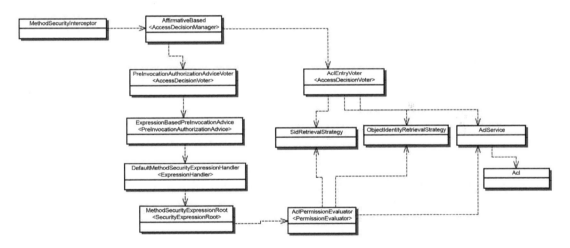

Figure 7-16. *A diagram showing the main classes and interfaces in the preprocessing phase of a method interception with ACL-based security*

@PreFilter invocations are handled by the PreInvocationAuthorization AdviceVoter, while @Secured annotations with ACL config attributes are handled by the AclEntryVoter. You can see in the diagram that, at the end of the processing, both paths reach the essential elements in the SidRetrievalStrategy, ObjectIdentityRetrievalStrategy, and AclService. In fact, the AclPermission Evaluator and the AclEntryVoter perform very similar functions.

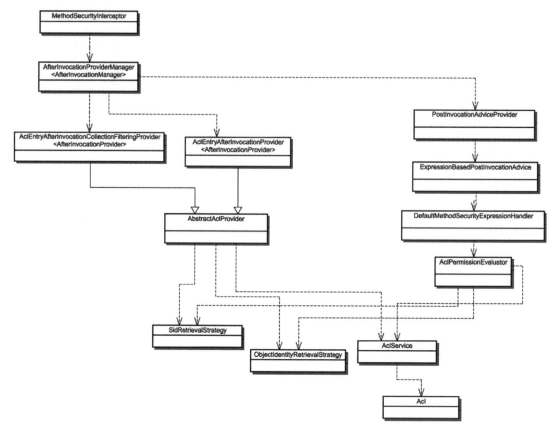

Figure 7-17. *A diagram showing the classes that participate in the postprocessing phase of a method interception with ACL-based security*

Again, you can see two branches. The branch on the left, where you can see the `AclEntryAfterInvocationProvider` and `AclEntryAfterInvocationCollection FilteringProvider`, is the branch that doesn't support SpEL expressions and is active when using `@Secured` and a static name for a config attribute, something like `ACL_ ALLOW_READ` or whatever, as you saw a couple of sections back. The right branch goes through the section that supports SpEL and both `@PostFilter` and `@PostAuthorize` annotations. You can see that these two branches map almost one-to-one to the branches in the preprocessing phase. Also, you can see that there is a high level of reuse in the system and that many classes are present in both the preprocessing and postprocessing phases.

We covered two different ways to handle ACL security, with the two branches we talked about in the previous paragraph. The one that uses @Secured is older and doesn't support SpEL expressions; the one using @PreFilter, @PreAuthorize, @PostAuthorize, and @PostFilter has existed since version 3.0 of Spring Security. They are newer options that support the use of SpEL expressions, so you will probably favor them over the other ones in your day-to-day use.

Securing the View Layer with ACLs

Another option you have for using ACLs to secure applications is to use the view-layer JSP tags to filter out domain objects for users who don't have the proper permissions to see them. We talked a bit about these tags in the web security chapter, but we intentionally left the ACL tags for more thorough treatment here. To use them in an example, let's continue with the code from the previous section, but let's make a couple of changes. First, in the ForumServiceImpl class, comment out the @PostFilter annotation in the getPosts method so that it doesn't filter out anything anymore. Then change the form.jsp file to look like Listing 7-24.

Listing 7-24. The form.jsp with Taglib ACL Security Applied for Filtering Domain Objects

```
<%@ page language="java" contentType="text/html; charset=ISO-8859-1"
    pageEncoding="ISO-8859-1"%>
<%@ taglib prefix="security"
    uri="http://www.springframework.org/security/tags"%>
<%@ taglib prefix="c" uri="http://java.sun.com/jsp/jstl/core"%>
<html>
<head>
<meta http-equiv="Content-Type" content="text/html; charset=ISO-8859-1">
<title>Posts</title>
</head>
```

```
<body>
<form method="post" action="/forum/post">
        New Post Content: <input type="text" name="postContent"/><br/>
        <input type="submit"/>
    </form>
    <c:forEach items="${posts}" var="post">
    <security:accesscontrollist  domainObject="${post}"
    hasPermission="READ">
    <form method="post" action="/forum/post/delete">
            ${post.content} <br />
            <input type="hidden" value="${post.id}" name="postId"/>
            <input type="submit" value="delete"/>
        </form>
    </security:accesscontrollist>
    </c:forEach>
</body>
</html>
```

This listing shows how simply you can secure domain objects on the view layer. In fact, it does a very similar job (in view terms) to what you get when you use the @PostFilter annotation.

The <accesscontrollist> tag depends on the configured org.springframework. security.access.PermissionEvaluator implementation that exists in the application context configuration. It will work only if there is only one bean of this type configured in the application context, because it will try to retrieve the bean by type. As you might recall, you have a configured PermissionEvaluator in your configuration of concrete type org.springframework.security.acls.AclPermissionEvaluator.

Now, if you restart the application and again execute the steps defined in Test Scenario 7.1, you should have exactly the same behavior from a presentation layer point of view as you had before when you first executed that scenario. The way it works is simple. Every time the tag is evaluated (in each iteration over the posts collection), the tag handler calls the PermissionEvaluator's hasPermission method, which returns a Boolean indicating whether or not permission has been granted. If permission is granted, the body of the tag is evaluated and rendered. If permission is not granted, the body of the tag is skipped.

The Cost of ACLs

This example shows that working with ACLs imposes a good deal of overhead in terms of the operations and logic you need to implement on top of your standard business operations. It's clear that storing a post is affected by the extra work that is necessary to store the corresponding ACL for that object, and retrieving a post is affected by the need to filter out certain elements of the collection based on the permissions.

This brief section will go inside the core class of the ACL Spring Security support to see how it works internally and how it might affect your application. This class is the org.springframework.security.acls.jdbc.JdbcMutableAclService.

JdbcMutableAclService is the class that deals with all the input and output to the database for everything regarding the ACL database schema. It's configured by default to work with HSQLDB, which is the database we have been using in the examples.

This class has different SQLs for the different things you do when you interact with the ACL system—like inserts into the different tables, deleting ACLs, updating values and, of course, selecting from the different tables. All of these operations are done using Spring Core's JdbcTemplate support.

Another important class is BasicLookupStrategy, the default implementation of LookupStrategy used in the framework to look up ACLs.

The first interesting operation you see is the method readAclsById, which exists in JdbcMutableAclService and delegates to a method of the same name in BasicLookupStrategy. This method tries to retrieve the requested ACL from the cache. If it finds the ACL in cache, the method will return this found ACL; if the ACL is not found in the cache, the implementation will query the database with a somewhat complex query with four joins, as Listing 7-25 shows. This query can get a bit more complex because the ACLs can be retrieved in batches of up to 50 elements (which is the default but is configurable by setting the property batchSize in the class BasicLookupStrategy) and, for each of these elements, the where clause adds an or operator to the query. The result from this query is then stored in the cache, which makes these ACLs available so that if another method calls readAclsById requesting one of the cached elements, the database doesn't need to be hit.

When you create a new post, readAclsById is called. Also, another select query is performed to retrieve the primary key of the objectIdentity represented by the domain object. And, of course, an "insert into acl_object_identity" is performed.

Also, in the same `createPost` method in `ForumServiceImpl`, when you call the `updateAcl` method, a "`delete from acl_entry`" is performed, followed by a batch "`insert into acl_entry`", followed by an "`update acl_object_identity`". Then all the caching entries for that Object Identity are cleared and a new call to the `readAclsById` is executed, which will query the database for the up-to-date information. You can see how the cost of deleting a post has increased considerably with the use of ACLs.

Deleting Post objects is also more costly because now it involves deleting ACE entries, deleting object identities, and clearing the cache for the relevant objects.

This section is not meant to scare you away from using ACLs. We simply want to make you aware that there is an extra cost (apart from the complexity of using it) you should take into consideration when creating your applications with the use of ACLs in mind. The more domain objects you have, the more ACL entries you will have as well. In a big application, you might be talking about millions of entries in the ACL support tables.

Listing 7-25. An ACL Retrieving Query That You Can Find in the Class org. springframework.security.acls.jdbc.BasicLookupStrategy

```
select acl_object_identity.object_id_identity, acl_entry.ace_order,  acl_
object_identity.id as acl_id,
acl_object_identity.parent_object, acl_object_identity.entries_inheriting,
acl_entry.id as ace_id, acl_entry.mask,
acl_entry.granting,  acl_entry.audit_success, acl_entry.audit_
failure,  acl_sid.principal as ace_principal,
acl_sid.sid as ace_sid,  acli_sid.principal as acl_principal, acli_sid.sid
as acl_sid, acl_class.class from
acl_object_identity left join acl_sid acli_sid on acli_sid.id = acl_object_
identity.owner_sid
left join acl_class on acl_class.id = acl_object_identity.object_id_class
left join acl_entry on acl_object_identity.id = acl_entry.acl_object_
identity
left join acl_sid on acl_entry.sid = acl_sid.id
where ( (acl_object_identity.object_id_identity = ? and acl_class.class = ?))
order by acl_object_identity.object_id_identity asc, acl_entry.ace_order asc
```

Summary

In this chapter, we explained in detail how to use Spring Security's support for ACLs. We showed how to configure support for ACLs in the Spring configuration file and how to use the @Secured, @PreAuthorize, @PreFilter, @PostAuthorize, and @PostFilter annotations to implement domain object–specific security. We also introduced some internal aspects of the framework and the main classes that are involved in its ACL functionality.

We examined different ways to make sure that secured domain objects don't show up in the presentation layer for a user who doesn't have appropriate permissions. You saw that this is achievable either with SpEL expressions at the @PostFilter business level or with the ACL Spring Security tag library directly in your JSP files. We also gave a quick overview of the different SQLs that are used by the ACL framework and how they might impact your application.

CHAPTER 8

Customizing and Extending Spring Security

Spring Security is a very extendable and customizable framework. This is primarily because the framework is built using object-oriented principles and design practices so that it is open for extension and closed for modification. In the previous chapter, you saw one of the major extension points in Spring Security—namely, the pluggability of different authentication providers. This chapter covers some other extension points in the framework that you can take advantage of to extend Spring Security's functionality or to modify or customize functionality that doesn't work exactly the way you need in your applications.

We will also briefly cover the Spring Security Extensions project (`http://static.springsource.org/spring-security/site/extensions.html`), an environment you can use to create extension modules for the core Spring Security project.

The next section defines what we consider to be some of the major extension points in Spring Security and describes how to use them to add or modify behavior in your security solution. Also, this chapter will show how to develop authentication and login applications using Spring Boot, Spring Security, Spring Data, Thymeleaf, and MongoDB.

Spring Security Extension Points

Spring Security offers a comprehensive set of extension points that can be customized (or completely overridden) with your own implementations and still leverage the core of the framework. Some of the extension points are evident, while some others are a bit more subtle and, in some cases, not even intended. However, because the framework is so flexible, you can take advantage of that flexibility to tweak its configuration to fit your intentions.

© Carlo Scarioni and Massimo Nardone 2019
C. Scarioni and M. Nardone, *Pro Spring Security*, https://doi.org/10.1007/978-1-4842-5052-5_8

Plugging into the Spring Security Event System

Spring Security supports an event model that is built on top of Spring Framework's own event model. You can use Spring's event model to develop applications that can listen to different events that happen within the framework and act accordingly.

We won't explain in any depth why an event model is such a powerful programming practice to have at your disposal. Instead, we'll just point out one big advantage: it allows you to decouple your applications, because in general the event producer or producers and the event consumer or consumers don't need to know anything about each other in order to operate correctly. In theory (and, indeed, in practice for events in general, although not for Spring events), you can have a completely heterogeneous application where you can write and evolve each module at its own pace without affecting other parts, and then integrate them all together through the exclusive use of events.

All Spring events should extend from the abstract class `org.springframework.context.ApplicationEvent`, and Spring Security's own events are no exception.

One of the main concrete implementations of the `ApplicationEvent` abstract class is `org.springframework.context.event.ApplicationContextEvent`, which itself serves as the parent class of a series of events that involve the life cycle of the application context (`ContextClosedEvent`, `ContextRefreshedEvent`, `ContextStartedEvent`, and `ContextStoppedEvent`).

To register your application to be notified of Spring events, you need one (or more) of the beans defined in your application to implement the interface `org.springframework.context.ApplicationListener<E extends ApplicationEvent>`. This interface defines a single method, `void onApplicationEvent(E event)`, that you can use to listen to a particular type of event in the application.

Publishing events is equally easy. You only need to define a bean in your Spring application context that implements the interface `org.springframework.context.ApplicationEventPublisherAware`, which again defines only one method:

```
void setApplicationEventPublisher(ApplicationEventPublisher
applicationEventPublisher)
```

This method is called automatically by Spring when the application starts up, and an instance of `ApplicationEventPublisher` (an implementation of it because it is an interface) is passed in. The instance of `ApplicationEventPublisher` that is passed in is normally the `ApplicationContext` instance itself that contains the application.

The default implementation of `ApplicationEventPublisher`'s `publishEvent` method (which lives in the class `AbstractApplicationContext`) delegates the publishing of the events to an implementation of `ApplicationEventMulticaster`— the only current implementation of which is `org.springframework.context.event.SimpleApplicationEventMulticaster`.

Broadcasting an event to all interested listeners is also straightforward. You simply need to create an instance of one of the implementing classes of `ApplicationEvent` (any subclass of it will do as an event) and then call the `ApplicationEventPublisher`'s `publishEvent(ApplicationEvent event)` method, passing your `ApplicationEvent` instance to it. Spring then takes care of ensuring that all the listeners registered for that particular event are notified of the event publication. By default, all listeners are invoked on the same thread as the publisher; however, you also could configure an `org.springframework.core.task.TaskExecutor` (which is an interface, so you could use an implementation class like `org.springframework.core.task.SimpleAsyncTaskExecutor`) to call the listeners in different threads. You will use this when you configure the listeners in the examples.

Spring Security comes with its own suite of `ApplicationEvent` implementations, so you can hook into different points of the security life cycle in an unobtrusive and decoupled way. The `ApplicationEvent` implementations that Spring Security provides are categorized as `Authorization`, `Authentication`, or `javax.servlet.http.Session` types, and they have descriptive names that hint what they do and where they are published. Here, we will give a concrete explanation of them and when they are published within the framework.

Events in Spring work as shown in Figure 8-1.

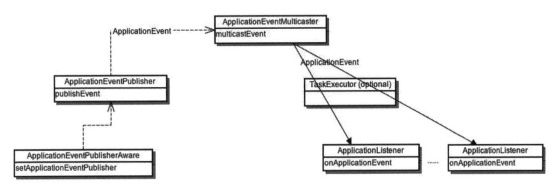

Figure 8-1. *Spring event mechanism. Spring Security has its own set of ApplicationEvent implementations*

Authorization-Related Events

These are events related to the different phases that an authorization process can go through—for example, informing a user when an authorization has failed. The events under this category are the following:

- `org.springframework.security.access.event.` `AbstractAuthorizationEvent`: This is the parent class of all the other authorization events. It doesn't really add any functionality on top of `ApplicationEvent`. It is more like a marker identifying all its subclasses as authorization events.

- `org.springframework.security.access.event.` `AuthenticationCredentialsNotFoundEvent`: This event is used to indicate that the `Authentication` object could not be obtained from the configured `SecurityContext`. This event is broadcast from the `AbstractSecurityInterceptor`'s `beforeInvocation` method after it decides that an invocation should have security but the interceptor doesn't find the required `Authentication` object in the security context. Simply put, this event is executed if the condition `SecurityContextHolder.getContext().getAuthentication() == null` is true.

- `org.springframework.security.access.event.` `AuthorizationFailureEvent`: This event indicates that the `Authentication` object's principal was not allowed access to a secured object because it lacked the required permissions to access it. This event is published by the `AbstractInterceptor`'s `beforeInvocation` and `afterInvocation` methods when it catches an `AccessDeniedException`. An `AccessDeniedException` can be thrown by the `org.springframework.security.access.` `AccessDecisionManager`'s decide method in the preprocessing phase of the interceptor, and by the `org.springframework.security.` `access.intercept.AfterInvocationProviderManager`'s decide method in the postprocess part of the interceptor.

- `org.springframework.security.access.event.AuthorizedEvent`:
  This event is published after access to a secured object has been
  granted and before actually invoking the secured object. This event is
  not published by default, and if you want it to be published, you need
  to set the property `publishAuthorizationSuccess` to `true` in the
  security interceptor.

- `org.springframework.security.access.event. LoggerListener`:
  This event outputs interceptor-related application events to
  Commons Logging, so all failures will be logged at the warning level,
  all with success events will be logged at the information level, and all
  public invocation events will be logged at the debug level.

- `level.org.springframework.security.access.event.`
  `PublicInvocationEvent`: This event is published by the
  `AbstractSecurityInterceptor`'s `beforeInvocation` method
  whenever a secured object receives an invocation to a nonsecured
  entry point (that is, a method without `ConfigAttribute` configured).
  In the case of method security, this means that when an object's
  security proxy is invoked, if the particular invoked method is
  not configured with security metadata, it is then handled as a
  nonsecured public call. However, instead of simply invoking the
  method, an event is broadcasted just before proceeding to inform
  to any listener interested in this fact that this (a public invocation)
  has happened. This could point to a case when you actually need
  to secure the endpoint and, thanks to the event, you will be notified
  that you haven't done so. After the event is published, no more
  preprocessing or postprocessing is executed for this invocation
  on the interceptor. If the property `rejectPublicInvocations`
  is set to `true` in the interceptor (the property is part of the
  `AbstractSecurityInterceptor` class), the event will not be
  published, and instead an `IllegalArgumentException` will be
  thrown saying that the particular invocation cannot be done without
  the `ConfigAttribute`(s) configured. This means that a configuration
  error needs to be taken care of.

More info can be found at https://docs.spring.io/spring-security/
site/docs/5.1.4.RELEASE/api/org/springframework/security/access/event/
AbstractAuthorizationEvent.html

Figure 8-2 shows these event classes and interfaces in UML (Unified Modeling
Language) form.

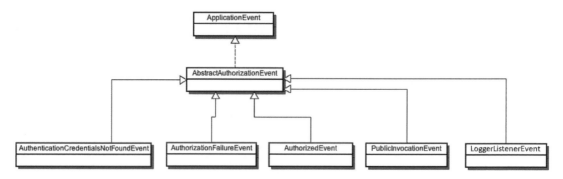

Figure 8-2. *Authorization-related events*

Authentication-Related Events

These events are related to the authentication process in the application and the
different phases this process goes through, such as informing interested listeners
of disabled accounts and expired credentials. Authentication events are published
by an implementation of org.springframework.security.authentication.
AuthenticationEventPublisher, which is invoked by the org.springframework.
security.authentication.ProviderManager class. By default, the configured
AuthenticationEventPublisher in the ProviderManager is an instance of
NullEventPublisher, which is a private static class defined inside the ProviderManager
class itself and which doesn't publish any events. There exists a default implementation
of the interface AuthenticationEventPublisher that you can use if you are configuring
the beans yourself, which is org.springframework.security.authentication.
DefaultAuthenticationEventPublisher. This instance is configured by default for the
web-layer security when using the <http> element.

The DefaultAuthenticationEventPublisher works in the following way: It has only
two public methods that it implements from the AuthenticationEventPublisher interface.
These methods are publishAuthenticationSuccess and publishAuthenticationFailure.
They are the two possible scenarios when attempting authentication; however, in the
case of authentication failure, there can be many reasons for it, as you can see from the

amount of AuthenticationFailureXXXEvent instances that we'll show you next. In the case of authentication failures, the DefaultAuthenticationEventPublisher will receive a call to the publishAuthenticationFailure method, and then it will query a mapping between the exception that was thrown when authentication was denied (like UsernameNotFoundException, for example) and the event that corresponds to such an exception (like AuthenticationFailureBadCredentialsEvent). Then an instance of this event will be created by reflection and will be published.

It is possible to add more mapping into the default mappings between exceptions and events using the method provided by the DefaultAuthenticationEventPublisher: setAdditionalExceptionMappings.

The authentication-related events currently in the framework are the following:

- org.springframework.security.authentication.event.
  AbstractAuthenticationEvent: This is the parent class of all other authentication-related events. It doesn't introduce any particular functionality, and it serves the basic function of classifying authentication events.

- org.springframework.security.authentication.event.
  AbstractAuthenticationFailureEvent: This is the parent class of all the authentication failure events. It extends AbstractAuthenticationEvent but adds a constructor that takes in the exception that was thrown when the authentication failure happened.

- org.springframework.security.authentication.event.
  AuthenticationFailureBadCredentialsEvent: This event is published when a BadCredentialsException is thrown by the system during authentication. This exception is thrown by the different AuthenticationProvider implementations when a check for the credentials of an Authentication object is not valid. The event is also published when a UsernameNotFoundException is thrown. This is thrown normally by UserDetailsService implementations when they can't find a user corresponding to the passed username and simply propagated by the AuthenticationProvider.

- `org.springframework.security.authentication.event.`
  `AuthenticationFailureCredentialsExpiredEvent`: This event
  is published when a `CredentialsExpiredException` is thrown.
  This exception is thrown, for example, by an implementation
  of `AbstractUserDetailsAuthenticationProvider` when the
  `UserDetails` object representing the user returns `false` from the
  method `isCredentialsNotExpired`.

- `org.springframework.security.authentication.event.`
  `AuthenticationFailureDisabledEvent`: This event is published
  when a `DisabledException` is thrown. This exception is thrown if
  the user account that is trying to log in has been disabled. It is used
  by `AbstractUserDetailsAuthenticationProvider` and also by
  `AccountStatusUserDetailsChecker` implementations evaluating if
  the `UserDetails.isEnabled` method returns `false`.

- `org.springframework.security.authentication.event.`
  `AuthenticationFailureExpiredEvent`: This event is published by
  the `ProviderManager` when an `AccountExpiredException` is thrown.
  This exception is thrown following the same logic as the previous
  case, but this time the `UserDetails.isAccountNonExpired` method is
  the one that is called. If it returns `false`, the exception is thrown.

- `org.springframework.security.authentication.event.`
  `AuthenticationFailureLockedEvent`: This event is published when
  a `LockedException` is thrown. This exception is thrown in the same
  places as the previous one (in preauthentication checking scenarios)
  and is thrown when the `UserDetails` representing the user returns
  `false` from its method `isAccountNonLocked`.

- `org.springframework.security.authentication.event.`
  `AuthenticationFailureProviderNotFoundEvent`: This event is
  different than the previous ones in that it is not related directly
  to the user attempting to log in. Instead, this event is published
  when a `ProviderNotFoundException` is thrown. This exception
  is thrown by the `ProviderManager` itself if none of the configured
  `AuthenticationProviders` configured in the `ProviderManager` are
  able to handle the authentication request.

- `org.springframework.security.authentication.event.`
  `AuthenticationFailureProxyUntrustedEvent`: This event indicates
  the authentication failure caused when the CAS user's ticket is
  generated by an untrusted proxy.

- `org.springframework.security.authentication.event.`
  `AuthenticationFailureServiceExceptionEvent`: This event
  gets published when an `AuthenticationServiceException` is
  thrown. This exception can be thrown by different parts of the
  system (for example, `UsernamePasswordAuthenticationFilter`
  and `DaoAuthenticationProvider`), and it is generally used for
  communicating that the authentication could not be processed due
  to some sort of system error—for example, if the user repository
  cannot be accessed.

- `org.springframework.security.authentication.event.`
  `AuthenticationSuccessEvent`: This event is simply published
  by the `DefaultAuthenticationEventPublisher` when its
  `publishAuthenticationSuccess` method is called.

- `org.springframework.security.authentication.event.`
  `InteractiveAuthenticationSuccessEvent`: This event is published
  directly by different filters in the web-layer security part of the
  framework, and not by the `DefaultAuthenticationEventPublisher`.
  It is published whenever a successful authentication is
  achieved by any of the filters that actively try authentication,
  like the `UsernamePasswordAuthenticationFilter` or the
  `RememberMeAuthenticationFilter`.

- `org.springframework.security.authentication.jaas.event.`
  `LoggerListener`: This event outputs authentication-related
  application events to Commons Logging so that all authentication
  events will be logged at the warning level.

More info can be found at `https://docs.spring.io/spring-security/site/`
`docs/5.1.4.RELEASE/api/org/springframework/security/authentication/event/`
`package-summary.html`

Figure 8-3 shows the mentioned event classes in a UML class diagram.

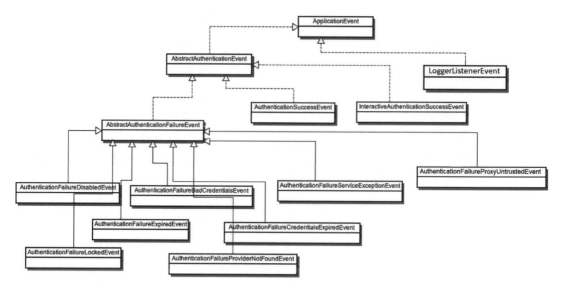

Figure 8-3. *Authentication-related event classes*

Session-Related Events

These events (org.springframework.security.core.session.SessionCreationEvent
and org.springframework.security.core.session.SessionDestroyedEvent),
which extend directly from ApplicationEvent, are related to the user session life
cycle. They are both published (actually, their concrete implementing subclasses
HttpSessionCreatedEvent and HttpSessionDestroyedEvent) by an instance of
HttpSessionEventPublisher, an implementation of the standard servlet interface
HttpSessionListener, which allows the HttpSessionEventPublisher to create session
life-cycle listeners. The implementation needs to be referenced in the web.xml file like
any other HttpSessionListener. The two session-related events map one-to-one to the
two methods defined by the HttpSessionListener interface. These methods are

```
void sessionCreated(HttpSessionEvent se)
void sessionDestroyed(HttpSessionEvent se)
```

This is all the theory you need to know about publishing and handling events in
Spring Security. Next you will see a very simple example where you put this knowledge
into practice to add behavior to your application based on listening to events.

This example will listen to only one type of event, but the configuration needed to
listen to more types is exactly the same. You implement the same interface but type it
differently in the generic type.

All you need do to start listening for events is implement the
ApplicationListener interface and configure the implementing bean in the
Spring application context. Listing 8-1 shows a simple implementation that logs
AuthenticationFailureBadCredentialsEvent events.

Listing 8-1. ApplicationListener That Listens to a
AuthenticationFailureBadCredentialsEvent and Logs It

```
package com.apress.pss.security;

import org.apache.commons.logging.Log;
import org.apache.commons.logging.LogFactory;
import org.springframework.context.ApplicationListener;
import org.springframework.security.authentication.event.
AuthenticationFailureBadCredentialsEvent;

public class LoggerBadCredentialsEvents implements ApplicationListener<Auth
enticationFailureBadCredentialsEvent>{

    private static Log LOG = LogFactory.getLog(LoggerBadCredentialsEvents.
    class);
    public void onApplicationEvent(
            AuthenticationFailureBadCredentialsEvent event) {
        LOG.warn("An attempt to login with bad credentials was made with
        username "+
event.getAuthentication().getName());

    }

}
```

The implementation of the listener is very straightforward. You need to implement
only the interface and type it with the class of the event that you want to listen to. Then if
you define a bean instance of the class LoggerBadCredentialsEvents in the application
context, it will automatically be wired into the Spring Framework event-handling system,
and every time an AuthenticationFailureBadCredentialsEvent is published, this
listener will be notified of it.

To define any other event handler, you do the same but type the handler class by the correct event that you want to listen to. Go ahead and try it yourself. It should be simple enough to test this functionality for different event types.

Your Own AuthenticationProvider and UserDetailsService

You saw in the previous chapter that Spring comes equipped with quite a few authentication options to adjust to a lot of different application requirements that you might have in your application. Looking at how these different authentication providers are set up in your application and the nice way they are contained in their own "modules," you might think that you should be able to use your own authentication provider. The truth is, of course, that you can, and here we will show you how with a simple example.

First of all, let's review how the authentication providers work in your application.

The main authentication entry point in Spring Security is the AuthenticationManager interface—in particular, the ProviderManager implementation. ProviderManager's main functionality is to iterate through a list of AuthenticationProvider implementations that are configured on it until one of them is able to authenticate the user (wrapped in one of the available Authentication implementation objects) or, in fact, until discovering that none of them can, at which point it throws an exception.

The standard way you saw in previous chapters for defining the ProviderManager and the AuthenticationProvider is the one shown in Listing 8-2. (Although the class names and the names of the elements in the XML file don't exactly match, the Spring Security namespace XML parsing mechanism takes care of matching the combination shown of the <authentication-manager> and <authentication-provider> elements to the classes mentioned before.) When you use the namespace to define an authentication manager and an authentication provider as shown in the listing, the framework instantiates two ProviderManager objects and sets one as the parent of the other. This scheme is used by the ProviderManager, which is able to establish a hierarchy of authentication managers. The child AuthenticationManager (in form of the ProviderManager class) is queried first for authentication. If it doesn't resolve the authentication request, it checks to see if it has a configured parent manager that it can query; if it does, it calls its authenticate method. This parent-child relationship is managed by Spring at startup time.

In the parent-child relationship of the `ProviderManager` instances, one of them has defined in the `AuthenticationProvider` list a `DaoAuthenticationProvider` instance, coming from the `<authentication-provider>` element, and the other has an `AnonymousAuthenticationProvider` configured, and this one is defined when the `<http>` element is used and the common filters are being defined. So they are the two providers that are used by default when you use the common definition from Listing 8-2.

Defining your own custom authentication provider is simple, as you just need to implement the interface `org.springframework.security.authentication.` `AuthenticationProvider`, which defines only two methods:

```
Authentication authenticate(Authentication authentication)
boolean supports(Class<?> authentication)
```

But implementing the interface is not the only option. You could easily extend `AbstractUserDetailsAuthenticationProvider` (the way that `DaoAuthenticationProvider` works) if the implementation you want to create depends on the `UserDetails` abstraction for authentication. The main method in the `AuthenticationProvider` is the `public Authentication` `authenticate(Authentication authentication)` method. This method, as you can see, receives an authentication and returns an authentication. The important difference between the two authentication objects (the one received and the one returned) is that the `Authentication` object it returns will return `true` in the method `isAuthenticated` (if authentication is successful, of course), indicating that a fully authenticated object is now in existence, while the `Authentication` object received in the method will have this method returning `false`. This is the logical way to work, as this method in an `Authentication` object (`isAuthenticated`) and its return value are what conceptually differentiate an `Authentication` object that is fully authenticated from one that is used only to wrap the user details before actually applying the authentication logic, or, indeed, any `Authentication` object that hasn't yet been fully authenticated and verified.

Sometimes, you might not need to implement a whole `AuthenticationProvider`, but instead you just might need to change the place from where `UserDetails` is obtained. That is the case, for example, when using the `InMemoryUserDetailsManager` for getting `UserDetails` stored in memory or using `JdbcUserDetailsManager` when getting `UserDetails` stored in a relational database. Of course, you can create a new `UserDetailsService` to retrieve this `UserDetails` from some other source, and that is something we'll show you in the upcoming examples. Figure 8-4 illustrates the relationship between the `AuthenticationProvider` (actually, the `AbstractUserDetailsAuthenticationProvider` implementation) and the `UserDetailsService`.

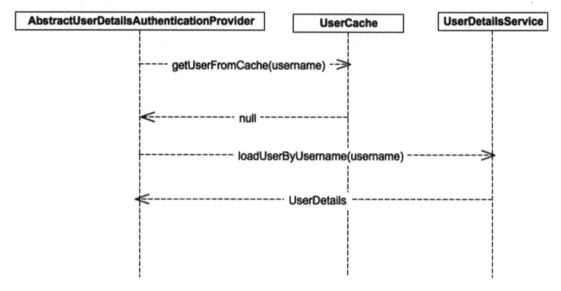

Figure 8-4. *The AbstractUserDetailsAuthenticationProvider and UserDetailsService relationship*

In Figure 8-4, both `AbstractAuthenticationProvider` and `UserDetailsService` can be replaced by custom implementations. The UserCache, by default, uses a `NullUserCache` implementation, which is a no-op cache. It can also be replaced easily, but we don't cover that here. The idea of the cache is to keep the `UserDetails` objects cached in case they need to be retrieved again. The authenticate method in the `AbstractUserDetailsAuthenticationProvider` will look first for `UserDetails` in this cache; if the authenticate method finds the `UserDetails in the cache`, it will use that `UserDetails` to try the authentication. If the authenticate method doesn't find `UserDetails in the cache`, it will query the configured `UserDetailsService` for the user and then store it on the cache for subsequent requests.

Listing 8-2. Common Definition of an AuthenticationManager and AuthenticationProvider. To Be Included in applicationContext-security.xml

```
<security:authentication-manager>
    <security:authentication-provider>
        <security:user-service>
            <security:user authorities="ROLE_XX" name="x" password="xx" />
        </security:user-service>
    </security:authentication-provider>
</security:authentication-manager>
```

The first example we'll show is how to create an authentication and login application using Spring Boot, Spring Security, Spring Data, Thymeleaf, and MongoDB.

The very first step is to create the Spring Boot Maven project using the Spring Initializr, which is the quickest way to generate Spring Boot projects. You just need to choose the language, build system, and JVM version for your project, and it will be automatically generated with all the dependencies needed.

Navigate to `https://start.spring.io/` and use the Spring Initializr web-based Spring project generator to create the Spring Boot Maven project named SpringSecurityMongoDB, as shown in Figure 8-5.

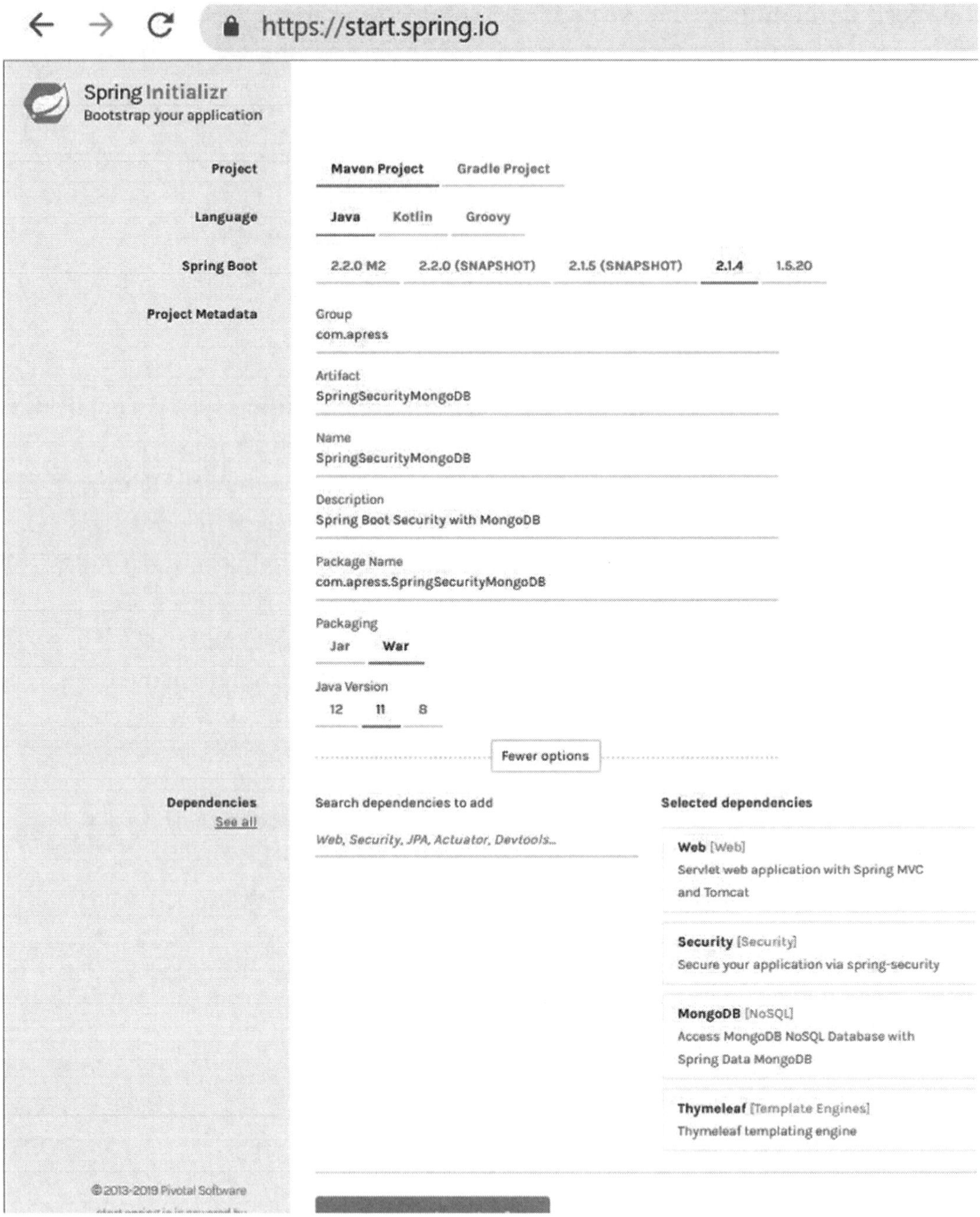

Figure 8-5. *Generate a Maven project using the Initializr web-based Spring project generator*

Select a Java v11 Maven project, using 2.1.4 Spring Boot version, and add the following dependencies: Web, Security, Thymeleaf, and MongoDB.

Fill in all of the required information and then click to generate the project. A project .zip file will be automatically generated. Download and unzip the file on your machine.

When opening the project with IntelliJ IDEA 2019, it will look Figure 8-6.

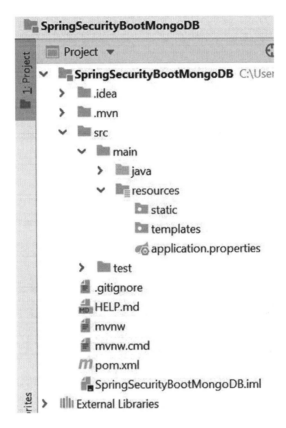

Figure 8-6. *Maven project structure*

The most important dependencies, which will be automatically updated in the `pom.xml` file, are shown in Listing 8-3.

Listing 8-3. Needed Dependencies

```
<dependency>
    <groupId>org.springframework.boot</groupId>
    <artifactId>spring-boot-starter-data-mongodb</artifactId>
</dependency>
```

```xml
<dependency>
    <groupId>org.springframework.boot</groupId>
    <artifactId>spring-boot-starter-security</artifactId>
</dependency>
<dependency>
    <groupId>org.springframework.boot</groupId>
    <artifactId>spring-boot-starter-web</artifactId>
</dependency>
<dependency>
    <groupId>org.springframework.boot</groupId>
    <artifactId>spring-boot-starter-thymeleaf</artifactId>
</dependency>
<dependency>
    <groupId>org.thymeleaf.extras</groupId>
    <artifactId>thymeleaf-extras-springsecurity5</artifactId>
</dependency>
```

The entire generated pom.xml file with the added dependencies is shown in Listing 8-4.

Listing 8-4. Pom.xml File and Dependencies

```xml
<?xml version="1.0" encoding="UTF-8"?>
<project xmlns="http://maven.apache.org/POM/4.0.0"
xmlns:xsi="http://www.w3.org/2001/XMLSchema-instance"
    xsi:schemaLocation="http://maven.apache.org/POM/4.0.0
    http://maven.apache.org/xsd/maven-4.0.0.xsd">
    <modelVersion>4.0.0</modelVersion>
    <parent>
        <groupId>org.springframework.boot</groupId>
        <artifactId>spring-boot-starter-parent</artifactId>
        <version>2.1.4.RELEASE</version>
        <relativePath/> <!-- lookup parent from repository -->
    </parent>
    <groupId>com.apress</groupId>
    <artifactId>SpringSecurityMongoDB</artifactId>
    <version>0.0.1-SNAPSHOT</version>
```

```xml
<name>SpringSecurityMongoDB</name>
<description>Demo project for Spring Boot</description>

<properties>
    <java.version>11</java.version>
</properties>

<dependencies>
        <groupId>org.springframework.boot</groupId>
        <artifactId>spring-boot-starter-data-mongodb</artifactId>
    </dependency>
    <dependency>
        <groupId>org.springframework.boot</groupId>
        <artifactId>spring-boot-starter-security</artifactId>
    </dependency>
    <dependency>
        <groupId>org.springframework.boot</groupId>
        <artifactId>spring-boot-starter-web</artifactId>
    </dependency>
    <dependency>
        <groupId>org.springframework.boot</groupId>
        <artifactId>spring-boot-starter-thymeleaf</artifactId>
    </dependency>
     <dependency>
        <groupId>org.thymeleaf.extras</groupId>
        <artifactId>thymeleaf-extras-springsecurity5</artifactId>
     </dependency>
    <dependency>
        <groupId>org.springframework.boot</groupId>
        <artifactId>spring-boot-starter-test</artifactId>
        <scope>test</scope>
    </dependency>
    <dependency>
        <groupId>org.springframework.security</groupId>
        <artifactId>spring-security-test</artifactId>
        <scope>test</scope>
    </dependency>
```

```
    </dependencies>
    <build>
        <plugins>
            <plugin>
                <groupId>org.springframework.boot</groupId>
                <artifactId>spring-boot-maven-plugin</artifactId>
            </plugin>
        </plugins>
    </build>
</project>
```

You will be using Spring Data to set up and use MongoDB. It is not really required, but because you are working with Spring it seems like a good idea. According to the Spring Data for MongoDB website (https://spring.io/projects/spring-data-mongodb), it "aims to provide a familiar and consistent Spring-based programming model for new datastores while retaining store-specific features and capabilities." So you have a Spring-based application and are using MongoDB, which is a good fit for it. The MongoDB dependency you need to add to the pom.xml file is

```
<dependency>
    <groupId>org.springframework.boot</groupId>
    <artifactId>spring-boot-starter-data-mongodb</artifactId>
</dependency>
```

Note   MongoDB can be used in embedded mode or as an external DB.

In this example, you will use the external installation of MongoDB. You can download it from its official site at www.mongodb.com/download-center.

After you download the .zip file, in our case mongodb-src-r4.0.8.zip, you can simply unpack the file somewhere and it is ready to run. To run the MongoDB server in Linux or Mac, just simply go to the bin directory of the directory you just unpacked and run the file ./mongod. If you're using Windows 10, just download the .zip file, unpack it, go to the installed folder, and run the command mongod to start it. Now MongoDB is started and up and running, as shown in Figure 8-7.

```
Command Prompt - mongo                                                    —   □   ×
C:\>cd C:\Program Files\MongoDB\Server\4.0\bin

C:\Program Files\MongoDB\Server\4.0\bin>mongo
MongoDB shell version v4.0.8
connecting to: mongodb://127.0.0.1:27017/?gssapiServiceName=mongodb
Implicit session: session { "id" : UUID("1ee8cb70-58fa-4fee-b45f-ac60cecee01d") }
MongoDB server version: 4.0.8
Server has startup warnings:
2019-04-12T11:51:45.548+0300 I CONTROL  [initandlisten]
2019-04-12T11:51:45.548+0300 I CONTROL  [initandlisten] ** WARNING: Access control is not enabled for the database.
2019-04-12T11:51:45.548+0300 I CONTROL  [initandlisten] **          Read and write access to data and configuration is u
nrestricted.
2019-04-12T11:51:45.548+0300 I CONTROL  [initandlisten]
---
Enable MongoDB's free cloud-based monitoring service, which will then receive and display
metrics about your deployment (disk utilization, CPU, operation statistics, etc).

The monitoring data will be available on a MongoDB website with a unique URL accessible to you
and anyone you share the URL with. MongoDB may use this information to make product
improvements and to suggest MongoDB products and deployment options to you.

To enable free monitoring, run the following command: db.enableFreeMonitoring()
To permanently disable this reminder, run the following command: db.disableFreeMonitoring()
---

> show dbs
admin   0.000GB
config  0.000GB
local   0.000GB
>
```

Figure 8-7. *MongoDB started*

Note   MongoDB is a very popular document-based database. It is part of many NoSQL solutions that have become so popular in the recent past. It is a very powerful and flexible tool. Its main power comes from the fact (at least from our perspective) that it combines a very scalable storage solution with a very intuitive document model built on top of known technologies (like JSON and JavaScript in the command-line interface). And it does this without forgetting about one of the best things of the SQL world, which is the flexibility given by the ability to execute dynamic queries, allowing you to query your database using very varied criteria and filtering options. This contrasts with, for example, key-value storage solutions that allow searching only by the key. As we said, MongoDB is a document store, where the documents are structured as JSON. MongoDB stores its documents in collections of documents called *collections*. We won't explain MongoDB any further, except for what is needed to create and run the example.

If you are interested in learning more about it, there is a lot of bibliography online that can help you out, starting with the project's website and, in particular, this link to current books on the topic: `https://docs.mongodb.com/?_ga=2.266750797.2128884934.1555058402-165371435.1555058402`.

For this example, you also use the MongoDB Compass tool which is a very easy MongoDB tool that you can download from `www.mongodb.com/download-center/compass?jmp=hero`. The MongoDB Compass tool dashboard is shown in Figure 8-8.

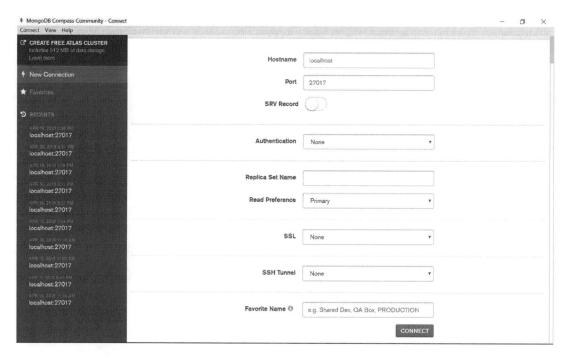

Figure 8-8. *MongoDB Compass tool*

Next, create the MongoDB database named `springsecuritymongodb` and two collections named `users` and `roles` needed for this example by completing the following steps:

1. Go to the directory where MongoDB was installed.

2. Go inside the `bin` folder.

3. Execute the `mongo` command.

4. Execute the commands shown in Figure 8-9.

```
Command Prompt - mongo                                                    —    □    ×
switched to db springsecuritymongodb
> db.createCollection("roles")
{ "ok" : 1 }
> db.roles.insert({"role":"ADMIN","_class":"com.apress.SpringSecurityMongoDB.domain.Role"});
WriteResult({ "nInserted" : 1 })
> db.roles.insert({"role":"USER","_class":"com.apress.SpringSecurityMongoDB.domain.Role"});
WriteResult({ "nInserted" : 1 })
> db.createCollection("users")
{ "ok" : 1 }
> db.users.insert({"email":"admin@admin.com","password":"$2a$10$DxuWIshcpvUAqDWyG.dlG.Ot5HjRlyNA8BJvJg49jEGyCGgCaZ0yu","
role":"ADMIN","roles":[{"$ref":"roles","$id":"5cd15d96333c2d2b2672ada2","$db":"undefined"}],"_class":"com.apress.SpringS
ecurityMongoDB.domain.User"});
WriteResult({ "nInserted" : 1 })
> db.roles.find().pretty()
{
        "_id" : ObjectId("5cd168ea333c2d2b2672adad"),
        "role" : "ADMIN",
        "_class" : "com.apress.SpringSecurityMongoDB.domain.Role"
}
{
        "_id" : ObjectId("5cd168f2333c2d2b2672adae"),
        "role" : "USER",
        "_class" : "com.apress.SpringSecurityMongoDB.domain.Role"
}
> db.users.find().pretty()
{
        "_id" : ObjectId("5cd16904333c2d2b2672adaf"),
        "email" : "admin@admin.com",
        "password" : "$2a$10$DxuWIshcpvUAqDWyG.dlG.Ot5HjRlyNA8BJvJg49jEGyCGgCaZ0yu",
        "role" : "ADMIN",
        "roles" : [
                DBRef("roles", "5cd15d96333c2d2b2672ada2", "undefined")
        ],
        "_class" : "com.apress.SpringSecurityMongoDB.domain.User"
}
>
```

Figure 8-9. *MongoDB looking at the newly created db, collections, users, and roles*

Basically, you need two collections. The roles collection includes just two records to define if the registered user has an ADMIN or USER credential to access the example. You do this by first creating the roles collection and then adding two records:

```
db.createCollection("roles")
db.roles.insert({"role":"ADMIN","_class":"com.apress.SpringSecurityMongoDB.
domain.Role"});
db.roles.insert({"role":"USER","_class":"com.apress.SpringSecurityMongoDB.
domain.Role"});
```

Then you create another collection named users where a new user with credential ADMIN is added:

```
db.createCollection("users")
db.users.insert({"email":"admin@admin.com","password":"$2a$10$qNYHb8JtRrRE
zSFKEwXfA.230HTujndUROqCTPsGP8.FqWetlSqmC","role":"ADMIN","roles":[{"$ref"
:"role","$id":"5cd04193dca5753dec0b07e9","$db":""}],"_class":"com.apress.
SpringSecurityMongoDB.domain.User"});
```

The roles ":[{"$ref":"role","$id":"5cd04193dca5753dec0b07e9","$db":""}]
will link this user admin to the ADMIN role in the roles collection so they can
authenticate as an admin. You have successfully created an admin user to be used as
admin for this example.

The idea is that a certain user is linked to a certain role, ADMIN or USER, and can
access part of the example based on that credential.

Please note that if you don't want to add the users via command lines, you can
also add them into MongoDB using the signup.html page we will explain later in this
chapter.

Now let's create the Spring Boot Security v5 and MongoDB example based on the
project you just created.

Add some properties to the application via the application.properties file:

```
spring.data.mongodb.database=springsecuritymongodb
spring.data.mongodb.host=localhost
spring.data.mongodb.port=27017

spring.freemarker.template-loader-path=/templates
spring.freemarker.expose-request-attributes=true
spring.freemarker.expose-spring-macro-helpers=true

spring.mvc.view.prefix=/resources/templates
spring.mvc.view.suffix=.html
server.error.whitelabel.enabled=false
```

You are telling the application which MongoDB database name to be used, the host,
and port number. Additionally, since you will use Freemarker templates in this example,
you add some info like where the templates are located and if the application can use
request attributes and macro helpers. You also define some Spring MVC view properties
and set server.error.whitelabel.enabled to false so that custom error page can be
created in the example.

Let's start to create the example. All the web resources will be created using the
HTML templates.

In general, the Spring Web Framework is built around the Model-View-Controller
(MVC) pattern, used to easily separate contents in an application. It allow us to use a lot
of different view technologies like

- Java Server Pages (JSP)

- Thymeleaf (to process HTML, XML, text, JavaScript, or CSS)

- FreeMarker (for XML files, configuration files, emails, and other text-based formats)

- Groovy (for generating any text format)

- Jade4j (for generating HTML files)

In this example, you will use Thymeleaf to process HTML files. Create the first HTML file named welcome.html, as shown in Listing 8-5.

Listing 8-5. welcome.html

```
<!DOCTYPE html>
<html>
    <head>
        <title>Spring Boot Security 5 and MongoDB Example</title>
    </head>
    <body>
            <h1>Welcome to Spring Boot Security 5 and MongoDB Example!</h1>
        <p>Please <a href="/login">login.</a></p>
    </body>
</html>
```

The next step is to create the example Java classes needed.

Your Spring Boot Security and MongoDB example will contain the following Java packages:

- configuration

- controller

- domain

- repositories

- service

You will now create the most important Java class of the example, SpringSecurityConfiguration, which is shown in Listing 8-6.

303

Listing 8-6. SpringSecurityConfiguration Java Class

```java
package com.apress.SpringSecurityMongoDB.configuration;

import com.apress.SpringSecurityMongoDB.service.CustomUserDetailsService;
import org.springframework.beans.factory.annotation.Autowired;
import org.springframework.context.annotation.Bean;
import org.springframework.context.annotation.Configuration;
import org.springframework.security.config.annotation.authentication.
builders.AuthenticationManagerBuilder;
import org.springframework.security.config.annotation.web.builders.
HttpSecurity;
import org.springframework.security.config.annotation.web.builders.
WebSecurity;
import org.springframework.security.config.annotation.web.configuration.
EnableWebSecurity;
import org.springframework.security.config.annotation.web.configuration.
WebSecurityConfigurerAdapter;
import org.springframework.security.core.userdetails.UserDetailsService;
import org.springframework.security.crypto.bcrypt.BCryptPasswordEncoder;
import org.springframework.security.web.util.matcher.AntPathRequestMatcher;

@Configuration
@EnableWebSecurity
public class SpringSecurityConfiguration extends
WebSecurityConfigurerAdapter {

    @Autowired
    private BCryptPasswordEncoder bCryptPasswordEncoder;

    @Autowired
    CustomizeAuthenticationSuccessHandler customizeAuthentication
    SuccessHandler;

    @Bean
    public UserDetailsService mongoUserDetails() {
        return new CustomUserDetailsService();
    }
```

```
    @Override
    protected void configure(AuthenticationManagerBuilder auth) throws
    Exception {
        UserDetailsService userDetailsService = mongoUserDetails();
        auth
                .userDetailsService(userDetailsService)
                .passwordEncoder(bCryptPasswordEncoder);

    }

    @Override
    protected void configure(HttpSecurity http) throws Exception {
        http
                .authorizeRequests()
                .antMatchers("/").permitAll()
                .antMatchers("/login").permitAll()
                .antMatchers("/signup").permitAll()
.antMatchers("/user/**").hasAnyAuthority("USER").anyRequest().authenticated()
.antMatchers("/admin/**").hasAnyAuthority("ADMIN").anyRequest()

.authenticated().and().formLogin().successHandler(customizeAuthenticationSu
ccessHandler)
                .loginPage("/login").failureUrl("/login?error=true")
                .usernameParameter("email")
                .passwordParameter("password")
                .and().logout()
                .logoutRequestMatcher(new AntPathRequestMatcher("/logout"))
.logoutSuccessUrl("/").and().exceptionHandling().accessDeniedPage("/
forbidden");
    }

    @Override
    public void configure(WebSecurity web) throws Exception {
        web
                .ignoring()
                .antMatchers("/resources/**");
    }
```

```
    @Bean
    public BCryptPasswordEncoder passwordEncoder() {
        BCryptPasswordEncoder bCryptPasswordEncoder = new
        BCryptPasswordEncoder();
        return bCryptPasswordEncoder;
    }
}
```

The application will include

- `BCryptPasswordEncoder`: To deal with the BCrypt password

- `CustomizeAuthenticationSuccessHandler`: For the custom login
  success handler

- `Configure(HttpSecurity http)`: All the info about what URLs to
  access and how. For instance, user and admin URLs will require
  `hasAnyAuthority("USER")` and `hasAnyAuthority("ADMIN")`.

- `Configure(WebSecurity web)`: The resources folder utilized for this
  example

The next Java class is `LoginController`. In order to start running the `welcome.html`
template you need to add the code in Listing 8-7.

Listing 8-7. LoginController Java Class

```
@RequestMapping(value = {"/","/welcome"}, method = RequestMethod.GET)
    public ModelAndView home() {
        ModelAndView modelAndView = new ModelAndView();
        modelAndView.setViewName("welcome");
        return modelAndView;
    }
```

The application is ready to be tested as simple welcome web page.

You can build the project using the Spring Boot configuration and run it on top of the
Tomcat Server v9, as shown in Figures 8-10 and 8-11.

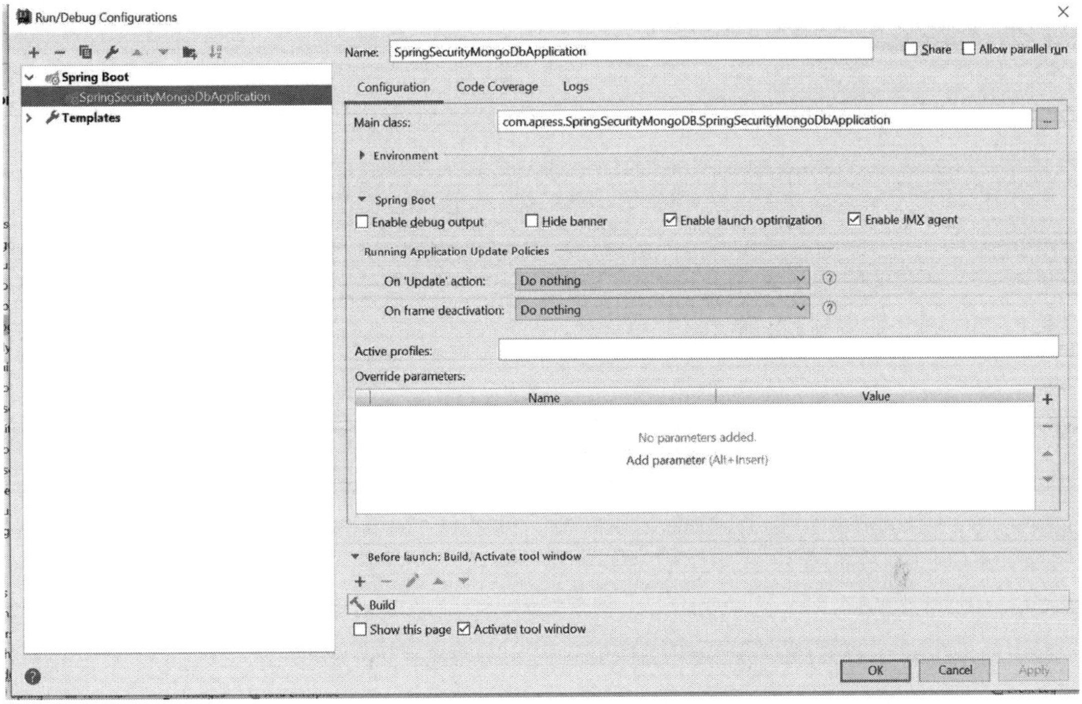

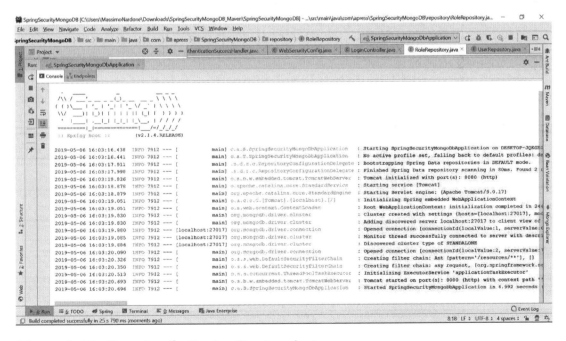

Figure 8-10. *Configure the running steps of your first Maven project*

Figure 8-11. *Running the Spring Boot project*

If you visit `http://localhost:8080/`, you will see the `welcome.html` page shown in Figure 8-12.

Welcome to Spring Boot Security 5 and MongoDB Example!

Please login.

Figure 8-12. *The welcome.html page*

You now have your first HTML file up and running. Now you can start building the rest of the example using MongoDB and Spring Security v5.

The next step is to create a Java class named `CustomizeAuthenticationSuccessHandler`, which will be used to handle the custom login success page; see Listing 8-8.

Listing 8-8. CustomizeAuthenticationSuccessHandler Java Class

```
package com.apress.SpringSecurityMongoDB.configuration;

import org.springframework.security.core.Authentication;
import org.springframework.security.core.GrantedAuthority;
import org.springframework.security.web.authentication.
AuthenticationSuccessHandler;
import org.springframework.stereotype.Component;

import javax.servlet.ServletException;
import javax.servlet.http.HttpServletRequest;
import javax.servlet.http.HttpServletResponse;
import java.io.IOException;

@Component
public class CustomizeAuthenticationSuccessHandler implements
AuthenticationSuccessHandler {

    @Override
    public void onAuthenticationSuccess(HttpServletRequest request,
                                        HttpServletResponse response,
                                        Authentication authentication)
```

```
        throws IOException, ServletException {
    response.setStatus(HttpServletResponse.SC_OK);

    for (GrantedAuthority auth : authentication.getAuthorities()) {
        if ("ADMIN".equals(auth.getAuthority())) {
            response.sendRedirect("/admin");
        }
        if ("USER".equals(auth.getAuthority())) {
            response.sendRedirect("/user");
        }
    }
}

}
```

This Java class simply checks if the authentication.getAuthorities of the user trying to login is equal to ADMIN and if so will redirect to the /admin page, or if it's USER and thus should redirect to the /user web page.

It was configured in the SpringSecurityConfiguration Java class via the configuration .authenticated().and().formLogin().successHandler(**customizeAuth enticationSuccessHandler**).

Now create the simple login.html page shown in Listing 8-9.

Listing 8-9. login.html Page

```
<!DOCTYPE html>
<html xmlns="http://www.w3.org/1999/xhtml"
xmlns:th="http://www.thymeleaf.org">
    <head>
        <title>Spinrg Boot Security 5 and MongoDB</title>
    </head>
    <body>
    <form th:action="@{/login}" method="post">
        <h1>Please login as user or admin:</h1>
        <div th:if="${param.error}">
            Invalid email and password.
        </div>
```

```html
        <label for="inputEmail">Email Address:</label>
        <input type="email" name="email" id="inputEmail"
        placeholder="Email" required="" /></br>
        <label for="inputPassword">Password:</label>
        <input type="password" name="password" id="inputPassword"
        placeholder="Password" required="" /><br>
        <button type="submit">Login</button></br></br>
    </form>
    <form th:action="@{/signup}" method="get">
        <button type="Submit">Signup as a new user</button>
    </form>
    </div>
    </body>
</html>
```

This login.html page will do three things:

1. Send the email address and password to the LoginController Java class as an HTTP POST method.

2. Check if the email and password are typed correctly.

3. Provide the signup option to add a new user to the MongoDB database.

To check if the credentials of the user are valid and where they should be redirected, create the Java Controller class named LoginController, as shown in Listing 8-10.

Listing 8-10. LoginController Java Class

```java
package com.apress.SpringSecurityMongoDB.controller;

import com.apress.SpringSecurityMongoDB.domain.User;
import com.apress.SpringSecurityMongoDB.service.CustomUserDetailsService;
import org.springframework.beans.factory.annotation.Autowired;
import org.springframework.security.core.Authentication;
import org.springframework.security.core.context.SecurityContextHolder;
import org.springframework.stereotype.Controller;
import org.springframework.validation.BindingResult;
import org.springframework.web.bind.annotation.RequestMapping;
```

```java
import org.springframework.web.bind.annotation.RequestMethod;
import org.springframework.web.servlet.ModelAndView;
import javax.validation.Valid;

@Controller
public class LoginController {

    @Autowired
    private CustomUserDetailsService userService;

    @RequestMapping(value = "/login", method = RequestMethod.GET)
    public ModelAndView login() {
        ModelAndView modelAndView = new ModelAndView();
        modelAndView.setViewName("login");
        return modelAndView;
    }

    @RequestMapping(value = "/signup", method = RequestMethod.GET)
    public ModelAndView signup() {
        ModelAndView modelAndView = new ModelAndView();
        User user = new User();
        modelAndView.addObject("user", user);
        modelAndView.setViewName("signup");
        return modelAndView;
    }

    @RequestMapping(value = "/signup", method = RequestMethod.POST)
    public ModelAndView createNewUser(@Valid User user, BindingResult
    bindingResult) {
        ModelAndView modelAndView = new ModelAndView();
        User userExists = userService.findUserByEmail(user.getEmail());
        if (userExists != null) {
            modelAndView.addObject("message", "There is already a user
            registered with the username provided");
            bindingResult
                    .rejectValue("email", "error.user",
                            "There is already a user registered with the
                            username provided");
        }
```

311

```java
        if (bindingResult.hasErrors()) {
            modelAndView.setViewName("signup");
        } else {
            userService.saveUser(user);
            modelAndView.addObject("successMessage", "User has been
            registered successfully");
            modelAndView.addObject("user", new User());
            modelAndView.setViewName("login");

        }
        return modelAndView;
    }

    @RequestMapping(value = "/admin", method = RequestMethod.GET)
    public ModelAndView admin() {
        ModelAndView modelAndView = new ModelAndView();
        Authentication auth = SecurityContextHolder.getContext().
        getAuthentication();
        User user = userService.findUserByEmail(auth.getName());
        modelAndView.addObject("currentUser", auth.getName());
        modelAndView.addObject("role", user.getRole());
        modelAndView.addObject("adminMessage", "Content Available Only for
        Authenticated Admins!");
        modelAndView.setViewName("admin");
        return modelAndView;
    }

    @RequestMapping(value = "/user", method = RequestMethod.GET)
    public ModelAndView user() {
        ModelAndView modelAndView = new ModelAndView();
        Authentication auth = SecurityContextHolder.getContext().
        getAuthentication();
        User user = userService.findUserByEmail(auth.getName());
        modelAndView.addObject("currentUser", auth.getName());
        modelAndView.addObject("role", user.getRole());
        modelAndView.addObject("userMessage", "Content Available Only for
        Authenticated Users!");
```

```
        modelAndView.setViewName("user");
        return modelAndView;
    }

    @RequestMapping(value = {"/","/welcome"}, method = RequestMethod.GET)
    public ModelAndView home() {
        ModelAndView modelAndView = new ModelAndView();
        modelAndView.setViewName("welcome");
        return modelAndView;
    }

    @RequestMapping(value = {"/forbidden"}, method = RequestMethod.GET)
    public ModelAndView forbidden() {
        ModelAndView modelAndView = new ModelAndView();
        modelAndView.setViewName("forbidden");
        return modelAndView;
    }

}
```

This Java class works as page controller that, based on the URL requested, will redirect to a page like welcome, forbidden, etc. When requesting the /admin or /user URL, the Java class will verify if the user credentials are ok to redirect to the preferred page. The modelAndView.addObject is used to collect information and messages to be displayed on the HTML pages.

All the page errors will be managed via the Java Controller class MyErrorController shown in Listing 8-11.

Listing 8-11. MyErrorController Java Class

```
package com.apress.SpringSecurityMongoDB.controller;

import org.springframework.boot.web.servlet.error.ErrorController;
import org.springframework.stereotype.Controller;
import org.springframework.web.bind.annotation.GetMapping;

import javax.servlet.http.HttpServletRequest;
import org.springframework.web.servlet.ModelAndView;
```

```java
@Controller
public class MyErrorController implements ErrorController {

    public MyErrorController() {}

    @GetMapping(value = "/error")
    public ModelAndView renderErrorPage(HttpServletRequest httpRequest) {

        ModelAndView errorPage = new ModelAndView("errorPage");
        String errorMsg = "";
        int httpErrorCode = getErrorCode(httpRequest);

        switch (httpErrorCode) {
            case 400: {
                errorMsg = "Http Error Code: 400. Bad Request";
                break;
            }
            case 401: {
                errorMsg = "Http Error Code: 401. Unauthorized";
                break;
            }
            case 404: {
                errorMsg = "Http Error Code: 404. Resource not found";
                break;
            }
            case 500: {
                errorMsg = "Http Error Code: 500. Internal Server Error";
                break;
            }
        }
        errorPage.addObject("errorMsg", errorMsg);
        return errorPage;
    }

    private int getErrorCode(HttpServletRequest httpRequest) {
        return (Integer) httpRequest
                .getAttribute("javax.servlet.error.status_code");
    }
```

```
@Override
public String getErrorPath() {
    return "/error";
}

}
```

This Java class in case of a whitelabel error will redirect to the `errorPage.html` page, which will display the error message received from the Java class. Notice that this will work when adding the following line in the `application.properties`:

```
server.error.whitelabel.enabled=false
```

The `errorPage.html` page looks like Listing 8-12.

Listing 8-12. errorPage.html Web Page

```
<!DOCTYPE html>
<html xmlns:th="http://www.thymeleaf.org">
<head>
    <title>Security with Spring Boot</title>
</head>
<body>
<h1>Error on page!</h1>
<div th:text="${errorMsg}"></div><br>
<a style="color: blue" th:href="@{/}">Home</a>
</body>
</html>
```

The `errorpage.html` page is shown in Figure 8-13.

Figure 8-13. *errorPage.html page*

If a forbidden page is requested, the `LoginController` Java class will redirect to the `forbidden.html` page, which is shown in Listing 8-13. This is configured in the `SpringSecurityConfiguration` Java class as follow:

```
exceptionHandling().accessDeniedPage("/forbidden");
```

Listing 8-13. forbidden.html Web Page

```
<!DOCTYPE html>
<html xmlns="http://www.w3.org/1999/xhtml"
      xmlns:th="http://www.thymeleaf.org"
      xmlns:sec="http://www.thymeleaf.org/thymeleaf-extras-springsecurity">
<head>
    <title>Security with Spring Boot</title>
</head>
<body>
<h1>Error on page!</h1>
Errortype: <div th:text="${currentError}"></div>
<a style="color: blue" th:href="@{/}">Home</a>
</body>
</html>
```

The `forbidden.html` page is shown in Figure 8-14.

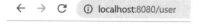

Access is Denied!

Home

Figure 8-14. *The forbidden.html page*

The next step is to create your needed models, named `User` and `Role`, which will store the MongoDB collections. First, create the `User` model shown in Listing 8-14.

Listing 8-14. The User Java Class

```java
package com.apress.SpringSecurityMongoDB.domain;

import org.springframework.data.annotation.Id;
import org.springframework.data.mongodb.core.index.IndexDirection;
import org.springframework.data.mongodb.core.index.Indexed;
import org.springframework.data.mongodb.core.mapping.DBRef;
import org.springframework.data.mongodb.core.mapping.Document;

import java.util.Set;

@Document(collection = "users")
public class User {

    @Id
    private String id;
    @Indexed(unique = true, direction = IndexDirection.DESCENDING)
    private String email;
    private String password;
    private String role;

    @DBRef
    private Set<Role> roles;

    public String getId() {
        return id;
    }

    public void setId(String id) {
        this.id = id;
    }

    public String getEmail() {
        return email;
    }

    public void setEmail(String email) {
        this.email = email;
    }
```

```java
    public String getPassword() {
        return password;
    }

    public void setPassword(String password) {
        this.password = password;
    }

    public String getRole() {
        return role;
    }

    public void setRole(String role) {
        this.role = role;
    }

    public Set<Role> getRoles() {
        return roles;
    }

    public void setRoles(Set<Role> roles) {
        this.roles = roles;
    }

    @Override
    public String toString() {
        return "User{" +
                "id=" + id +
                ", email='" + email.replaceFirst("@.*", "@***") +
                ", password='" + password.substring(0, 10) +
                ", role=" + role +
                '}';
    }

}
```

Basically this User Java class will manage getting and adding user data from and to the MongodDB. For instance, for an email address, the following code will get the email and set the email value to the MongoDB database:

```java
public String getEmail() {
    return email;
}

public void setEmail(String email) {
    this.email = email;
}
```

You do the same to create the Role model, shown in Listing 8-15.

Listing 8-15. The Role Java Class

```java
package com.apress.SpringSecurityMongoDB.domain;

import org.springframework.data.annotation.Id;
import org.springframework.data.mongodb.core.index.IndexDirection;
import org.springframework.data.mongodb.core.index.Indexed;
import org.springframework.data.mongodb.core.mapping.Document;

@Document(collection = "roles")
public class Role {

    @Id
    private String id;
    @Indexed(unique = true, direction = IndexDirection.DESCENDING)

    private String role;

    public String getId() {
        return id;
    }

    public void setId(String id) {
        this.id = id;
    }
```

```java
    public String getRole() {
        return role;
    }

    public void setRole(String role) {
        this.role = role;
    }

}
```

Again, like for the User Java class, get and set will be used to get data and set data from and to the MongoDB database.

The next step is to create two Java repository interfaces, one for User and one for Role, to find email and role values from the database. They are shown in Listings 8-16 and 8-17.

Listing 8-16. The User Java Interface

```java
package com.apress.SpringSecurityMongoDB.repository;

import com.apress.SpringSecurityMongoDB.domain.User;
import org.springframework.data.mongodb.repository.MongoRepository;

public interface UserRepository extends MongoRepository<User, String> {

    User findByEmail(String email);

}
```

Listing 8-17. The Role Java Interface

```java
package com.apress.SpringSecurityMongoDB.repository;

import com.apress.SpringSecurityMongoDB.domain.Role;
import org.springframework.data.mongodb.repository.MongoRepository;

public interface RoleRepository extends MongoRepository<Role, String> {

    Role findByRole(String role);
}
```

The next step is to create the SpringSecurityMongoDbApplication, which is used
to set the new registered user the credential value of ADMIN or USER, as shown in
Listing 8-18.

Listing 8-18.   The login.html Page

```java
package com.apress.SpringSecurityMongoDB;

import com.apress.SpringSecurityMongoDB.domain.Role;
import com.apress.SpringSecurityMongoDB.repository.RoleRepository;
import org.springframework.boot.CommandLineRunner;
import org.springframework.boot.SpringApplication;
import org.springframework.boot.autoconfigure.SpringBootApplication;
import org.springframework.context.annotation.Bean;

@SpringBootApplication
public class SpringSecurityMongoDbApplication {

    public static void main(String[] args) {
        SpringApplication.run(SpringSecurityMongoDbApplication.class, args);
    }

    @Bean
    CommandLineRunner init(RoleRepository roleRepository) {

        return args -> {

            Role adminRole = roleRepository.findByRole("ADMIN");
            if (adminRole == null) {
                Role newAdminRole = new Role();
                newAdminRole.setRole("ADMIN");
                roleRepository.save(newAdminRole);
            }

            Role userRole = roleRepository.findByRole("USER");
            if (userRole == null) {
                Role newUserRole = new Role();
                newUserRole.setRole("USER");
                roleRepository.save(newUserRole);
            }
```

```
        };
    }
}
```

The SpringSecurityMongoDbApplication class receives the user credential value from the login.html page and creates and sets it for the user via the following lines:

For Role:

```
            Role newUserRole = new Role();
            newUserRole.setRole("USER");
            roleRepository.save(newUserRole);
```

For User:

```
            Role newAdminRole = new Role();
            newAdminRole.setRole("ADMIN");
            roleRepository.save(newAdminRole);
```

The next Java class is CustomUserDetailsService, which is a Java service class needed for user functions to implement the Spring Security User Details Service. It is shown in Listing 8-19.

Listing 8-19. The CustomUserDetailsService Java Class

```
package com.apress.SpringSecurityMongoDB.service;

import com.apress.SpringSecurityMongoDB.domain.Role;
import com.apress.SpringSecurityMongoDB.domain.User;
import com.apress.SpringSecurityMongoDB.repository.RoleRepository;
import com.apress.SpringSecurityMongoDB.repository.UserRepository;
import org.springframework.beans.factory.annotation.Autowired;
import org.springframework.security.core.GrantedAuthority;
import org.springframework.security.core.authority.SimpleGrantedAuthority;
import org.springframework.security.core.userdetails.UserDetails;
import org.springframework.security.core.userdetails.UserDetailsService;
import org.springframework.security.core.userdetails.
UsernameNotFoundException;
import org.springframework.security.crypto.bcrypt.BCryptPasswordEncoder;
import org.springframework.stereotype.Service;
```

```java
import java.util.*;

@Service
public class CustomUserDetailsService implements UserDetailsService {

    @Autowired
    private UserRepository userRepository;
    @Autowired
    private RoleRepository roleRepository;
    @Autowired
    private BCryptPasswordEncoder bCryptPasswordEncoder;

    public User findUserByEmail(String email) {
        return userRepository.findByEmail(email);
    }

    public void saveUser(User user) {
        user.setPassword(bCryptPasswordEncoder.encode(user.getPassword()));
        String getroletype;
        getroletype = user.getRole();
        Role userRole = roleRepository.findByRole(getroletype);
        user.setRoles(new HashSet<>(Arrays.asList(userRole)));
        userRepository.save(user);
    }

    @Override
    public UserDetails loadUserByUsername(String email) throws
    UsernameNotFoundException {

        User user = userRepository.findByEmail(email);
        if(user != null) {
            List<GrantedAuthority> authorities = getUserAuthority(user.
            getRoles());
            return buildUserForAuthentication(user, authorities);
        } else {
            throw new UsernameNotFoundException("username not found");
        }
    }
```

```java
    private List<GrantedAuthority> getUserAuthority(Set<Role> userRoles) {
        Set<GrantedAuthority> roles = new HashSet<>();
        userRoles.forEach((role) -> {
            roles.add(new SimpleGrantedAuthority(role.getRole()));
        });

        List<GrantedAuthority> grantedAuthorities = new ArrayList<>(roles);
        return grantedAuthorities;
    }

    private UserDetails buildUserForAuthentication(User user,
    List<GrantedAuthority> authorities) {
        return new org.springframework.security.core.userdetails.User(user.
        getEmail(), user.getPassword(), authorities);
    }
}
```

This Java class is used when you need to

- Load user information like an email address or the user
  GrantedAuthority list via findUserByEmail() and
  loadUserByUsername()

- Save a new user via saveUser()

- Get a user authority via getUserAuthority()

- Build a user for authentication via buildUserForAuthentication()

Note that you return a new org.springframework.security.core.userdetails.
User() to store the user authentication credential including email, password, and
authorities.

Now finally you can create your login.html page; see Listing 8-20.

Listing 8-20. The login.html Page

```html
<!DOCTYPE html>
<html xmlns="http://www.w3.org/1999/xhtml" xmlns:th="http://www.thymeleaf.org">
<head>
    <title>Spinrg Boot Security 5 and MongoDB</title>
</head>
```

```html
<body>
<form th:action="@{/login}" method="post">
    <h1>Please login as user or admin:</h1>
    <div th:if="${param.error}">
        Invalid email or password.
    </div>
    <label for="inputEmail">Email Address:</label>
    <input type="email" name="email" id="inputEmail" placeholder="Email"
    required="" /></br>
    <label for="inputPassword">Password:</label>
    <input type="password" name="password" id="inputPassword"
    placeholder="Password" required="" /><br>
    <button type="submit">Login</button></br></br>
</form>
<form th:action="@{/signup}" method="get">
    <button type="Submit">Signup as a new user</button>
</form>
</div>
</body>
</html>
```

The login.html page collects the info needed to login such as email and password and sends it via the POST method to the /login URL, which via the LoginController Java class will be validated using the following lines:

```java
@RequestMapping(value = "/login", method = RequestMethod.GET)
public ModelAndView login() {
ModelAndView modelAndView = new ModelAndView();
modelAndView.setViewName("login");
return modelAndView;
```

The login.hmtl page is shown in Figure 8-15.

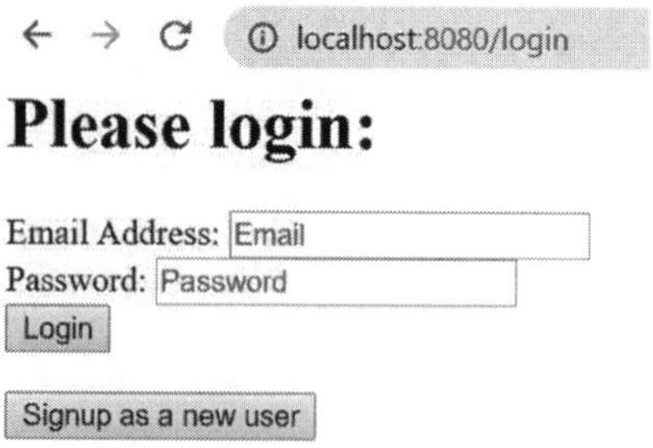

Figure 8-15. *The login.html page*

If the email or password values are invalid, the error message "Invalid email and password" will be displayed as shown in Figure 8-16.

Figure 8-16. *Invalid email and password*

If the user is authenticated as User, she will be redirected to the user.html page, which is shown in Listing 8-21.

Listing 8-21. The user.html Page

```
<!DOCTYPE html>
<html xmlns:th="http://www.thymeleaf.org"
     xmlns:sec="http://www.thymeleaf.org/extras/spring-security">

<html>
    <head>
        <title>Spring Security 5 and MongoDB.</title>
    </head>
    <body>
            <h1>Welcome [[${#httpServletRequest.remoteUser}]]!</h1>
            <h2>You are succesfully logged as an authenticated User!</h2>
```

```
    <div sec:authorize="isAuthenticated()">
        This content is only shown to authenticated users.
    </div>

    <div sec:authorize="hasAnyAuthority('USER')">
        This content is only shown to users with authority "USER".
    </div>

</br>
    <form action="/logout" method="post">
        <input type="submit" value="Sign Out"/>
    </form>

    </body>
</html>
```

Note that you used sec:authorize="isAuthenticated()" and sec:authorize="has
AnyAuthority('USER')" via Thymeleaf to determine if the user is actually authenticated
and if she has USER as her authority.

The user.html page is shown in Figure 8-17.

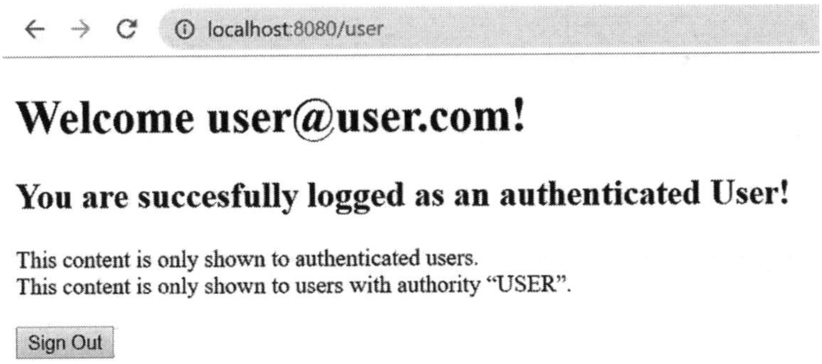

← → C ① localhost:8080/user

Welcome user@user.com!

You are succesfully logged as an authenticated User!

This content is only shown to authenticated users.
This content is only shown to users with authority "USER".

Sign Out

Figure 8-17. *The user.html page*

Click the Sign Out button to log out.

If the user is authenticated as ADMIN, she will be redirected to the admin.html page,
which is shown in Listing 8-22.

Listing 8-22. The admin.html Page

```
<!DOCTYPE html>
<html xmlns:th="http://www.thymeleaf.org"
      xmlns:sec="http://www.thymeleaf.org/extras/spring-security">

<html>
    <head>
        <title>Spring Security 5 and MongoDB.</title>
    </head>
    <body>
            <h1>Welcome [[${#httpServletRequest.remoteUser}]]!</h1>
            <h2>You are succesfully logged as an Admin!</h2>

            <div sec:authorize="isAuthenticated()">
                N1: This content is only shown to authenticated users.
            </div>
            <div sec:authorize="hasAnyAuthority('ADMIN')">
                N2: This content is only shown to administrators.
            </div>

            <p>Click <a href="/allusers">here</a> to show all registered
            users.</p>

    </br>
            <form action="/logout" method="post">
                <input type="submit" value="Sign Out"/>
            </form>

    </body>
</html>
```

As you did for the user.html page, here in the admin.html page you use sec:auth
orize="isAuthenticated()" and sec:authorize="hasAnyAuthority('ADMIN')" via
Thymeleaf to determine if the user is actually authenticated and if she has ADMIN as her
authority.

The admin.html page is shown in Figure 8-18.

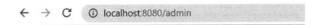

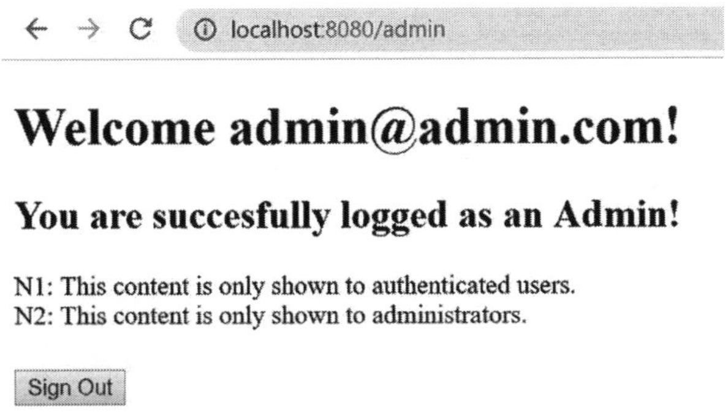

Welcome admin@admin.com!

You are succesfully logged as an Admin!

N1: This content is only shown to authenticated users.
N2: This content is only shown to administrators.

Sign Out

Figure 8-18. *The admin.html page*

Click the Sign Out button to log out.

Now if you wish to create a new user in the MongoDB, you select click the "Signup as a new user" button on the login.html page and send via the HTTP GET method to the /signup page which via the LoginController Java class will be validated using the following lines:

```
@RequestMapping(value = "/signup", method = RequestMethod.GET)
public ModelAndView signup() {
    ModelAndView modelAndView = new ModelAndView();
    User user = new User();
    modelAndView.addObject("user", user);
    modelAndView.setViewName("signup");
    return modelAndView;
}
```

If you want to add a new user in the MongoDB database, you invoke the singup.html page shown in Listing 8-23.

Listing 8-23. The signup.html Page

```
<!DOCTYPE html>
<html xmlns="http://www.w3.org/1999/xhtml"
xmlns:th="http://www.thymeleaf.org">
<head>
```

```html
<html>
    <head>
        <title>Spring Boot Security 5 and MongoDB Example</title>
    </head>
    <body>
            <form class="form-signin" action="/signup" method="post">
                <h1>Add a new user to the MongoDB.</h1></br>

                <label>Email Address:</label>
                <input type="email" name="email" id="inputEmail"
                placeholder="Emailaddress" required="" /></br>
                <label for="inputPassword" >Password:</label>
                <input type="password" name="password" id="inputPassword"
                placeholder="Password" required="" /></br>

                <label>Role:</label>
                <select name="role" id="role" required>
                    <option value="USER">USER</option>
                    <option value="ADMIN">ADMIN</option>
                </select>
                </br>
                <button class="btn btn-lg btn-primary btn-block"
                type="submit">Add new user</button>
            </form>
    </body>
</html>
```

Signup.hmtl will trigger the LoginController for the /signup HTTP POST method as shown here:

```java
@RequestMapping(value = "/signup", method = RequestMethod.POST)
public ModelAndView createNewUser(@Valid User user, BindingResult
bindingResult) {
    ModelAndView modelAndView = new ModelAndView();
    User userExists = userService.findUserByEmail(user.getEmail());
    if (userExists != null) {
        modelAndView.addObject("message", "Username provided is already
        registered in the db! ");
```

```
        bindingResult
                .rejectValue("email", "error.user",
                        "Username provided is already registered in
                        the db!");
    }
    if (bindingResult.hasErrors()) {
        modelAndView.setViewName("signup");
    } else {
        userService.saveUser(user);
        modelAndView.addObject("successMessage", "New user has been
        registered successfully");
        modelAndView.addObject("user", new User());
        modelAndView.setViewName("login");

    }
    return modelAndView;
}
```

In this case, the `LoginController` class using the `/signup` HTTP POST method will

- Check if the user email address is already registered in the MongoDB database, display the message "Username provided is already registered in the db!", and redirect again to `/signup`.

- Or trigger the creation of a new user and display the message "New user has been registered successfully".

The `signup.html` page is shown in Figure 8-19.

Figure 8-19. The signup.html page

Your final and complete project will look like Figure 8-20.

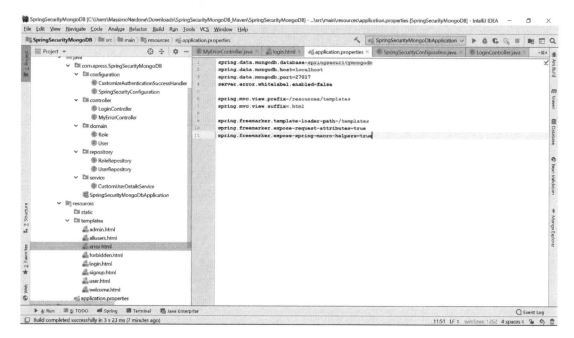

Figure 8-20. *Complete project overview*

You completed your example but we'll describe better password encryption and error handling next.

Password Encryption

One thing you might have noticed in this example and all the previous examples is that you are storing and retrieving passwords in plain text. Spring Security offers an abstraction to encrypt passwords in the form of the interface that was in Spring Security v4 as `org.springframework.security.authentication.encoding.PasswordEncoder` but changed in Spring Security v5 to `org.springframework.security.crypto.password.PasswordEncoder` in the core framework.

Since Spring Security v5 it was declared the PasswordEncoder in `org.springframework.security.authentication.encoding` was deprecated so this interface was removed since it was not designed for a randomly generated salt.

Also, Spring Security v5 changed how encoded passwords are handled since, before v5, every application could only work with one password encoding algorithm.

Before Spring Security v5, the default `PasswordEncoder` was `NoOpPasswordEncoder` which required plain text passwords. `PasswordEncoder` is now replaced with `BCryptPasswordEncoder`.

Then of course we could face right away problems like, how do we deal with old applications using old password encodings that cannot easily migrate? And what happens when the password storage changes again?

Since Spring Security v5, a concept of password encoding delegation named `DelegatingPasswordEncoder` was introduced, which generally allow us to use different encodings for different passwords.

DelegatingPasswordEncoder works so that any password is encoded using the current password storage recommendations, allows for validating passwords in modern and legacy formats, and allows for upgrading the encoding in the future.

Spring Security v5 automatically recognizes the algorithm using an identifier prefixing the encoded password. The general format for a password is *{id}* *encodedPassword.* Here are some examples of encoded password:

```
{noop}password
{bcrypt}$1c$23$TeLobXCxerA5EDFqwKJFn.KUT2VCdsaAwD67WETa9A.7Hrt123Kea
{sha256}123ghjss67239nsgewt6772ghsjd22789sa2jkalsaldsdj72349378sadsajdsljd
32874732salkdf
{pbkdf2}hdsfjhdsfurehyuhhfsjdhfhfkjhdsfkjhdfkjshdfösakfucxvhkjvhcoiweshfjd
sfewtsrewrwyir
{scrypt}?shdf4Md3234hlkf843Lhhdsjfsd7982374293hsdkjfshdfh91273fgsjjdhfgssj
fdggfsdllflsdlfsdfsdUp4of4g24hHnazw==$0AOec05+bXxvuu/1qZ6NUOc/9bdYSrN1oD?
```

As you saw for the bcrypt example, the `{bcrypt}` prefix was used to tell Spring Security to use the bcrypt password encoder. In case of a password hash with no prefix, the delegation process uses a default encoder, which is by default the `StandardPasswordEncoder`.

So the password will have `PasswordEncoder id = bcrypt` and `encodedPassword = $1c$23$TeLobXCxerA5EDFqwKJFn.KUT2VCdsaAwD67WETa9A.7Hrt123Kea` so when matching it would delegate to `BCryptPasswordEncoder`.

Note that you can easily construct an instance of `DelegatingPasswordEncoder` using `PasswordEncoderFactories` like this:

```
PasswordEncoder passwordEncoder = PasswordEncoderFactories.
createDelegatingPasswordEncoder();
```

So, how does the password matching work? It works based upon the {id} and the mapping of the id to the PasswordEncoder provided in the constructor, as you saw before.

In general, by default, the result of invoking matches(CharSequence, String) with a password and an id that is not mapped (including a null id) will trigger the IllegalArgumentException. You can customize this behavior by using Delegating PasswordEncoder.setDefaultPasswordEncoderForMatches(PasswordEncoder).

Finally, the Java configuration for BCrypt could be like this:

```
import org.springframework.security.crypto.bcrypt.BCryptPasswordEncoder;
@Bean
    public BCryptPasswordEncoder passwordEncoder() {
        BCryptPasswordEncoder bCryptPasswordEncoder = new
        BCryptPasswordEncoder();
        return bCryptPasswordEncoder;
    }
```

Handling Errors and Entry Points

Spring Security has a very nice error-handling mechanism built in. It offers a comprehensive set of exceptions that map to the most common cases of security errors you could expect to have in a system. Continuing with Spring Security's great single-responsibility architecture, the handling of error conditions is mostly encapsulated in one single class. This class is (and you have studied it before) the org.springframework. security.web.access.ExceptionTranslationFilter, and it basically deals with two types of exceptions: AccessDeniedException and AuthenticationException. If any other exception is caught by this filter, it will simply rethrow it as a RuntimeException.

Spring Security offers a couple of extension points you can use to plug in functionality in the form of a custom entry point and a custom access-denied handler. Basically, what happens is that when an AuthenticationException is caught by the filter, an AuthenticationEntryPoint's "commence" method is called with the HTTP request, the HTTP response, and the exception. The particular AuthenticationEntryPoint implementation that is configured in the application can decide what to do with the exception and, more importantly, what to do with the HTTP response. By default, the implementation used is org.springframework.security.web. authentication.LoginUrlAuthenticationEntryPoint, which redirects to the login URL, which, as you already know, is /login in the root of your application.

The entry point is invoked when an `AuthenticationException` is thrown or when an `AccessDeniedException` is thrown and the current `Authentication` object is anonymous.

As another artificial example, you will implement an entry point that will add a cookie each time an authentication attempt is made from the client side and then show the basic authentication scheme in the browser. This means you will set a cookie in the response that will increment its value every time the entry point is invoked. Then the cookie is sent back to the server every time with the new value. This means that the counter for the attempts is not stored in the server at all; it is stored just in the client cookie and is sent back and forth between the client and the server. So the server receives the cookie, increments its value, and then sends it back. It is not really innovative in any way, but it allows us, again, to show that you can override the entry point to do different things.

Most likely, the entry point is overridden when a different kind of authentication scheme is being used. For example, one of the standard entry points applies when using authentication schemes that require showing a login page, while others (in particular the `BasicAuthenticationEntryPoint`) are used to set up particular values in the response to inform the browser how to treat it. In most cases, the implementation of an entry point goes hand in hand with the implementation of a new security filter. If you take a look at the implementations provided by the framework, you can see this clear relationship in `BasicAuthenticationEntryPoint` – `BasicAuthenticationFilter`, `LoginUrlAuthenticationEntryPoint` – `UsernamePasswordAuthenticationFilter` (kind of; this one is not as one-to-one), `CasAuthenticationEntryPoint` – `CasAuthenticationFilter`, and some others. Basically, the entry points set the groundwork and then the filter processes the subsequent request.

Figure 8-21 shows the relationship between the `ExceptionTranslationFilter` and the `AuthenticationEntryPoint`.

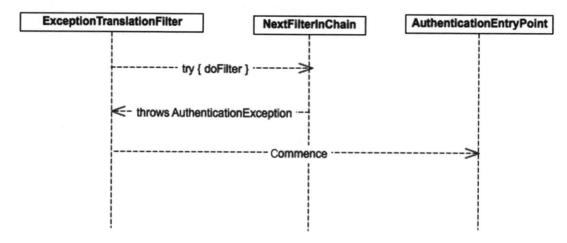

Figure 8-21. *The ExceptionTranslationFilter and AuthenticationEntryPoint relationship*

Listing 8-24 shows an example of entry-point implementation, and Listing 8-25 shows the configuration needed to make it work. It is a very simple implementation, but it is actually a little more complex than the standard `BasicAuthenticationEntryPoint`.

Listing 8-24. AuthenticationEntryPoint Implementation That Creates an Attempts Cookie and a Basic Authentication Response

```
package com.apress.pss.security;

import java.io.IOException;

import javax.servlet.ServletException;
import javax.servlet.http.Cookie;
import javax.servlet.http.HttpServletRequest;
import javax.servlet.http.HttpServletResponse;

import org.springframework.security.core.AuthenticationException;
import org.springframework.security.web.AuthenticationEntryPoint;

public class AttemptsAuthenticationEntryPoint implements
AuthenticationEntryPoint{

    public void commence(HttpServletRequest request,
        HttpServletResponse response, AuthenticationException
        authException)
```

```
    throws IOException, ServletException {
    response.addHeader("WWW-Authenticate", "Basic realm=\"theapp\"");
    response.addHeader("Set-Cookie",
      "authentication_attempts="+(getDeniesCookie(request)+1)+"; Max-
      Age=3600; Version=1");
    response.sendError(HttpServletResponse.SC_UNAUTHORIZED,
      authException.getMessage());

  }

  private int getDeniesCookie(HttpServletRequest request) {
    for(Cookie cookie:request.getCookies()){
        if(cookie.getName().equals("authentication_attempts")){
            return Integer.parseInt(cookie.getValue());
        }
    }
    return 0;
  }

}
```

The code in Listing 8-25 has a lot in common with the code from `org.springframework.security.web.authentication.www.BasicAuthenticationEntryPoint` because it also tells the browser in the response to start a new basic authentication input process. The main difference is, of course, in the retrieval and processing of the `authentication_attempts` cookie. The cookie is first retrieved from the request in the private method getDeniesCookie. Then the value of this cookie (which is assumed to be an integer) is increased by one and reset in the response header in the following line:

```
response.addHeader("Set-Cookie",
  "authentication_attempts="+(getDeniesCookie(request)+1)+"; Max-Age=3600;
  Version=1");
```

Listing 8-25. Spring Configuration Needed to Use a Custom Entry Point

```
......
<security:http auto-config="true" entry-point-
ref="attAuthenticationEntryPoint">
        <security:intercept-url pattern="/*" access="ROLE_USER" />
    </security:http>
...
<bean id="attAuthenticationEntryPoint" class="com.apress.pss.security.
AttemptsAuthenticationEntryPoint"/>
```

If a different kind of exception than the ones mentioned before is thrown (particularly, an AccessDeniedException for a fully authenticated user), an AccessDeniedHandler is invoked instead of the AuthenticationEntryPoint.

The default AccessDeniedHandler implementation that is invoked is AccessDeniedHandlerImpl, which also by default will set a 403 error status in the response and let the browser render its default 403 page. However, you can also configure an errorPage property in the handler to determine that a forward (an internal dispatching mechanism inside the application, different from a redirect) is made to a customized error page, which is probably the most common personalization you will do when using the AccessDeniedHandler.

You can also define your own implementation of AccessDeniedHandler, and that is what you will do here to illustrate the point, but you will also use a custom errorPage property much as you would use it in the AccessDeniedHandlerImpl.

The implementation, as in the previous example, will simply add an extra header in the response in the form of a cookie that specifies the number of "access-denied" responses received from the particular computer and browser from where the requests are coming. Listing 8-26 shows an example of the implementation of the handler.

Listing 8-26. Handler Java Class

```
package com.apress.pss.security;

import java.io.IOException;

import javax.servlet.RequestDispatcher;
import javax.servlet.ServletException;
import javax.servlet.http.Cookie;
```

```java
import javax.servlet.http.HttpServletRequest;
import javax.servlet.http.HttpServletResponse;

import org.springframework.security.access.AccessDeniedException;
import org.springframework.security.web.WebAttributes;
import org.springframework.security.web.access.AccessDeniedHandler;

public class CookieAccessDeniedHandler implements AccessDeniedHandler {

    private static final String ACCESS_DENIES = "access_denies";

    private String errorPage;

    public void handle(HttpServletRequest request,
            HttpServletResponse response,
            AccessDeniedException accessDeniedException) throws
            IOException,
            ServletException {
        if (!response.isCommitted()) {
            response.addCookie(new Cookie(ACCESS_DENIES,
                String.valueOf(getDeniesCookie(request)+1)));
            if (errorPage != null) {
                request.setAttribute(WebAttributes.ACCESS_DENIED_403,
                accessDeniedException);
                response.setStatus(HttpServletResponse.SC_FORBIDDEN);
                RequestDispatcher dispatcher = request.getRequestDispatcher
                (errorPage);
                dispatcher.forward(request, response);
            } else {
                response.sendError(HttpServletResponse.SC_FORBIDDEN,
                accessDeniedException.getMessage());
            }
        }
    }
```

```java
    private int getDeniesCookie(HttpServletRequest request) {
        for(Cookie cookie:request.getCookies()){
            if(cookie.getName().equals(ACCESS_DENIES)){
                return Integer.parseInt(cookie.getValue());
            }
        }
        return 0;
    }

}
```

As mentioned, the code is mostly the same as the `AccessDeniedHandlerImpl`. You just added the cookie in the response, which will be set to incremental values every time this handler is invoked. You can see that there is also the logic for processing the `errorPage property` in case it is set. A servlet dispatcher forward will be done to this error page URL, which means that it will have access to the same request that is used inside this class.

Changing the Security Interceptor

The security interceptor is a class you rarely find yourself modifying or replacing because the default implementations cover the most common scenarios of filter security and method-level security. However, you can extend it for use in different kinds of applications that don't strictly fit into the web app-business method services scheme. For example, Spring Integration has its own security interceptor implementation in the form of the `org.springframework.integration.security.channel.ChannelSecurityInterceptor`. Instead of working with simple method invocations or filter invocations, it works with a different abstraction, which is the `org.springframework.integration.security.channel.ChannelInvocation`. This means that it basically intercepts "send" and "receive" calls on a determined secured channel. Spring Integration also uses the class `org.springframework.integration.security.channel.ChannelSecurityMetadataSource` as the `org.springframework.security.access.SecurityMetadataSource` implementation for message channels.

The creation of a different security interceptor, as the Spring Integration example shows, is basically for when you want to add Spring Security's authorization support to applications that don't follow the standard web-service way of doing things. However, keep in mind that a previous authentication mechanism must be in place, as the security interceptor will look for the different components that it needs to grant access to a resource. This means that an Authentication object must exist in the SecurityContext, the AccessDecisionManager must be configured, and so on. Listing 8-27 shows the security interceptor implementation from Spring Integration.

Listing 8-27. ChannelSecurityInterceptor Java Class

```
/*
 * Copyright 2002-2019 the original author or authors.
 *
 * Licensed under the Apache License, Version 2.0 (the "License");
 * you may not use this file except in compliance with the License.
 * You may obtain a copy of the License at
 *
 *       https://www.apache.org/licenses/LICENSE-2.0
 *
 * Unless required by applicable law or agreed to in writing, software
 * distributed under the License is distributed on an "AS IS" BASIS,
 * WITHOUT WARRANTIES OR CONDITIONS OF ANY KIND, either express or implied.
 * See the License for the specific language governing permissions and
 * limitations under the License.
 */

package org.springframework.integration.security.channel;

import java.lang.reflect.Method;

import org.aopalliance.intercept.MethodInterceptor;
import org.aopalliance.intercept.MethodInvocation;

import org.springframework.security.access.SecurityMetadataSource;
import org.springframework.security.access.intercept.
AbstractSecurityInterceptor;
import org.springframework.security.access.intercept.
InterceptorStatusToken;
import org.springframework.util.Assert;
```

```java
/**
 * An AOP interceptor that enforces authorization for MessageChannel send
   and/or receive calls.
 *
 * @author Mark Fisher
 * @author Oleg Zhurakousky
 * @see SecuredChannel
 */
public final class ChannelSecurityInterceptor extends
AbstractSecurityInterceptor implements MethodInterceptor {

        private final ChannelSecurityMetadataSource securityMetadataSource;

        public ChannelSecurityInterceptor() {
          this(new ChannelSecurityMetadataSource());
        }

        public ChannelSecurityInterceptor(ChannelSecurityMetadataSource
        securityMetadataSource) {
          Assert.notNull(securityMetadataSource, "securityMetadataSource
          must not be null");
          this.securityMetadataSource = securityMetadataSource;
        }

        @Override
        public Class<?> getSecureObjectClass() {
          return ChannelInvocation.class;
        }

        public Object invoke(MethodInvocation invocation) throws Throwable {
          Method method = invocation.getMethod();
          if (method.getName().equals("send") || method.getName().
          equals("receive")) {
                  return this.invokeWithAuthorizationCheck(invocation);
          }
          return invocation.proceed();
        }
```

```
private Object invokeWithAuthorizationCheck(MethodInvocation
methodInvocation) throws Throwable {
  Object returnValue = null;
  InterceptorStatusToken token = super.beforeInvocation(new Channel
  Invocation(methodInvocation));
  try {
          returnValue = methodInvocation.proceed();
  }
  finally {
          returnValue = super.afterInvocation(token, returnValue);
  }
  return returnValue;
}

@Override
public SecurityMetadataSource obtainSecurityMetadataSource() {
  return this.securityMetadataSource;
}

}
```

In this code, you can see that `ChannelInvocation` wraps a `MethodInvocation` before calling the `beforeInvocation` method on the parent class. Apart from wrapping, it will also do some inner processing to make the current executing channel available to be queried for `ConfigAttributes`. Also note that the interceptor will do its security validations only if the method being invoked is one of the standard "send" and "receive" methods of Spring Integration.

The `ChannelSecurityMetadataSource` that is being used in the code is the one that will be queried for obtaining the security metadata attributes. It is the one that knows how to extract this information from Spring Integration Channels and the related `org.springframework.integration.security.channel.ChannelAccessPolicy`.

It is very unlikely you will override the security interceptor in your own applications. However, it is good to know that you could do it and also understand why you would want to do it.

As the example for Spring Integration shows, one reason you would want to replace a security interceptor (or add an additional one) is because you have certain abstractions, to which you want to apply interception-based security, that don't fit either URL interception or simple method interceptions. You want to give a more meaningful name to your interception logic and also filter certain things that are not filtered by default with the default implementations. This is what the Spring Integration example is doing. It is intercepting `MessageChannel` communication, which is the domain element that makes sense in its context. However, in the end, it is basically intercepting methods and filtering to intercept only the methods `send` and `receive`, which again are the ones that make sense in the particular context.

Spring Security Extensions Project

There is a whole project dedicated to the development of Spring Security extensions, where people from the community can develop their own extensions on top of Spring Security. In this way, they can decouple these extensions from the main Spring Security project, allowing it to evolve independently. The home of this extensions project is `https://spring.io/projects/spring-security`.

If you visit this page, you will see that currently there are two extensions projects in existence: Kerberos integration and SAML2 integration. There is also the OAuth integration, which lives on its own as an individual project. You can find it at `https://docs.spring.io/spring-security/oauth/`.

Each project in Spring Security Extensions can implement as many parts of the framework as it needs in order to work correctly. This means that many of the extension points that we defined in this chapter (and some others) could be overridden in a particular extension in order to do its work.

Summary

In this chapter, we showed how the modularity in the architecture of Spring Security pays off when you want to customize or extend its behavior. We showed how to create a Spring Boot Web Application using Spring Security v5 and MongoDB. We also showed some of the different and most common extension points that Spring Security offers so that you can adapt its functionality to your particular application while keeping the core functionality, making the work easier for you by leveraging this functionality. After reading this chapter, and with all the theory and practice from previous chapters, you should feel confident enough to implement functionality that goes beyond the out-of-the-box offerings of the framework.

CHAPTER 9

Integrating Spring Security with Other Frameworks and Languages

This chapter will explore Spring Security in the context of other application frameworks and languages that run on the JVM.

You saw in previous chapters that the two main ways of using Spring Security are in the web layer in the shape of filters and in the business layer with Spring AOP. This means that you could use Spring Security in any application that is built on top of the Servlet technology or in any application that is willing to use Spring and Spring AOP to handle its object life cycles and interactions.

In the following sections, you'll see examples of both cases. We'll start by looking at a couple of popular Java frameworks (one of which is also Spring-based) and how to use Spring Security with them. These frameworks are the popular Struts 2 web framework and Spring Web Flow, another member of the SpringSource suite.

After studying these two frameworks, we'll take a brief look at a few Java Virtual Machine (JVM) programming languages (and some of their related frameworks) and how to use Spring Security with them. We'll be looking at Groovy in the context of its web-development framework Grails, JRuby in the context of Rails, and Scala embedded in a Spring Web Application.

We will not go into any of these frameworks or languages in much detail, because that would be beyond the scope of this book. The purpose of this chapter is simply to explain how to use Spring Security in a wider context.

© Carlo Scarioni and Massimo Nardone 2019
C. Scarioni and M. Nardone, *Pro Spring Security*, https://doi.org/10.1007/978-1-4842-5052-5_9

Spring Security with Struts 2

Struts 2 is a popular Java web framework built by merging the original Struts project and the WebWork project. Struts 2 was always intended to be a complete evolution from the original Struts framework, adapted to a new generation of powerful web frameworks, and it really kept little of the original Struts principles and implementations.

Struts 2 is widely used and is as good a candidate as any other external servlet-based framework to integrate with Spring and Spring Security.

Struts 2 is an MVC (model view controller) framework built on top of the standard Java servlets technology, so many of the web-based security principles you have read about in this book apply without modification. If you want to use only the URL-level, web-based security you studied in Chapter 5, you just need to configure your `web.xml` and your Spring Security filter chain accordingly or you can implement using the WebApplicationInitializer.

More information about the Struts 2 releases can be found at `https://struts.apache.org/releases.html`. In this book, Struts version 2.5.20 will be used.

As with the rest of frameworks and languages in this chapter, we won't explain Struts 2 in any depth (because there are many good books available on that subject). We'll explain just enough so that you can use Spring Security with it. In fact, we assume that if you are reading this section it, is probably because you are already using Struts 2 and want to integrate Spring Security with it. However, to explain a little more, Figure 9-1 shows the big picture of how Struts 2 works.

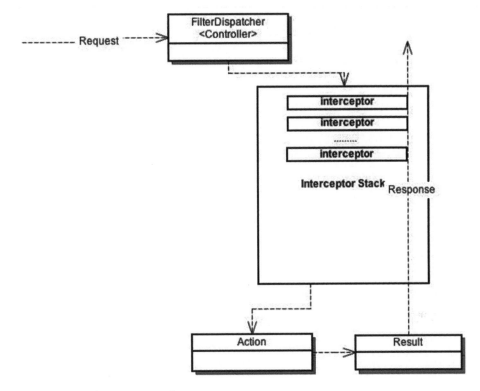

Figure 9-1. *How Struts 2 works*

When a request comes to the application, a front controller (http://en.wikipedia.org/wiki/Front_Controller) implemented in a servlet filter takes care of the request. It sends the request through a set of configured interceptors that perform different kinds of functionality before and after the action is invoked. The action is then invoked, which carries with it all the business logic required by the current request. After the action finishes, a result object representing the view is created and the interceptor stack is invoked in inverse order as before (while returning the result) until a response is finally returned to the client.

The first step for you to do is of course download the libraries to include in your Maven project from this link:

https://struts.apache.org/download.cgi#struts-ga.

Struts 2 can be download in a full distribution, including everything, or just as a separate set of libraries, sources, documentation, etc.

You'll be using Maven to build this project. So let's create a new Maven project as shown in Figure 9-2. Then follow the prompts by selecting a new *starter project* at the first prompt and selecting some relevant `groupId` and `artifactId` names. (We chose `com.apress.pss.struts` and `struts-example`, respectively, as shown in Figure 9-2. You can use the same to follow along in the examples easily).

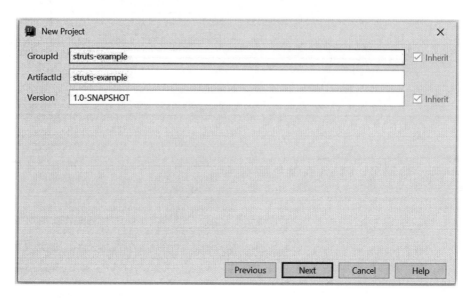

Figure 9-2. The Struts project

Now create a simple, functional Struts 2 web application with the components you need to create the test, including Spring integration (although it uses an old DTD version of the configuration XML file). The file structure after executing that command is shown in Figure 9-3.

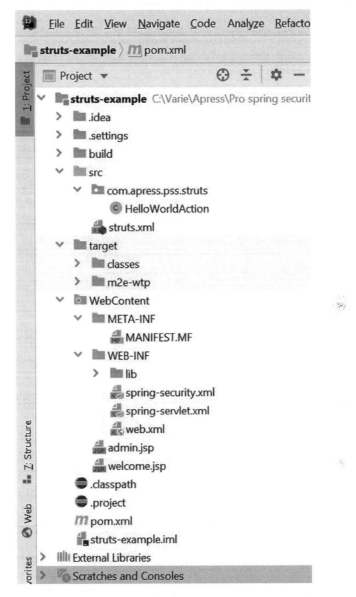

Figure 9-3. *Struts 2 application file structure after executing the Maven command*

In Figure 9-3, you can see that there is a file named `struts.xml`; this is the main Struts 2 configuration file, and you can see its contents in Listing 9-1.

Listing 9-1. The struts.xml File

```
<?xml version="1.0" encoding="UTF-8"?>
<!DOCTYPE struts PUBLIC
        "-//Apache Software Foundation//DTD Struts Configuration 2.5//EN"
        "http://struts.apache.org/dtds/struts-2.5.dtd">
 <struts>
 <constant name="struts.action.excludePattern" value="/j_spring_security_
 check.*,.*\\.j_spring_security_check"/>
   <package name="default" namespace="/" extends="struts-default">
     <action name="welcome">
      <result>welcome.jsp</result>
     </action>
     <action name="helloWorld" class="com.apress.pss.struts.
     HelloWorldAction">
        <result name="SUCCESS">admin.jsp</result>
     </action>
     <action name="logout">
      <result>welcome.jsp</result>
     </action>
   </package>
 </struts>
```

In Listing 9-1, the action, `"helloWorld"`, doesn't define a class name on the attribute `class`. In this case, it defines a simple string that identifies a Spring bean in the `spring-security.xmlspring-security.xml` that you'll see later. When a request comes in, the framework looks at the definitions from this file to determine how to handle the particular request. (This definition is simplistic, but it's good enough to make the point.) If it sees the name of a class in the `action` attribute, the framework instantiates a new object of that class to handle the request. If the framework detects that it is not a class, it looks for a bean with that ID in the Spring configuration and gets the object from there. All this is possible in the framework thanks to the `struts2-spring-plugin` plugin, which enhances Struts 2 with Spring functionality and makes it possible to define actions (and other components such as interceptors) in Spring beans.

Please notice the usage of struts-2.5.dtd as Structs 2.5 version.

What you'll do now is rewrite the default `spring-security.xml`, replace it with the one from Listing 9-2, and add the familiar dependencies from Listing 9-3 to the `pom.xml` file.

Listing 9-2. The spring-security.xml File for the Struts 2 Application

```
<?xml version="1.0" encoding="UTF-8"?>
<beans:beans xmlns="http://www.springframework.org/schema/security"
xmlns:xsi="http://www.w3.org/2001/XMLSchema-instance"
xmlns:beans="http://www.springframework.org/schema/beans"
            xsi:schemaLocation="
    http://www.springframework.org/schema/security
      http://www.springframework.org/schema/security/spring-security-
      4.2.xsd
    http://www.springframework.org/schema/beans
      http://www.springframework.org/schema/beans/spring-beans-4.3.xsd"
>
<global-method-security pre-post-annotations="enabled"></global-method-
security>
   <http auto-config="false" use-expressions="true">
       <intercept-url pattern="/welcome" access="permitAll"/>
       <intercept-url pattern="/**" access="isAuthenticated()"/>
       <form-login authentication-success-handler-ref="awareAuthentication
       SuccessHandler" />

   <logout logout-success-url="/logout" logout-url="/j_spring_security_
   logout" invalidate-session="true"/>
   </http>
   <beans:bean class="org.springframework.security.web.
   authentication.SavedRequestAwareAuthenticationSuccessHandler"
   name="awareAuthenticationSuccessHandler"/>
   <beans:bean id ="passwordEncoder" class = "org.springframework.
   security.crypto.password.NoOpPasswordEncoder" factory-method =
   "getInstance" />
```

```
    <authentication-manager>
        <authentication-provider>
            <user-service>
                <user name="admin" password="admin123" authorities=
                "ROLE_USER"/>
                <user name="massimo" password="massimo123"
                authorities="ROLE_USER"/>
            </user-service>
        </authentication-provider>
    </authentication-manager>
</beans:beans>
```

Listing 9-3. Spring Security Dependencies in the pom.xml File

```
<properties>
        <springframework.version>5.1.5.RELEASE</springframework.version>
        <springsecurity.version>5.1.5.RELEASE</springsecurity.version>
    </properties>

    <dependencies>
        <!-- Spring -->
        <dependency>
            <groupId>org.springframework</groupId>
            <artifactId>spring-core</artifactId>
            <version>${springframework.version}</version>
        </dependency>
        <dependency>
            <groupId>org.springframework</groupId>
            <artifactId>spring-web</artifactId>
            <version>${springframework.version}</version>
        </dependency>
        <dependency>
            <groupId>org.springframework</groupId>
            <artifactId>spring-webmvc</artifactId>
            <version>${springframework.version}</version>
        </dependency>
```

```xml
<!-- Spring Security -->
<dependency>
    <groupId>org.springframework.security</groupId>
    <artifactId>spring-security-web</artifactId>
    <version>${springsecurity.version}</version>
</dependency>
<dependency>
    <groupId>org.springframework.security</groupId>
    <artifactId>spring-security-config</artifactId>
    <version>${springsecurity.version}</version>
</dependency>
```

Next, you need to add the Spring Security filter to the web.xml. This filter should execute before the Struts 2 filter, so an authentication object is populated before reaching the action. Remember that Struts 2 works with filters and not with servlets. Listing 9-4 shows the web.xml file you can use as a test. Note that we removed some filter definitions we don't care to use in the example.

Listing 9-4. The web.xml with the Spring Security Filter and Struts 2 Filter

```xml
<?xml version="1.0" encoding="UTF-8"?>
<web-app xmlns="http://xmlns.jcp.org/xml/ns/javaee"
        xmlns:xsi="http://www.w3.org/2001/XMLSchema-instance"
        xsi:schemaLocation="http://xmlns.jcp.org/xml/ns/javaee
        http://xmlns.jcp.org/xml/ns/javaee/web-app_4_0.xsd"
        version="4.0">
<display-name>struts-example</display-name>

 <!-- Welcome file lists -->
   <welcome-file-list>
       <welcome-file>index.jsp</welcome-file>
   </welcome-file-list>

       <context-param>
               <param-name>contextConfigLocation</param-name>
               <param-value>classpath:spring-security.xml</param-value>
       </context-param>
```

```
<filter>
    <filter-name>struts2</filter-name>
    <filter-class>org.apache.struts2.dispatcher.filter.
    StrutsPrepareAndExecuteFilter</filter-class>
</filter>
<filter-mapping>
    <filter-name>struts2</filter-name>
    <url-pattern>/*</url-pattern>
</filter-mapping>

    <!-- Spring MVC -->
<servlet>
  <servlet-name>spring</servlet-name>
  <servlet-class>org.springframework.web.servlet.DispatcherServlet
  </servlet-class>
  <load-on-startup>1</load-on-startup>
</servlet>
<servlet-mapping>
  <servlet-name>spring</servlet-name>
  <url-pattern>/</url-pattern>
</servlet-mapping>

<listener>
  <listener-class>org.springframework.web.context.ContextLoaderListener
  </listener-class>
</listener>

<!-- Spring Security -->
<filter>
  <filter-name>springSecurityFilterChain</filter-name>
  <filter-class>org.springframework.web.filter.DelegatingFilterProxy
  </filter-class>
</filter>
```

```
<filter-mapping>
  <filter-name>springSecurityFilterChain</filter-name>
  <url-pattern>/*</url-pattern>
</filter-mapping>

  <servlet>
      <servlet-name>jspSupportServlet</servlet-name>
      <servlet-class>org.apache.struts2.views.JspSupportServlet</servlet-
      class>
      <load-on-startup>5</load-on-startup>
  </servlet>

</web-app>
```

Next, we simplified the `.jsp` files inside the `jsp` folder like this: the file `helloWorld.jsp` just contains the string "This is your first "Secured" Struts2 Application!" inside, nothing else.

Struts 2 has a built-in system to handle the exceptions that might be thrown in your application. This mechanism would get in the way of Spring Security's exception-handling system, which depends on `AccessDeniedException`, among other exceptions, to be thrown to alter the flow of execution. For example, when showing a login form, you need to deactivate the Struts 2 exception-handling mechanism. To do that in the file `struts.xml`, you add the line `<constant name="struts.handle.exception" value="false" />` just below the other line that contains a defined `<constant>` element.

Finally, you need to secure your action. Make your `HelloWorldAction` look like Listing 9-5.

Listing 9-5. HelloWorldAction Secured

```
package com.apress.pss.struts;

import javax.servlet.http.HttpServletRequest;
import org.apache.struts2.ServletActionContext;

        public class HelloWorldAction {
              private String username;
```

```java
    public String execute() {
        HttpServletRequest request =
        ServletActionContext.getRequest();
        this.setUsername(request.getUserPrincipal().getName());
         return "SUCCESS";
}
    public String getUsername() {
        return username;
    }
    public void setUsername(String username) {
        this.username = username;
    }
}
```

Now if you restart your application and visit http://localhost:8080/struts-example/helloWorld, you'll be presented with the standard Spring Security login form. If you use the login username **admin** and password **admin123**, you'll be able to access the page. Figure 9-4 shows the login, the HelloWorld. and the logout page.

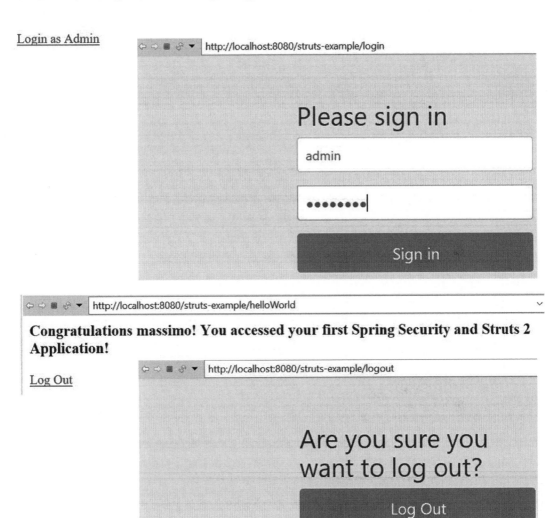

Figure 9-4. *The secured Struts 2 application and the accessed action*

Spring Security with Spring Web Flow

Spring Web Flow is a framework, built on top of Spring MVC, that allows you to link different steps of a web-driven process into a fluent workflow. In other words, it allows you to define in a declarative way the different steps that a web application can go through while you are interacting with it. Basically, you use it to define a set of rules and transitions between the user interface (UI) parts of a web application and the back-end process that each transition should trigger. Please check this link for all information about Spring Web Flow: `https://projects.spring.io/spring-webflow/`.

When you create a new Maven project, you need to add the Spring MF dependency like this:

```
<dependency>
    <groupId>org.springframework.webflow</groupId>
    <artifactId>spring-webflow</artifactId>
    <version>2.5.1.RELEASE</version>
</dependency>
```

Graphically, Spring Web Flow works, in a simplified form, as shown in Figure 9-5. The example is a fake web page for a simplified product. The boxes represent various states (the View state, Action state, Decision state, Subflow state, and others), and the arrows represent transitions.

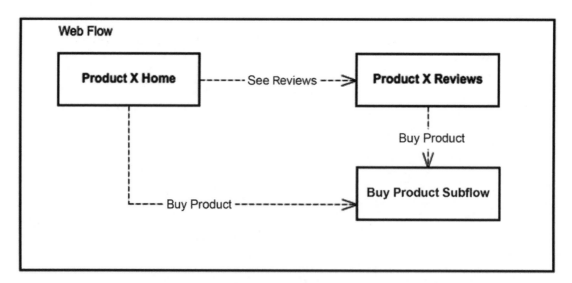

Figure 9-5.   *The Simple Spring Web Flow scheme shows that, from a product page, you can go to the review page or buy the product*

To implement this simple flow with Spring Web Flow, you'll create a new project. As is the case for most of the examples, you'll use Maven to build and manage your project. So let's do it. Let's create a new Maven project, as shown in Figure 9-6.

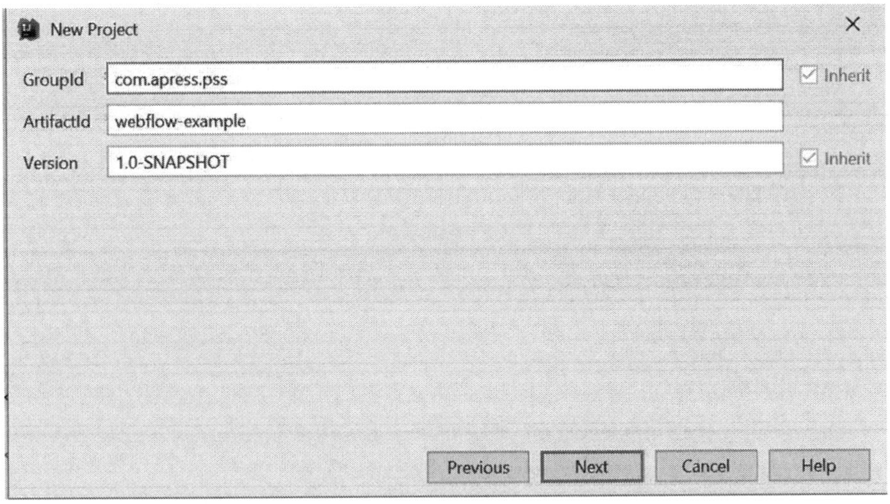

Figure 9-6. *New Spring Web Flow Maven project*

Now you'll create all the configuration files. Replace the pom.xml file in the new project with the one shown in Listing 9-6, and replace the web.xml file with the one shown in Listing 9-7. Then, in the WEB-INF directory, create the files shown in Listings 9-8 and 9-9 with the names spring-servlet.xml and spring-security.xml, respectively.

Listing 9-6. The pom.xml File with Spring Security and Spring Web Flow Dependencies

```
<project xmlns="http://maven.apache.org/POM/4.0.0"
xmlns:xsi="http://www.w3.org/2001/XMLSchema-instance"
xsi:schemaLocation="http://maven.apache.org/POM/4.0.0
http://maven.apache.org/xsd/maven-4.0.0.xsd">
  <modelVersion>4.0.0</modelVersion>
  <groupId>com.apress.pss</groupId>
  <artifactId>webflow-example</artifactId>
  <version>0.0.1-SNAPSHOT</version>
  <packaging>war</packaging>

  <properties>
      <springframework.version>5.1.5.RELEASE</springframework.version>
      <springsecurity.version>5.1.5.RELEASE</springsecurity.version>
  </properties>
```

```xml
<dependencies>
    <!-- Spring Web flow-->
    <dependency>
        <groupId>org.springframework.webflow</groupId>
        <artifactId>spring-webflow</artifactId>
        <version>2.5.1.RELEASE</version>
     </dependency>

    <!-- Spring -->
    <dependency>
        <groupId>org.springframework</groupId>
        <artifactId>spring-core</artifactId>
        <version>${springframework.version}</version>
    </dependency>
    <dependency>
        <groupId>org.springframework</groupId>
        <artifactId>spring-web</artifactId>
        <version>${springframework.version}</version>
    </dependency>
    <dependency>
        <groupId>org.springframework</groupId>
        <artifactId>spring-webmvc</artifactId>
        <version>${springframework.version}</version>
    </dependency>

    <!-- Spring Security -->
    <dependency>
        <groupId>org.springframework.security</groupId>
        <artifactId>spring-security-web</artifactId>
        <version>${springsecurity.version}</version>
    </dependency>
    <dependency>
        <groupId>org.springframework.security</groupId>
        <artifactId>spring-security-config</artifactId>
        <version>${springsecurity.version}</version>
    </dependency>
```

```xml
    <dependency>
        <groupId>javax.servlet</groupId>
        <artifactId>javax.servlet-api</artifactId>
        <version>4.0.1</version>
    </dependency>
    <dependency>
        <groupId>javax.servlet.jsp</groupId>
        <artifactId>javax.servlet.jsp-api</artifactId>
        <version>2.3.3</version>
    </dependency>
    <dependency>
        <groupId>javax.servlet</groupId>
        <artifactId>jstl</artifactId>
        <version>1.2</version>
    </dependency>
    <dependency>
        <groupId>taglibs</groupId>
        <artifactId>standard</artifactId>
        <version>1.1.2</version>
    </dependency>
  </dependencies>

<build>
  <sourceDirectory>src</sourceDirectory>
  <resources>
    <resource>
      <directory>src</directory>
      <excludes>
        <exclude>**/*.java</exclude>
      </excludes>
    </resource>
  </resources>
  <plugins>
    <plugin>
      <artifactId>maven-compiler-plugin</artifactId>
      <version>3.8.0</version>
```

```xml
        <configuration>
          <source>11</source>
          <target>11</target>
        </configuration>
      </plugin>
      <plugin>
        <artifactId>maven-war-plugin</artifactId>
        <version>3.2.3</version>
        <configuration>
          <warSourceDirectory>WebContent</warSourceDirectory>
        </configuration>
      </plugin>

    </plugins>
    <finalName>webflow-example</finalName>
  </build>
</project>
```

Listing 9-7. The web.xml for Spring Web Flow and Spring Security

```xml
<web-app id="WebApp_ID" version="2.4"
        xmlns="http://java.sun.com/xml/ns/j2ee"
        xmlns:xsi="http://www.w3.org/2001/XMLSchema-instance"
        xsi:schemaLocation="http://java.sun.com/xml/ns/j2ee
  http://java.sun.com/xml/ns/j2ee/web-app_2_4.xsd">

  <display-name>Spring MVC Application</display-name>

  <!-- Spring MVC -->
  <servlet>
    <servlet-name>spring</servlet-name>
    <servlet-class>org.springframework.web.servlet.DispatcherServlet
    </servlet-class>
    <load-on-startup>1</load-on-startup>
  </servlet>
  <servlet-mapping>
```

```xml
    <servlet-name>spring</servlet-name>
    <url-pattern>/</url-pattern>
  </servlet-mapping>

  <listener>
    <listener-class>org.springframework.web.context.ContextLoaderListener
    </listener-class>
  </listener>

  <context-param>
    <param-name>contextConfigLocation</param-name>
    <param-value>
      /WEB-INF/spring-security.xml
    </param-value>
  </context-param>

  <!-- Spring Security -->
  <filter>
    <filter-name>springSecurityFilterChain</filter-name>
    <filter-class>org.springframework.web.filter.DelegatingFilterProxy
    </filter-class>
  </filter>

  <filter-mapping>
    <filter-name>springSecurityFilterChain</filter-name>
    <url-pattern>/*</url-pattern>
  </filter-mapping>

    <welcome-file-list>
    <welcome-file>welcome.jsp</welcome-file>
    </welcome-file-list>
</web-app>
```

You should already be familiar with the content of Listing 9-7. It is a web.xml file that includes Spring's ContextLoaderListener, which loads the Spring application-context file given in context-param "contextConfigLocation". It also defines Spring's DispatcherServlet servlet, which takes care of setting up Spring

363

MVC by loading the appropriate configuration file. You also define the already familiar springSecurityFilterChain filter. Both the security filter and the dispatcher servlet are configured to handle every URL in the system.

Note   In Spring MVC, the name of the DispatcherServlet servlet is important because that name will match the name of the Spring configuration file that will be used in the application to configure the application. For example, in this case, by defining the DispatcherServlet with the name "spring", Spring will expect to find a file with the name spring-servlet.xml in the WEB-INF folder where the beans for the web layer should be defined.

Listing 9-8. The spring-servlet.xml File That Imports the Flow

```
<beans xmlns="http://www.springframework.org/schema/beans"
       xmlns:context="http://www.springframework.org/schema/context"
       xmlns:xsi="http://www.w3.org/2001/XMLSchema-instance"
       xsi:schemaLocation="
        http://www.springframework.org/schema/beans
        http://www.springframework.org/schema/beans/spring-beans-3.0.xsd
        http://www.springframework.org/schema/context
        http://www.springframework.org/schema/context/spring-context-
        3.0.xsd">

  <bean
          class="org.springframework.web.servlet.view.
          InternalResourceViewResolver">
      <property name="prefix">
          <value>/WEB-INF/</value>
      </property>
      <property name="suffix">
          <value>.jsp</value>
      </property>
  </bean>

    <import resource="example-webflow.xml" />
</beans>
```

This file is very simple, and its only job is to import another file (the example-webflow.xml file), which will contain the entire Spring Web Flow configuration. This configuration will remain in a different file just to keep it separated from the main servlet file.

Listing 9-9. The spring-security.xml File

```
<?xml version="1.0" encoding="UTF-8"?>
<beans:beans xmlns="http://www.springframework.org/schema/security"
xmlns:xsi="http://www.w3.org/2001/XMLSchema-instance"
xmlns:beans="http://www.springframework.org/schema/beans"
            xsi:schemaLocation="
    http://www.springframework.org/schema/security
      http://www.springframework.org/schema/security/spring-security-
      4.2.xsd
    http://www.springframework.org/schema/beans
      http://www.springframework.org/schema/beans/spring-beans-4.3.xsd">

<global-method-security pre-post-annotations="enabled"></global-method-
security>
    <http auto-config="true" use-expressions="true">
        <intercept-url pattern="/main" access="permitAll"/>
        <intercept-url pattern="/**" access="isAuthenticated()"/>
        <form-login authentication-success-handler-ref="awareAuthentication
        SuccessHandler" />

    <logout logout-success-url="/logout" logout-url="/j_spring_security_
    logout" invalidate-session="true"/>
    </http>
    <beans:bean class="org.springframework.security.web.authentication.
    SavedRequestAwareAuthenticationSuccessHandler" name="awareAuthenticatio
    nSuccessHandler"/>
    <beans:bean id ="passwordEncoder" class = "org.springframework.
    security.crypto.password.NoOpPasswordEncoder" factory-method =
    "getInstance" />
```

```
    <authentication-manager>
        <authentication-provider>
            <user-service>
                <user name="admin" password="admin123" authorities=
                "ROLE_USER"/>
            </user-service>
        </authentication-provider>
    </authentication-manager>
</beans:beans>
```

This is another file you should be able to understand easily by now. Listing 9-9 shows a very basic Spring Security configuration. You are defining just a single user with role ROLE_ USER, which will be enough for your tests. You are not defining any URL security rules here because that is not what you want to do in this Spring Web Flow example. You want to add security at the flow level (its states), and that is what we will show you how to do.

Now you need to define the web-flow configuration of the application as well as the actual web flows themselves. Again, this will be a simplistic example just to show how the functionality works. The example will be based on Figure 9-6. Listing 9-10 shows the web-flow configuration file, and Listing 9-11 shows your only flow definition.

Listing 9-10. The example-webflow.xml in the WEB-INF Folder

```
<?xml version="1.0" encoding="UTF-8"?>
<beans xmlns="http://www.springframework.org/schema/beans"
       xmlns:xsi="http://www.w3.org/2001/XMLSchema-instance"
       xmlns:flow="http://www.springframework.org/schema/webflow-config"
       xsi:schemaLocation="
       http://www.springframework.org/schema/webflow-config
       http://www.springframework.org/schema/webflow-config/spring-webflow-
       config.xsd
       http://www.springframework.org/schema/beans
       http://www.springframework.org/schema/beans/spring-beans-4.3.xsd">

    <bean class="org.springframework.webflow.mvc.servlet.
    FlowHandlerMapping">
        <property name="flowRegistry" ref="activationFlowRegistry"/>
    </bean>
```

```
<flow:flow-builder-services id="flowBuilderServices"
                         view-factory-creator="mvcViewFactoryCreator"/>

<bean id="mvcViewFactoryCreator" class="org.springframework.webflow.
mvc.builder.MvcViewFactoryCreator">
    <property name="viewResolvers" ref="jspViewResolver"/>
</bean>

<flow:flow-registry id="activationFlowRegistry" flow-builder-services="
flowBuilderServices">
    <flow:flow-location id="product" path="/WEB-INF/flows/product.xml"/>
</flow:flow-registry>

<bean class="org.springframework.webflow.mvc.servlet.
FlowHandlerAdapter">
    <property name="flowExecutor" ref="activationFlowExecutor"/>
</bean>
<flow:flow-executor id="activationFlowExecutor" flow-
registry="activationFlowRegistry"/>

</beans>
```

This file defines the general configuration for Spring Web Flow. The main part of the file is the element flow-registry and its attribute flow-builder-services. This element is where the location of the flows in the application are defined. Currently, you'll define only one flow, which will be in the product.xml file. Also, note the way your views will get resolved when referenced in a view state in a flow. The class org. springframework.webflow.mvc.builder.MvcViewFactoryCreator is the one that will resolve view locations. By default, it will resolve view files by looking in the flow definition directory for files whose names are the names of the view states concatenated with .jsp at the end. This simply means that if a view is named *review*, it will look for a file named *review.jsp*.

Listing 9-11. The product.xml Simple Flow in the /WEB-INF/flows/ Folder

```xml
<?xml version="1.0" encoding="UTF-8"?>
<flow xmlns="http://www.springframework.org/schema/webflow"
      xmlns:xsi="http://www.w3.org/2001/XMLSchema-instance"
      xsi:schemaLocation="http://www.springframework.org/schema/webflow
                          http://www.springframework.org/schema/webflow/
                          spring-webflow.xsd">

    <view-state id="activation">
        <transition on="activate" to="success"/>
        <transition on="cancel" to="failure"/>
    </view-state>

    <view-state id="success" />

    <view-state id="failure" />

</flow>
```

This is the actual flow definition. You are simply defining three view states here. As we said before, each of these view states will map to a physical view file in the application. The view files, by default behavior, should be located in the same directory as this flow file and should be named according to the view states concatenated with `.jsp` at the end. So you should have in the `WEB-INF/flows/products` directory files named `activation.jsp`, `success.jsp`, and `failure.jsp`. They are shown in Listings 9-12, 9-13, and 9-14, respectively.

Listing 9-12. The activation.jsp for the Main View State

```html
<html>
<body>
<h2>Hello Spring WebFlow!</h2>
<h2>Activate Spring WebFlow:</h2>
<form method="post" action="${flowExecutionUrl}">

    <input type="hidden" name="_eventId" value="activate">
    <input type="submit" value="Proceed" />

</form>
<form method="post" action="${flowExecutionUrl}">
```

```
<input type="hidden" name="_eventId" value="cancel">
<input type="submit" value="Cancel" />

</form>
</body>
</html>
```

Listing 9-13. *The success.jsp for the Review State*

```
<html>
<body>
<h2>Spring WebFlow Activation Successful!</h2>
</body>
</html>
```

Listing 9-14. *The failure.jsp for the Buy View State of the Flow*

```
<html>
<body>
<h2>Spring WebFlow Activation Failed!</h2>
</body>
</html>
```

In the previous three `.jsp` files, you defined the three view states in your web flow. Listings 9-12 and 9-13 have transition triggers in the form of the `eventId` parameter in the `href` links. `${flowExecutionUrl}` makes reference to the current executing state of the flow. So, in the case of the main state the first time you access the page, the value of `${ flowExecutionUrl }` is `/product?execution=e1s1`, making the full URL to the next flow states something like `/product?execution=e1s1}&_eventId=review`.

If you visit `http://localhost:8080/product`, you'll be taken to the main view state. That view displays `activate.jsp`, where you will have one button to activate and one to cancel the activation, as Figure 9-7 shows. The moment you click the activate button you activate the Spring Web Flow process and the `success.jsp` opens.

Let's use Spring Security to do just that. Spring Security and Spring Web Flow integrate nicely because both are part of the Spring portfolio.

Securing flows with Spring Security is easy. First, you need to add to the current `<webflow:flow-executor>` element from the file `example-webflow.xml` (the element in Listing 9-15) and add the content shown in Listing 9-16 somewhere in the same file.

369

Listing 9-15. The flow-executor with Spring Security Listener

```
<webflow:flow-execution-listeners>
    <webflow:listener ref="securityFlowExecutionListener" />
</webflow:flow-execution-listeners>
```

Listing 9-16. The Spring Security Listener Bean

```
<bean id="securityFlowExecutionListener"
    class="org.springframework.webflow.security.
    SecurityFlowExecutionListener" />
```

Figure 9-7. *The activation.jsp, which is the entry point into the web flow*

By implementing the preceding content, you integrate Spring Security into Spring Web Flow. All you need to do now is decide which parts of the flow to secure and what constraints to define to secure them. But before that, we'll explain briefly what this SecurityFlowExecutionListener is doing for Spring Web Flow.

Spring Web Flow offers an abstraction in the form of the interface org. springframework.webflow.execution .FlowExecutionListener, which allows you to implement classes to listen to or observe the life cycle of a flow execution. When a listener implementation is registered for the flows, it can intercept the flow execution at different points in its life cycle. In that sense, it is similar to the AOP concepts you studied before.

org.springframework.webflow.security.SecurityFlowExecutionListener is a listener implementation that intercepts three particular points in the life cycle of the flow: sessionCreating, stateEntering, and transitionExecuting. In each of these interceptions, the listener delegates to a configured org.springframework.security. access.AccessDecisionManager like the ones we explained in different parts of this book. If an `AccessDecisionManager` implementation is not provided when the bean is defined, a new role-based access decision manager will be created on the fly.

So now you want to secure the view-state `"activation"` and allow access to it only to authenticated users with role `ROLE_USER`. To do that, you simply define the element `<secured attributes="ROLE_USER" />` as a child of the `"activation"` `<view-state>` element. After you do that, if you restart the application and try to access the "buy" state, you'll find yourself presented with the familiar Spring Security login screen. If you log in with the username **admin** and the password **admin123**, you'll be able to reach the "buy" state. The resulting "buy" state view is shown in Figure 9-8.

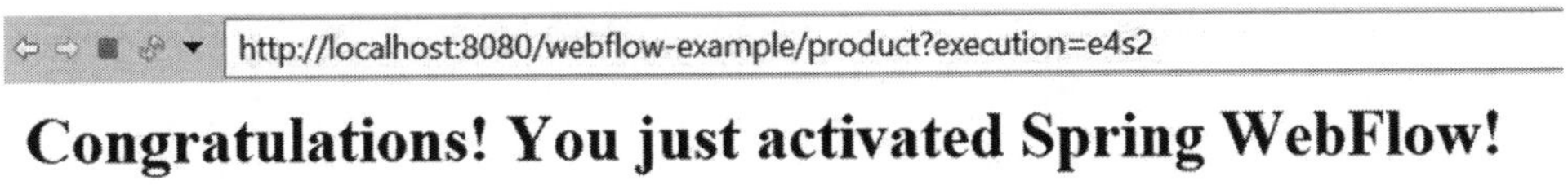

Congratulations! You just activated Spring WebFlow!

Figure 9-8. *Spring Web Flow Activation page*

You could also secure the whole flow if you want by having the `<secured>` element be a direct child of the `<flow>` element. This means that, to access any state of the flow, a user needs to have the required permissions. Go ahead and try it yourself; it should be very straightforward.

Spring Security in Other JVM Languages

We are not experts in any of the languages that follow, and maybe we won't use them in the examples in the most idiomatic way. (We know Ruby best because we often use it both at work and during leisure time. It's one of our favorite languages.) However, our objective is just to show that, with some tweaking, you can integrate Spring Security into projects that are written in a language other than Java.

You'll see that the support for Spring Security in other JVM languages is sometimes straightforward and comprehensive (like when using Groovy and its Grails framework); at other times, you might need to roll your own integration solution to support it. In the upcoming sections, we give a brief overview of how to integrate Spring Security into what we consider to be the three major JVM languages other than Java: Groovy, JRuby, and Scala.

Remember that ultimately Spring Security is no more than a set of Java libraries built on top of Spring Framework, which allows you to plug authentication/authorization security mechanisms into your applications. So it should be possible to integrate it into any Java (Java JVM) application you have. Of course, not all functionality will apply to all applications. For example, the filter chain won't make sense in a non-web application.

Spring Security and Ruby (JRuby)

Ruby is definitely one of our favorite languages, and we spend a lot of time working with it. It combines great syntax with great language constructs, and it's a pleasure to work with. Ruby is an object-oriented dynamic language with a focus on productivity, concision, and simplicity.

The standard Ruby interpreter is written in C and was known as *MRI Ruby* until version 1.9. From version 1.9 forward, the official interpreter is known as the *YARV interpreter*.

Ruby is an incredibly popular language, and most of its popularity stems from the widespread use of its incredible web framework, Ruby on Rails (RoR), also known simply as *Rails*.

Rails is an MVC framework that places great emphasis on convention over configuration practices. It's a very productive framework you can use to develop simple web applications in a fast and easy way if you follow the conventions enforced by the framework.

We won't give an in-depth explanation of either Ruby or Rails because that would be beyond the scope of this book. We also assume that if you're reading this section, you probably know about them and just want to learn how to integrate Spring Security into them, or to learn if it's at all possible. However, we'll try to give small explanations of Ruby concepts when we use them in the examples.

JRuby is a fully functional implementation of the Ruby programming language written in Java. You can use it to run Ruby programs inside a Java virtual machine and interact with your other JVM languages—mainly, of course, Java.

What we'll show in this section is a simple tutorial for integrating Spring Security into a Rails application and for deciding if it's even worth doing.

In the JRuby case, there is no plugin like the one you find in Grails. In fact, the integration between Java and Ruby is not as smooth as the integration between Java and Groovy. Basically, you'll have to roll your own implementation to make the integration work.

First things first. Let's install JRuby. The JRuby version used for this book is version 9.2.6.0. You'll use the simple installation here: just downloading a file, uncompressing it, and adding its executables to the path. The following is the procedure we used on a Windows machine (which should be similar to other operating systems):

1. Go to the directory where you want to install JRuby.

2. Download and install the file from https://s3.amazonaws.com/ jruby.org/downloads/9.2.6.0/jruby_windows_x64_9_2_6_0. exe into the following directory: c:\jruby-9.2.6.0.

3. You should have access to JRuby now. Execute jruby -v, and you should get the version of JRuby you just installed, as shown in Figure 9-9.

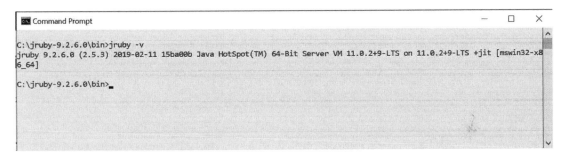

Figure 9-9. *JRuby version page*

4. Next, install Rails: jruby -S gem install rails, as shown in Figure 9-10.

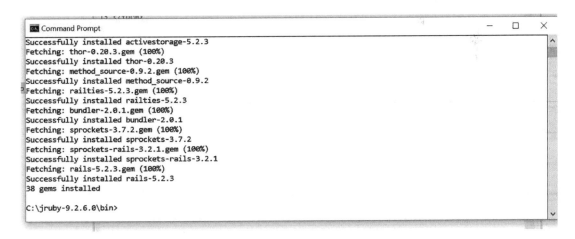

Figure 9-10. *Installing Rails*

5. Now create your Rails application. As in the rest of the book, this
    will be an application with very little functionality just to show you
    how to use Spring Security. Let's call this application simply *demo*.
    From a directory of your choice, write the following command:
    `rails new demo`.

You now have a new basic Rails application in the system. You can run it by going to
the directory `demo` that you just created from the command line and entering `rails s`.
That command will start a WEBrick server and run the application on that server. If you
are following the example, you should be able to visit `http://localhost:3000` on your
computer and access the default Rails application home page.

In the process of creating the Rails application, a lot of infrastructure code and a
well-defined directory structure was generated for you. If you take a look at the `demo`
directory (which is the root of your application), you'll see what we mean.

Anyway, as we said before, we won't go into any depth examining the Rails
framework or Ruby itself. We'll simply show with a rudimentary example how you could
approach integrating Spring Security into a Ruby on Rails application. We are assuming
you already know Ruby and Rails.

Web-Layer Security in Rails

When you ran your Rails application in the previous section, you ran it with a Ruby
server (WEBrick). This server doesn't know anything about Java servlets, so you might
guess that it's not possible to run Spring Security web-layer security with this server—
and you would be correct. What you need to do is run your Rails application in a
standard Java web container, and that is what you'll do next.

First, install *warbler*, a gem you use to create standard WAR files from your Rails
application. To install warbler, use the command `jruby -S gem install warbler`.
After warbler is installed, you can execute `jruby -S warble` in the root directory of your
application and it will create `demo.war`.

That's good, but let's not deploy it just yet. Let's add some functionality to it first, and
then let's add Spring Security-level security.

You'll add two simple routes to your application. One will return the string SECURED
and will be accessible only to logged-in users. The other one will return the string
UNSECURED and will be available to any user.

Let's create a pair of controllers: one for admin users and one for standard users. You'll call these controllers simply AdminsController and StandardsController. Type the following two commands in the root of your demo application to generate them:

```
rails g controller admins
rails g controller standards
```

The execution of those commands generates output describing the artifacts that got generated. You'll then edit those controllers to look like Listings 9-17 and 9-18. You can find the controllers in the standard Rails location in the app/controllers directory.

Listing 9-17. AdminsController with a Secured Action

```
class AdminsController < ApplicationController
  def secured
    render :text => "This is top secret code"
  end
end
```

Listing 9-18. StandardsController with an Unsecured Action

```
class StandardsController < ApplicationController
  def unsecured
    render :text => "Anybody can read this meaningless message"
  end
end
```

The next thing you need to do is to copy all the Java libraries you need to use into the lib directory of your Rails application:

```
aopalliance-1.0.jar
commons-codec-1.3.jar
commons-logging-1.1.1.jar
javax.servlet-api-4.0.1.jar
spring-aop-5.1.8.RELEASE.jar
spring-asm-5.1.8.RELEASE.jar
spring-beans-5.1.8.RELEASE.jar
spring-context-5.1.8.RELEASE.jar
spring-core-5.1.8.RELEASE.jar
```

```
spring-expression-5.1.8.RELEASE.jar
spring-jdbc-5.1.8.RELEASE.jar
spring-security-config-5.1.5.RELEASE.jar
spring-security-core-5.1.5.RELEASE.jar
spring-security-crypto-5.1.5.RELEASE.jar
spring-security-web-5.1.5.RELEASE.jar
spring-tx-5.1.8.RELEASE.jar
spring-web-5.1.8.RELEASE.jar
```

The next step is to enable your Rails application to be run in a standard Java web server, such as Tomcat. For that, you'll use the gem *warbler*. Warbler is a JRuby exclusive gem you use to convert different kinds of Ruby applications into standard Java packaging artifacts, such as JAR and WAR files. In your case, you'll obviously be creating a WAR file.

Warbler uses internally the gem `jruby-rack` and packs it into the WAR-based application. This gem is the core of the integration between Ruby Rack–based applications (such as Rails applications) and Java web servlet–based applications, which is what you need.

Jruby-rack works as a translation layer. It first initializes the Ruby part of the application with a servlet listener (`org.jruby.rack.rails.RailsServletContextListener`), and then, on each request, it intercepts the calls to the server with a servlet filter, `org.jruby.rack.RackFilter`. When this filter gets the `HttpServletRequest`, it will translate these Java-based requests into Rack requests that will pass through to the Rails application, as these are the requests Rails will understand as it is built on the Rack model. Of course, there is a lot more detail regarding warbler and `jruby-rack`, but for the moment, the explanations presented here should be enough for you to continue with the example. In Figure 9-11, you can see a graphical illustration of how `jruby-rack` works.

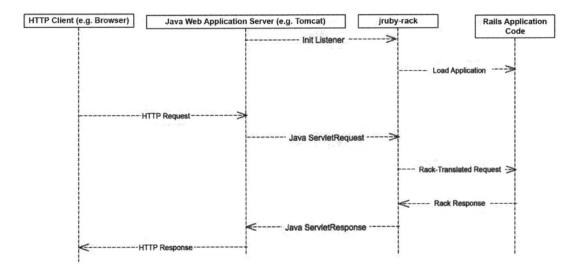

Figure 9-11. A jruby-rack mapping of the Java and Ruby worlds

To use warbler with Spring Security, you need to change the web.xml file that gets automatically generated by it. To do this, you need to copy the web.xml.erb that comes with warbler (which resides in the gem installation directory of Ruby and which is ~/. rvm/gems/jruby-1.8/gems/warbler-1.3.6/web.xml.erb on my computer) into the config directory of your demo application. Then you need to edit it and make it look like Listing 9-19. By doing this, you are including the Spring Security configuration in your web.xml file as you did in previous chapters.

Next, copy the applicationContext-security.xml file from Listing 9-20 into the root of your demo application. Here you have your familiar Spring Security configuration from Chapter 2, with a few modifications. You are simply securing the URL /admin/* for members of the Scarvarez family.

Then you need to edit warbler's configuration file. To do that, you execute the command jruby -S warble config in the root of your application. That execution generates a warble.rb file inside the config directory of the application. Make sure that that file looks like Listing 9-21. In the file, you are ensuring JRuby will be compatible with Ruby 1.9 and that the Spring configuration file will be included in the WEB-INF directory in the generated WAR file when warbler builds this file.

That's all you need, so let's create the WAR file again. From the root directory of your application, execute JRUBY_OPTS=--1.9 warble. This command doesn't work in Windows. You should execute just warble and set the JRUBY_OPTS variable separately. This generates the WAR file with your Rails application embedded on it. Deploy it to your web application server. (We deployed it to Tomcat 9.)

After it is deployed, you can visit the corresponding URLs. On our computer, the behavior is as follows: When we visit http://localhost:8080/demo/standard/message, we see the message "Anybody can read this meaningless message."

However, if we visit http://localhost:8080/demo/admin/message, the familiar login page is shown. After we log in with the username **massimo** and the password **nardone**, we see the following message on the page: "This is top secret code." This is the behavior we expected. We have secured our Rails application with basic web-layer security.

Listing 9-19. The web.xml.erb in the config Folder, Including Configuration for Spring Security

```
<!DOCTYPE web-app PUBLIC
  "-//Sun Microsystems, Inc.//DTD Web Application 2.3//EN"
  "http://java.sun.com/dtd/web-app_2_3.dtd">
<web-app>
<% webxml.context_params.each do |k,v| %>
<context-param>
<param-name><%= k %></param-name>
<param-value><%= v %></param-value>
</context-param>
<% end %>
  <!-- Spring MVC -->
  <servlet>
    <servlet-name>spring</servlet-name>
    <servlet-class>org.springframework.web.servlet.DispatcherServlet</
    servlet-class>
    <load-on-startup>1</load-on-startup>
  </servlet>
  <servlet-mapping>
    <servlet-name>spring</servlet-name>
    <url-pattern>/</url-pattern>
  </servlet-mapping>

  <listener>
    <listener-class>org.springframework.web.context.ContextLoaderListener</
    listener-class>
  </listener>
```

```xml
<context-param>
  <param-name>contextConfigLocation</param-name>
  <param-value>
    /WEB-INF/applicationContext-security.xml
  </param-value>
</context-param>

<!-- Spring Security -->
<filter>
  <filter-name>springSecurityFilterChain</filter-name>
  <filter-class>org.springframework.web.filter.DelegatingFilterProxy</
  filter-class>
</filter>

<filter-mapping>
  <filter-name>springSecurityFilterChain</filter-name>
  <url-pattern>/*</url-pattern>
</filter-mapping>

<filter>
  <filter-name>RackFilter</filter-name>
  <filter-class>org.jruby.rack.RackFilter</filter-class>
</filter>

<filter-mapping>
  <filter-name>springSecurityFilterChain</filter-name>
  <url-pattern>/*</url-pattern>
</filter-mapping>

<filter-mapping>
  <filter-name>RackFilter</filter-name>
  <url-pattern>/*</url-pattern>
</filter-mapping>

<% if webxml.jndi then [webxml.jndi].flatten.each do |jndi| %>
<resource-ref>
  <res-ref-name><%= jndi %></res-ref-name>
  <res-type>javax.sql.DataSource</res-type>
```

```
    <res-auth>Container</res-auth>
</resource-ref>
<% end; end %>
</web-app>
```

Listing 9-20. The applicationContext-security.xml Security for /admin/* URLs

```
<?xml version="1.0" encoding="UTF-8"?>
<beans:beans xmlns="http://www.springframework.org/schema/security"
xmlns:xsi="http://www.w3.org/2001/XMLSchema-instance" xmlns:beans="http://
www.springframework.org/schema/beans"
            xsi:schemaLocation="
    http://www.springframework.org/schema/security
      http://www.springframework.org/schema/security/spring-security--
      4.2.xsd
    http://www.springframework.org/schema/beans
      http://www.springframework.org/schema/beans/spring-beans-4.3.xsd">

    <security:http auto-config="true">
        <security:intercept-url pattern="/admin/*" access="ROLE_SCARVAREZ_
        MEMBER" />
    </security:http>
    <security:authentication-manager>
        <security:authentication-provider>
            <security:user-service>
                <security:user authorities="ROLE_NARDONE_MEMBER"
                name="massimo" password="nardone" />
                <security:user authorities="ROLE_NARDONE_MEMBER"
                name="luna" password="nardone" />
                <security:user authorities="ROLE_NARDONE_MEMBER" name="leo"
                password="nardone" />
                <security:user authorities="ROLE_NARDONE_MEMBER"
                name="neve" password="nardone" />
            </security:user-service>
        </security:authentication-provider>
    </security:authentication-manager>
</beans>
```

380

Listing 9-21. The warble.rb Configuration File

```
Warbler::Config.new do |config|
    config.dirs = %w(app config lib log vendor tmp)
    config.includes = FileList["db"]
    config.webinf_files += FileList["applicationContext-security.xml"]
    config.webxml.jruby.compat.version = "1.9"
end
```

Spring Security, Groovy, and Grails

Groovy is one of the strongest contenders for the number one spot in the non-Java JVM language space. It has a great community and currently is supported and managed by the SpringSource people.

Groovy is a programming language that tries to combine the power of Java with the elegance and developer-friendly characteristics of some dynamic programming languages—taking ideas mainly from well-known and much-loved languages such as Python and Ruby. Groovy successfully creates an environment where different kinds of programmers, with some practice, can feel at home (experienced Java developers and Ruby developers, for example).

Groovy has many advantages when you compare it with other JVM languages— the main ones being, in our opinion, the easy transition from Java to Groovy and the interoperability between the two languages.

With regard to the transition part, it is easy to take a Java program and make it a Groovy program. As a matter of fact, you don't have to do anything. A Java program is already a valid Groovy program. This is good from one point of view but bad from another. Even when you can compile a Java program as a Groovy one, it doesn't make sense. Ultimately, you are using Groovy to take advantage of the great features it has compared to Java. Those great features include a lot of metaprogramming techniques, new powerful constructs like closures, faster development cycles, and a clearer and more concise and developer-friendly syntax.

Grails is a web framework written in Groovy and intended to be used with Groovy. It is built on top of the Spring Framework and is heavily influenced by Ruby on Rails. Grails is an attempt to make a friendlier and lighter framework in a JVM-based language that can be picked up quickly. Also, it offers better and more concise ways to develop applications. At the same time, it is built upon some of the strongest Java libraries and frameworks, such as Spring and Hibernate.

Let's install Groovy library for the example and specify the Groovy SDK. Download the standard Groovy SDK tool from the official distributions available at `http://groovy-lang.org/download.html`. Unpack it into any directory and specify this directory as the library home. In our case, it is `C:\apache-groovy-sdk-2.5.6`. Now you can create your new example.

Using Grails to Secure the Web Layer with URL Rules

Grails and Spring Security integration is incredibly simple because Spring Security is the default security solution for Grails applications and a comprehensive plugin exists to support it. Here, you'll create a simple Grails application, and you'll learn how to secure it with Spring Security. As usual, we'll introduce this application in a step-by-step process.

Download and install the latest version of Grails if you still don't have it. You can download it from its homepage at `http://grails.org/`. We are running this example with version 3.3.9 of Grails.

To install it, simply unzip the downloaded the `grails-3.3.9.zip` file (in our case, it is `C:\grails-3.3.9`) and then set the environment variable `GRAILS_HOME` to point to the new expanded directory. Also, add to your `PATH` environment variable the path `GRAILS_HOME/bin`.

At the command line, go to any directory where you want to create the application and execute `grails create-app demo-grails` to create the application.

Next, generate a couple of controllers: a secured controller and an unsecured controller. Execute `grails create-controller secured` inside the generated application directory. And then execute `grails create-controller unsecured`.

Now you need to create an action in each controller and make them look like Listings 9-22 and 9-23. Put these files in the directory `grails-app/controllers/demo/grails` of your application.

Run the application now with `grails run-app` and visit either `http://localhost:8080/demo-grails/secured/message` or `http://localhost:8080/demo-grails/unsecured/message`, and you should be able to access both URLs without a problem. The next logical step is to secure the secured URL.

As we said before, Grails is built on top of Spring, so it's only logical that an integration with Spring Security should be straightforward. Grails is built in a clever modular way so that you can add functionality in the form of plugins. Let's install the Spring Security plugin by executing `grails install-plugin spring-security-core` (which, in our current version, installs the version 1.2.7.3). Then execute the command `grails s2-quickstart demo.security User Role` to generate the needed models to support users and roles in the application.

Next, you'll create a couple of test users to try out security. Open the file `BootStrap.groovy` (in the `grails-app/conf` directory), and make it look like the code in Listing 9-24. Here you are creating two users: one with role `ROLE_ADMIN` and the other one with the role `ROLE_USER`. You can see that this code uses the classes generated in the previous step, `User` and `Role`.

As with previous examples, you'll secure certain URLs so that they are accessible only for users with a specific role. To do this in Grails, you need to add the code from Listing 9-25 to the end of the file `Config.groovy` (which resides in the directory `grails-app/conf`). The code is self-explanatory. It simply tells Grails to use an intercept URL map for security. This map defines URL paths with wildcards (in Ant-style syntax, which we covered before for standard Java rules) and the roles that are allowed to access such URLs.

Run the application by executing the command `grails run-app` in the root directory. Now, if you try to access `http://localhost:8080/demo-grails/unsecured/message` or `http://localhost:8080/demo-grails/secured/message`, you'll get redirected to a login page. If you log in with the username **luna** and the password **password**, you'll be granted access to the secured URL and not the unsecured one. However, if you log in with the username **neve** and the password **password**, you'll be granted access to `http://localhost:8080/demo-grails/unsecured/message` but you'll get an "access denied" error when trying to access `http://localhost:8080/demo-grails/secured/message`. You can see that you have properly secured access to the URLs.

The first thing that is hard to see from this example is that you are actually using Spring Security. We say this because you haven't defined any filters, any authentication managers, any voters, any user service, or any authentication provider. Actually, you haven't defined any Spring bean at all. You could easily assume that something else is used under the covers because there is nothing specific to Spring Security here. This is a good thing, and one of the nice features of Grails. The use of plugins gives you sensible common defaults and leaves you only with the responsibility of defining the things that are exclusive to your business problem. In the case of security, you need to define your users, their passwords, and the roles and access permissions for your application.

Listing 9-22. SecuredController with a Secured Message in the Grails Application

```
package demo.grails

class SecuredController {

    def message() {
        render "Incredibly confidential message"
    }
}
```

Listing 9-23. UnsecuredController with an Unsecured Message in the Grails Application

```
package demo.grails

class UnsecuredController {

    def message() {
        render "message for everyone"
    }
}
```

Listing 9-24. BootStrap.groovy Setting Up a Couple of Test Users with Security Roles Assigned to Them

```
import demo.security.Role
import demo.security.User
import demo.security.UserRole

class BootStrap {

    def init = { servletContext ->
        def adminRole = new Role(authority: 'ROLE_ADMIN').save(flush: true)
        def userRole = new Role(authority: 'ROLE_USER').save(flush: true)

        def testAdmin = new User(username: 'luna', enabled: true, password:
        'password')
        testAdmin.save(flush: true)
```

```
    def testUser = new User(username: 'neve', enabled: true, password:
    'password')
    testUser.save(flush: true)

    UserRole.create testAdmin, adminRole, true
    UserRole.create testUser, userRole, false

}
def destroy = {
}
}
```

Listing 9-25. An Excerpt from Config.groovy, Where We Add the URLs That Need
to Be Secured

```
grails.plugins.springsecurity.securityConfigType = "InterceptUrlMap"
grails.plugins.springsecurity.interceptUrlMap = [
    '/secured/**':    ['ROLE_ADMIN'],
    '/unsecured/**':  ['ROLE_USER'],
 ]
```

Grails' Spring Security plugin gives you more access to the functionality offered
by Spring Security and, of course, it also allows you to customize it by overriding the
defaults. One of the things it supports is the use of SpEL for access rules. To test this
in the context of this example, and with the simplest security SpEL expression we can
think of, simply replace the security section introduced in the file Config.groovy (from
Listing 9-25) with the content from Listing 9-26. In this listing, as you can see, you are
using the security expression hasRole, which you studied in previous chapters. Note
that this is a simple example with hasRole, but here you have access to the full suite
of expressions offered by Spring Security SpEL support. For example, you could use
authentication.name == 'luna' as an expression instead of hasRole.

Listing 9-26. An Excerpt from Config.groovy, Which Uses SpEL Instead of Simple Roles

```
grails.plugins.springsecurity.securityConfigType = "InterceptUrlMap"
grails.plugins.springsecurity.interceptUrlMap = [
    '/secured/**':    ["hasRole('ROLE_ADMIN')"],
    '/unsecured/**':  ["hasRole('ROLE_USER')"],
 ]
```

Using Grails Security at the Method Level

Grails' Spring Security plugin supports method-level security the same way as it does with Java. This means you can put @grails.plugins.springsecurity secured annotations (or the standard Spring Security @Secured annotation as well) in your controller classes and Spring Security will make sure they are secured according to those annotations. Doing this is very simple. Let's keep working on the application from the last section. First, replace the current content of the file Config.groovy (in the grails-app/conf directory) from the line that reads grails.plugins.springsecurity. securityConfigType = "InterceptUrlMap" onward with the simple line grails. plugins.springsecurity.securityConfigType = "Annotation". Then replace the content of class SecuredController (in the grails-app/controllers/demo/grails directory) with the content of Listing 9-27 and the content of class UnsecuredController (in the grails-app/controllers/demo/grails directory) with the content of Listing 9-28. After you do this, if you restart the application, you should get the same access constraints that you got in the previous section when you secured the URLs.

Listing 9-27. SecuredController with the @Secured Annotation

```
package demo.grails

import grails.plugins.springsecurity.Secured;

class SecuredController {

    @Secured(["ROLE_ADMIN"])
    def message() {
        render "Incredibly confidential message"
    }
}
```

Listing 9-28. UnsecuredController with the @Secured Annotation

```
package demo.grails

import grails.plugins.springsecurity.Secured;

class UnsecuredController {

    @Secured(["ROLE_USER"])
    def message() {
        render "message for everyone"
    }
}
```

In these last two sections, we just scratched the surface of the functionality available using Grails' Spring Security plugin. You can do virtually everything you can do using the standard Java support. For a comprehensive guide to using the Grails plugin, take a look at its official page at `http://plugins.grails.org/plugin/grails/spring-security-core`.

Spring Security and Scala

Scala is probably the strongest language (in the sense of number of adopters and the liveliness of the community around it) running on top of the Java Virtual Machine apart from Java itself. (Scala also has a version that runs on the .NET platform.) Scala is a very powerful, general-purpose programming language that tries to merge the best of the object-oriented and functional programming paradigms.

Scala is a language that aims to provide a concise and elegant alternative to the world of enterprise Java programming, while keeping the type safety of Java. As we said, it comes with functional programming features built in, adding a whole new layer of power for the seasoned object-oriented programmer that increases productivity.

We are not experts in Scala or functional programming (far from it as we have just recently started to look at them) but we will give you the core definitions and the main characteristics of both and show you how to use them with Spring and Spring Security.

Functional programming is a paradigm in which programs are composed of functions that receive inputs and produce outputs, while also avoiding the use of state and mutability. This is in clear contrast to object-oriented programming, where the main abstraction is the object and its internal state, and mutability is a very common thing.

387

By not allowing mutability and state, functional programming presents itself as a good alternative for programming concurrent programs, because programmers don't need to worry about synchronization between concurrent processes or threads.

In Scala, functions can be passed around (as function parameters or function return values) as simple values. In this sense, they behave pretty much like any other simple value (for example, a string), and this is an important concept in a functional programming language. In Scala, functions are first-class objects.

According to the literature, Scala's name comes from the words *scalable language*. This implies that Scala supports object-oriented and functional programming paradigms and that it is suitable for simple scripting tasks or full enterprise applications. Combining this capability with an elegant and concise syntax makes the language scalable in terms of the number of domains and uses that it can address.

Let's install Scala now. There are two ways of installing Scala: as via the IntelliJ IDEA plugin or via a manual installation. For manual installation, you just go to its home page (`www.scala-lang.org/download/`) and download the latest version (2.13.0 at the time of this writing). Uncompress the downloaded file in your directory of choice and configure it.

Let's install Scala via the plugin, as shown in Figure 9-12.

Figure 9-12. *Scala IDE plugin installation for IntelliJ IDEA*

OK, that was your introduction to Scala! It was a very simple introduction, we know. However, as we said, covering the language in depth is outside the scope of this book and there are a lot of great books dedicated to the topic. We're assuming here that you probably know the language better than we do and you are just interested in how to use Spring Security with it.

The next thing you'll do is create the project by combining Scala with Spring and Spring Security. See Figure 9-13.

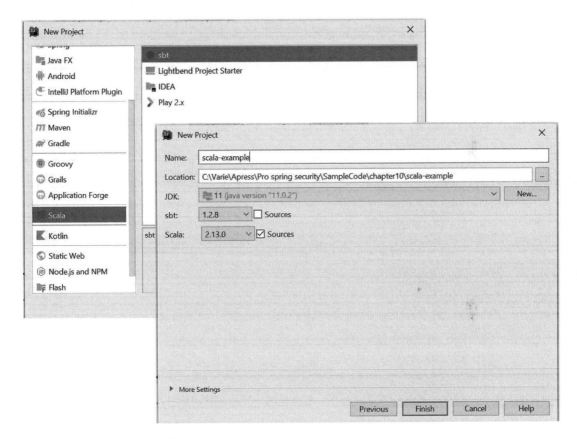

Figure 9-13. *New Scala project*

Convert the Scala project to a Maven project, and in the generated `pom.xml` file, add the Scala dependency shown in Listing 9-29.

Listing 9-29. Scala Maven Dependency

```
<dependency>
    <groupId>org.scala-tools</groupId>
    <artifactId>maven-scala-plugin</artifactId>
    <version>2.15.2</version>
</dependency>
```

Next, of course, you need to add the Spring dependencies to the pom.xml file. You should know how to do this by now. You also need to add the Scala plugin in the plugin sections. In the end, your pom.xml file should look like Listing 9-30.

Listing 9-30. The pom.xml File in the Scala Maven Project

```
<project xmlns="http://maven.apache.org/POM/4.0.0" xmlns:xsi="http://www.
 w3.org/2001/XMLSchema-instance"
        xsi:schemaLocation="http://maven.apache.org/POM/4.0.0
        http://maven.apache.org/maven-v4_0_0.xsd">
    <modelVersion>4.0.0</modelVersion>
    <groupId>com.apress.pss</groupId>
    <artifactId>scala-example</artifactId>
    <packaging>war</packaging>
    <version>1.0-SNAPSHOT</version>
    <name>scala-example Maven Webapp</name>
    <url>http://maven.apache.org</url>
    <repositories>
      <repository>
            <id>scala-tools.org</id>
            <name>Scala-tools Maven2 Repository</name>
            <url>http://scala-tools.org/repo-releases</url>
      </repository>
    </repositories>
    <pluginRepositories>
      <pluginRepository>
            <id>scala-tools.org</id>
            <name>Scala-tools Maven2 Repository</name>
            <url>http://scala-tools.org/repo-releases</url>
```

```xml
    </pluginRepository>
  </pluginRepositories>
  <dependencies>
    <dependency>
            <groupId>org.scala-tools</groupId>
            <artifactId>maven-scala-plugin</artifactId>
            <version>2.15.2</version>
    </dependency>
    <dependency>
            <groupId>org.scala-lang</groupId>
            <artifactId>scala-library</artifactId>
            <version>2.11.7</version>
    </dependency>
    <dependency>
            <groupId>javax.servlet</groupId>
            <artifactId>javax.servlet-api</artifactId>
            <version>4.1.0</version>
    </dependency>
    <dependency>
            <groupId>junit</groupId>
            <artifactId>junit</artifactId>
            <version>4.5</version>
            <scope>test</scope>
    </dependency>
    <dependency>
            <groupId>org.springframework.security</groupId>
            <artifactId>spring-security-core</artifactId>
            <version>5.1.5.RELEASE</version>
    </dependency>
    <dependency>
            <groupId>org.springframework.security</groupId>
            <artifactId>spring-security-config</artifactId>
            <version>5.1.5.RELEASE</version>
    </dependency>
    <dependency>
```

```
            <groupId>org.springframework.security</groupId>
            <artifactId>spring-security-web</artifactId>
            <version>5.1.5.RELEASE</version>
    </dependency>
    <dependency>
            <groupId>commons-logging</groupId>
            <artifactId>commons-logging</artifactId>
            <version>1.1.1</version>
    </dependency>
    <dependency>
            <groupId>commons-codec</groupId>
            <artifactId>commons-codec</artifactId>
            <version>1.3</version>
    </dependency>
    <dependency>
            <groupId>org.springframework</groupId>
            <artifactId>spring-webmvc</artifactId>
            <version>5.1.5.RELEASE</version>
    </dependency>
</dependencies>
<build>
  <finalName>scala-example</finalName>
  <sourceDirectory>src/main/scala</sourceDirectory>
  <testSourceDirectory>src/test/scala</testSourceDirectory>
  <plugins>
        <plugin>
                <groupId>org.scala-tools</groupId>
                <artifactId>maven-scala-plugin</artifactId>
                <executions>
                        <execution>
                                <id>scala-compile-first</id>
                                <phase>process-resources</phase>
                                <goals>
                                        <goal>add-source</goal>
                                        <goal>compile</goal>
```

```xml
                                </goals>
                        </execution>
                        <execution>
                                <id>scala-test-compile</id>
                                <phase>process-test-resources
                                </phase>
                                <goals>
                                        <goal>testCompile</goal>
                                </goals>
                        </execution>
                </executions>
        </plugin>
    </plugins>
    </build>
</project>
```

This will be a simple web application with Spring MVC, and it will have a very simple Service layer. The big difference from the applications you saw in other chapters is that both the Controller layer and the Service layer will be written in Scala instead of Java. We'll show you how to add security to the method level, but, as you'll see, it is almost the same as with Java. Let's start with the code for the controller. In the package com. apress.pss.scala.web in a source folder with the path src/main/scala, create the ScalaController class shown in Listing 9-31.

Listing 9-31. ScalaController

```scala
package com.apress.pss.scala.web;
import org.springframework.beans.factory.annotation.Autowired
import org.springframework.web.bind.annotation.RequestMapping
import org.springframework.web.bind.annotation.RequestMethod
import org.springframework.stereotype.Controller
import com.apress.pss.scala.service.ScalaServiceFacade
import javax.servlet.http.HttpServletResponse
import javax.servlet.http.HttpServletRequest

@RequestMapping(Array("/enter"))
class ScalaController(service: ScalaServiceFacade) {
```

393

```scala
@RequestMapping(value = Array("/scala"), method =
Array(RequestMethod.GET))
def scalaRequest(request:HttpServletRequest,
response:HttpServletResponse) = {
 val value = service.scalaService
 response.getWriter().write(value)
 }
}
```

In the controller, you are defining a simple method that returns (writes on the response, actually) whatever the service returns. Note the use of the annotation @RequestMapping in the example. With Scala, you cannot use a simple string to set the value of array-based annotation values. You need to set a real array with just one element as the value. For the rest, the example is very much like the Java version, with some syntax modifications.

Then, in the package com.apress.pss.scala.service, create the ScalaService class shown in Listing 9-32.

Listing 9-32. ScalaService Class

```scala
package com.apress.pss.scala.service;
import org.springframework.stereotype.Service
import org.springframework.security.access.annotation.Secured

trait ScalaServiceFacade {
    def scalaService: String
}

class ScalaService extends ScalaServiceFacade{
  @Secured(Array("ROLE_USER"))
  def scalaService() = "Service accessed"
}
```

Again, the code in this listing is straightforward. It is a service class with a simple method that returns a string. Notice how you are using the @Secured annotation here. Again, you are using the Array function (actually, what you are indirectly calling here is the apply method of the Array companion object, which allows you to create a new instance of the Array class) and passing the string that will be the only element of the array. With Scala, you can't use the convenient technique of passing a simple string for this value as you did in the Java version.

Note also the use of the `trait` just before the class definition and then the class extending that trait. A `trait` in Scala is somewhat the equivalent of the interfaces in Java, but it has a lot more power. Although not shown in this example, a trait can have fully implemented methods as well as the traditional abstract (definition only) methods typical of Java interfaces, and your class can extend more than one trait "inheriting" the functionality defined in all of them without needing to implement the already implemented methods.

This technique, also called *mixin*, is in no way exclusive to Scala because other languages also have constructs that fulfil the same purpose. For example, in Ruby you can use modules to achieve more or less the same outcome that you get with Scala traits. Again, we won't go into any details about this. For this example, you can think of a trait simply as a Java interface that you use from the controller to access the service.

Next, you need to make your configuration. By now you should be very familiar with configuring a Spring Security Web Application. So we will simply show you the files next and won't go into the details of any of them. Note that we are referencing Scala classes just as we used to reference Java classes before in our beans. It is great that interoperability between Java and Scala is so nicely achieved. Listing 9-33 shows the `web.xml` file. Listing 9-34 shows the `applicationContext-security.xml`. Listing 9-35 shows the file `scala-servlet.xml`. All files should live under the `WEB-IF` directory of your application.

Listing 9-33. The web.xml File for the Scala Project

```
<web-app id="WebApp_ID" version="2.4"
        xmlns="http://java.sun.com/xml/ns/j2ee" xmlns:xsi=
        "http://www.w3.org/2001/XMLSchema-instance"
        xsi:schemaLocation="http://java.sun.com/xml/ns/j2ee
   http://java.sun.com/xml/ns/j2ee/web-app_2_4.xsd">

        <display-name>Spring MVC Application</display-name>

        <!-- Spring MVC -->
        <servlet>
          <servlet-name>scala</servlet-name>
```

```
    <servlet-class>org.springframework.web.servlet.
    DispatcherServlet</servlet-class>
    <load-on-startup>1</load-on-startup>
  </servlet>
  <servlet-mapping>
    <servlet-name>scala</servlet-name>
    <url-pattern>/</url-pattern>
  </servlet-mapping>

  <listener>
    <listener-class>org.springframework.web.context.
    ContextLoaderListener</listener-class>
  </listener>

  <context-param>
    <param-name>contextConfigLocation</param-name>
    <param-value>
            /WEB-INF/applicationContext-security.xml
    </param-value>
  </context-param>

  <!-- Spring Security -->
  <filter>
    <filter-name>springSecurityFilterChain</filter-name>
    <filter-class>org.springframework.web.filter.
    DelegatingFilterProxy</filter-class>
  </filter>

  <filter-mapping>
    <filter-name>springSecurityFilterChain</filter-name>
    <url-pattern>/*</url-pattern>
  </filter-mapping>

</web-app>
```

Listing 9-34. The applicationContext-security.xml for the Scala Project

```xml
<?xml version="1.0" encoding="UTF-8"?>

<beans:beans xmlns="http://www.springframework.org/schema/security"
xmlns:xsi="http://www.w3.org/2001/XMLSchema-instance" xmlns:beans="http://
www.springframework.org/schema/beans"
                xsi:schemaLocation="
    http://www.springframework.org/schema/security
        http://www.springframework.org/schema/security/spring-security--
        4.2.xsd
    http://www.springframework.org/schema/beans
        http://www.springframework.org/schema/beans/spring-beans-4.3.xsd">

<global-method-security secured-annotations="enabled"></global-method-
security>

        <beans:bean class="org.springframework.security.web.authentication.
        SavedRequestAwareAuthenticationSuccessHandler" name="awareAuthentic
        ationSuccessHandler"/>
        <beans:bean id ="passwordEncoder" class = "org.springframework.
        security.crypto.password.NoOpPasswordEncoder" factory-method =
        "getInstance" />

        <beans:bean id="scalaService" class="com.apress.pss.scala.service.
        ScalaService"/>

        <http auto-config="true" />

        <authentication-manager>
          <authentication-provider>
                <user-service>
                        <user name="luna" authorities="ROLE_USER"
                                                password="nardone" />
                        <user name="leo" authorities="ROLE_ADMIN"
                                                password="nardone" />
                </user-service>
          </authentication-provider>
        </authentication-manager>
</beans:beans>
```

Listing 9-35. The scala-servlet.xml File with the Controller Definition

```
<beans xmlns="http://www.springframework.org/schema/beans"
        xmlns:context="http://www.springframework.org/schema/context"
        xmlns:xsi="http://www.w3.org/2001/XMLSchema-instance"
        xsi:schemaLocation="
    http://www.springframework.org/schema/beans
    http://www.springframework.org/schema/beans/spring-beans-3.0.xsd
    http://www.springframework.org/schema/context
    http://www.springframework.org/schema/context/spring-context--
    3.0.xsd">

<bean class="org.springframework.web.servlet.view.
InternalResourceViewResolver">
        <property name = "prefix" value="/WEB-INF/views/" />
        <property name = "suffix" value=".jsp" />
</bean>

<bean id="scalaController" class="com.apress.pss.scala.web.
ScalaController">
        <constructor-arg ref="scalaService"/>
</bean>
</beans>
```

Now you can exercise your project. From the root of the project in the command line, execute the command mvn clean install jetty:run to run the application. It should run without any problem.

Next, if you try to access http://localhost:8080/scala-example/enter/scala, you'll be presented with the login screen you have seen so many times before.

If you log in with the username **luna** and the password **nardone**, you should be able to access the application and see the page shown in Figure 9-14.

Service accessed

Figure 9-14. *Successfully accessing the secured Scala application*

That's all we are going to say about integrating with Scala. You can see that for a simple application like this it's not really that different from integrating with Java itself. Actually, beyond the syntactic differences, it's probably just about the same. Of course, in this example you are starting with a Spring application and defining the different components (controllers and services) in Scala. It could be more of a challenge to integrate if you are using a Scala-specific framework. All you need to remember is that to secure methods, those methods need to belong to Spring-managed beans. To secure URLs, the URLs need to be accessed in a servlet-based web application.

Summary

In this chapter, we showed you, at a fairly high level, how to integrate Spring Security into various frameworks and languages. The chosen framework was Spring's own Spring Web Flow, and the illustrative languages chosen were JRuby and Groovy, with their web frameworks Rails and Grails, respectively.

We showed you that integrating Spring Security into these different frameworks and languages can be straightforward (as with Grails) or not so straightforward (as with JRuby or Scala). However, through the JVM, in theory, you could integrate Spring Security into anything you need to secure.

Here is the main takeaway from this chapter, regardless of the frameworks or languages used: Spring Security is, ultimately, just a Java library (a couple of simple .jar files). You can integrate it into any Java (as in JVM) project that you want. You simply have to remember what you can do with it and use the parts that make sense for your particular problem. For instance, using web-layer security wouldn't make sense in a Swing application, or even in a web application that doesn't use standard servlet filters (such as the Play framework).

APPENDIX A

Reference Material

This appendix contains reference material for Spring Security v5.

Tools utilized in this book:

- Java SE Development Kit (JDK) 11: `www.oracle.com/technetwork/java/javase/downloads/jdk11-downloads-5066655.html`

- Maven 3.6: `https://maven.apache.org/download.cgi`

- Spring Security 5.1.5 release: `https://github.com/spring-projects/spring-security/releases/tag/5.1.5.RELEASE`

- IntelliJ IDEA 2019.2: `www.jetbrains.com/idea/download/#section=windows`

- Apache Tomcat Server and plugin v9: `https://tomcat.apache.org/download-90.cgi`

- JRuby 9.2.6.0: `https://s3.amazonaws.com/jruby.org/downloads/9.2.6.0/jruby_windows_x64_9_2_6_0.exe`

- Rails 4.1: `http://installrails.com/steps/railsinstaller_windows`

Spring Security references:

- Spring Security official source code web page: `https://github.com/spring-projects/spring-security`

- GitHub web page to report bugs and enhancement requests: `https://github.com/spring-projects/spring-security/issues`

- Spring official web page: `https://spring.io`

© Carlo Scarioni and Massimo Nardone 2019
C. Scarioni and M. Nardone, *Pro Spring Security*, https://doi.org/10.1007/978-1-4842-5052-5

- Spring Security official web page: `https://spring.io/projects/spring-security`

- Spring Security official documentation web page: `https://docs.spring.io/spring-security/`

- Apache 2 License (Spring Security is an open source tool released under the Apache 2.0 license): `www.apache.org/licenses/LICENSE-2.0.html`

  Spring Security on Twitter:

  - @SpringSecurity

  - @SpringCentral

  - To ask and check questions related to Spring Security: `https://stackoverflow.com`

Spring Security example references:

- `https://spring.io/guides`

- `www.springboottutorial.com`

- `www.tutorialspoint.com/spring_boot/`

- `www.baeldung.com/security-spring`

- `www.javacodegeeks.com/spring-security-tutorials`

Index

A

X, Y, Z